GIO PONTI

The Complete Work 1923-1978

Testina, watercolour on paper with enameled frame, 1942.

Lisa Licitra Ponti

GIO PONTI

The Complete Work 1923—1978

Foreword by Germano Celant

With 630 illustrations, 90 in colour

Thames and Hudson

Acknowledgments

I am grateful to Nives Ciardi, protectress of my texts, Giovanna Rosselli, my all-knowing sister, Vincenzo Fidomanzo, an acrobat of research, Marco Romanelli, who specially contributed to the bibliographical notes, and Marianne Lorenz, eye of *Domus*.
Basic, precious help in collecting the data for this work on Gio Ponti — still a work in progress — has been given me by Angela Baguzzi, Mariateresa Galli, Virna Tagliatti in Milan; Cile Bach and Jeanne Winder in Denver, Marianne Lamonaca Loggia in New York.
I specially thank Arturo Carlo Quintavalle and his CSAC (Centro Studi e Archivio della Comunicazione, Università di Parma, Dipartimento Progetto), Elena Maggini and her Museo delle Porcellane di Doccia, and the *Domus* Archives. And all those who helped me during these years, whether knowing it or not.

L.L.P.

Author's note

The descriptions that accompany Gio Ponti's works are largely intended as a testimony to the way Ponti thought about his work, before all trace of this is lost.
They represent a first step toward allowing today's reader to make a connection between *now* and *then*.
The photographic documentation is also taken, almost in its entirety, from Gio Ponti's studio.
For this description of his work a chronological sequence has been decided on, divided up by decades; in appearance, this is not a Pontian approach, but it does take into account the progress of the works as a whole, whatever the variations in their scale, and this is Pontian.
Alongside Ponti's works, I have given space to the history of *Domus* and *Stile*, for they present us with a picture of Ponti's relationship with his contemporaries.
Notes and bibliographic references on the different works are grouped at the end of the book. Abbreviations used in the Notes and Critical Apparatus appear on p. 270.

L.L.P.

Editorial conception: Passigli Progetti, Milano
Art Direction: Anthony Mathews
Editorial consultant: Andrea Branzi
English translation: Huw Evans

First published in Great Britain in 1990 by
Thames and Hudson Ltd, London

© 1990 Passigli Progetti

Printed and bound in Italy

for Luigi, Matteo, Salvatore

Massimo Campigli, *La famiglia Ponti*, oil on canvas, 1934.

Painting on perspex, 1979.

Contents

Gio Ponti, writing desk, 1953.
This is my masterpiece: I call it my jumping horse: I mean it is a piece of furniture that is very simple but not formally inert.

List of works reproduced
The works are listed alphabetically by decade

The sixties

The seventies

The substantiality of the impalpable
Gio Ponti

The substantiality of Gio Ponti's work is made manifest in something that resembles insubstantiality. At its most extreme — a point where a vast amount of energy is liberated — it actually loses all solidity. The whole of his work has been an effort to get rid of any hint of linear development or the monolithic, which would have given his research a misleading and unwieldy coherence. He has fostered — and to a considerable extent sustained — a movement or a way of thinking and operating that sets out to condense and fix the flows of creativity, to render the transparent plain and solid, to glorify moments of transition, and to increase the brilliance and the flowing intensity of fragile and elegant forms. As a result he has attempted to give expression to insubstantiality, to make it concrete, and to give itself a sensual and theoretical density and depth, with a vibrancy that has never previously been attained. Even a cursory look at the ceramic works he produced in the twenties for Richard-Ginori will show how Ponti has made use of the effects of impalpability and of glowing light to create a depth and an intensity that are a source of brilliance, as if the manipulation of such reflections and glows had made it possible for him to congeal the impalpable. The same thing happened with the objects and furnishings for the Schejola apartment of 1929, where the lightening of mass and bulk and the simplification of forms and junctures has created the impression that they are floating, about to glide off into the surroundings. Hence the frequent use of

mirrors, the crossing and resurrection of voids, the liquefaction of supports — we are reminded of the increasing slenderness of the legs he designed for his chairs and tables, armchairs and closets. This ability to impart an impression of lightness was to serve in the future as a metaphor of Ponti's imagery.

In his ceramics and majolica for Richard-Ginori, the introduction of a quality of airiness and transparency is also to be seen on the gilded surfaces, strewn with soft and rippling colors, that turn into centers of visual activity, areas of luminous reflection, enchanted and radiant solids. On top of these float figures whose poses are lively and seductive, fusing sensuality and seduction, and therefore movement and mutation. At times suspended in empty space, Ponti's women and youths are the condensation of a vitrified, almost dreamlike libido. Their forms, floating without visible support, dance and flex to follow the swelling and the sensual curves of bowls and vases, bonbonnières and ink stands, taking on almost voluptuous connotations.

Here is another manifestation of that sense of vibration and palpitation which shaped the Milanese architect's dream of rendering forms continually present; forms that in order to come alive have to render visible the invisible, that is to say, to continue to pursue transformation and mutation in a flight toward the unknown. Thus we can begin to understand how E. Persico, as far back as 1934, in *L'Italia letteraria*, declared Ponti to «have something in common with the *novecentista* style, with Carlo Carrà and Giorgio de Chirico.» Evidently he was referring not only to the quest for the spirit of classicism, but also to their mutual yearning for an impatient fullness of art, for an intense spirituality that would promote progressions and expansions of thought. The result would be changes of style and emancipation from any rigid definition of tendency, whether that of futurism and metaphysical art, return to order and rationalism, or neoclassicism and art déco. Each one sought instead to draw on the language — of art or architecture, of theater or design — in order to make use of its dynamism. For this reason they all allowed themselves to be seduced by those sources of visual and plastic nourishment that were capable of arousing, whether coherent or not, their cultural appetite. Moreover, Gio Ponti was also linked to Carrà and de Chirico by a thirst for supersaturation, a tendency to overdo things, with the attendant risk of a redundancy of image, going beyond the bounds of even fantasy's restraint. Their work is reminiscent of a bunch of grapes, where the richness and profusion of the stalks, as well as of the grapes of language themselves, makes the harvest an abundant one.

It could be said that these artists delighted in reviving the idea of an archipelago of images or of objects, in which each island, petrified and friable but ever-changing, provides a refuge for vegetation in a perpetual state of mutation.

The way in which the islands designed by Ponti emerged can be seen again in the theoretical crystallization of the «Italian-style house» with which the magazine *Domus* was launched on its publishing career in 1928. Here the horizon of the coasts from which he would take his bearings during the voyage to come was clearly outlined. In it we recognize the idea of a house as «beautiful as a crystal, but hollowed out like a cave filled with stalagtites»; perfect, therefore, but open to continual growth, based on the fortuitousness of natural events, that is, those of expression and imagination. Here once again we find the theme of transparency or insubstantiality that grows and becomes solid. It is brought in to give substance to the solidity of domestic limits, identified with the focus of a «good taste» that was still to be found in the lightness and essence of the modern, as well as in the quality and memory of the ancient. And the clarity of his work and his thought is condensed both in the printed pages of magazines, from *Domus* to *Stile*, and in the materials of so many objects of everyday use, whose vitality, it should be remembered, always depends on the consistency of almost impalpable materials, such as glass and light. These turn into an image of décor in the «furnished window,» one of Ponti's true architectural trademarks, in which the luminous and transparent insubstantiality is transmuted into material and form, leading to displacements of volume and combinations of color that become functions and essences of habitation. The desire for openness that underlies his airy creativity permeates the whole of Ponti's universe in all its manifestations. The epiphany of the window, a passageway for wind and light, is to be found again in all his interiors from Casa Vanzetti (1930) to Villa la Diamantina (1955), but also turns up in the Ferrari fabrics (1930), such as the «Morosi alla finestra» taffeta, and even in the «Luminous Pictures» (1960). The same evocation of another depth, opening onto unknown conditions, typical of an architecture as kaleidoscopic as that of the Milanese architect, is behind his use of reflection. In his interiors one always finds «a glimmering space,» linked to the theme of the mirror. What he was looking for was the split or inverted image of a figure or a luminous outline, a search that could find expression in the use of paint or in the diversified flow of energy in an object like the La Pavoni coffee machine (1948), where the inverted reflection captures the vertical to horizontal position of the boiler, reconciling its industrial epidermis with its animated surface. Similar Pontian processes are doubtless at work in the condensation of light, in his glassware and lamps, where transparency hardens and turns into barricaded space and absolute limpidity.

These few references to Ponti's immensely varied output demonstrate the importance of the role which the solidification of the impalpable and of the lightweight plays in his imagery. Yet giving substance and weight to the immaterial or tangibility to the transparent introduces the game of ambiguity, the dialectics of contradiction. Here everything was open and the quality of ambiguity in Ponti's work was destined to produce hostile reactions. Nevertheless, ambiguity and ambivalence have always been his strong points, simply because they allowed him to avoid the absoluteness of architectural ideology, whether cloaked in rationalist purism or in traditionalist conservatism. The novelty of his position, for which he was «condemned» on many occasions, did not in fact consist in the illusion of an abstract linearity, but in the fluidity, directed as much at the modern as at the ancient, of a not-knowing and a not-recognizing, which he tied to daily experience, and which changed on the basis of the dizzy whirl of events. In this sense he could be accused of uncertainty, but even this criticism fits into his synthesis, which admitted a plurality of meanings nurtured on hesitation and indecision, only to be unleashed once the contingent target had been identified.

In fact the metaphor that we should adopt to «define» (if that is at all possible) his mode of operation is that of a rejection of demarcation, in which the imagination or the process of designing leads to a conceivable and tangible «whole.» Hence Ponti works on the "mixture," wherever the limits are vague, shifting from one language to the other, from graphics to design, from architecture to cultural organization, from craft-based production to industrial production, from ceramics to furnishings... as if he were moving through a landscape thronged with figures or playing with a kaleidoscope — the light we see again, in diamond or hexagonal shapes, marking Taranto Cathedral (1970). The result is to produce a multitude of figures out of the fusion of the same patterns and materials. Through these diversified narrations he surpasses himself, dancing on his own reflections and reverberations, rising and falling because he is working on the scansion of identity.

Another distinctive element is the passage of fluids, clearly visible in the aqueous outpouring of the Pirelli skyscraper (1956). This vertical jet of solid lightness can be identified with water itself. The building is dematerialized, playing on the reflections of the glass and turning into a «mirage» of architecture. Its laminar presence turns on their head all the visual concreteness and static quality of rationalist parallelepipeds and gives further form to the tower of insubstantiality, to the point where it recalls the shape or the impalpability of a veil suspended in the sky: something exciting and transparent, within or behind which are concealed the sensuality of the body and the movement of life.

The motif of the vehemence of the void and of immaterial energy is already present in the «diamondline» automobile body, on an Alfa Romeo chassis, of 1952—54, in which the sense of speed and of penetration by air sustain the essence of the design. With it, Ponti shook the image of the automobile out of its decorative complacency, typical of an Americanized baroque, and rendered its forms and functions absolute, allowing them to breathe visibly and making them light and open. He establishes a link between internal and external flows. He evokes mobility not just through the wheels, but through the circulation of transparency. The same subtle agitation informs the «Superleggera» (1957), a malleable but not fragile object, freed of all weight and every load. This stands out in fact for its extraordinary reductionism, which lends an essential quality to the fusion between materials and use.

We are talking about an object that no longer plays the role of a piece of furniture, but becomes a nonsubstance that tends to overturn the anchoring function of the chair. We are talking about a densification of lightness that finds an epidermal equivalent in the sanitary appliances he designed for Ideal Standard in 1953, where the opacity of the surfaces and the dullness of the function are exalted in a glazed and gleaming skin, backed up by the formal mutation of the object. If these products recall the superficiality or simplicity of consumption, the ornate and astonishing appearance of the Sabattini flatware (1956) or the representations of animals in the De Poli enamels (1956), as well as the explosive development, on the level of the iconography of design, of the Lucano apartment (1952), are evidence of an elusive focus.

The appearance of the figures and images brings to light a depth of childishness and an effusion of fantasy that verges on the excessive. Ostensibly used as ornamentation, they are actually indicative of a force of liberation and provocation that carries on with the investigation of an astounding process of dematerialization and centrifugal refraction of design and architecture.

It still needs emphasizing that the procedure of transformation adopted by Gio Ponti builds on a coherent and consistent image, based on a single root. The extreme poles of difference coexist, since he works on the spatio-temporal contiguity of experience, in which a motif rediscovered later on sets off a chain of associations and memories. In the work of the Milanese architect this experience is linked to the element of irrationality contained in the idea of «sacred,» that is to say in that category of the interpretation of the irrational and the spiritual, wherein lies the territory of morality and ethics. Through this belief in a primal and primitive cause, Ponti got away from rational, and rationalist, linearity and worked on the conceptually ineffable, finding figures that he used to «designate» every single moment, while remaining conscious of the overall sense of creation. He made an effort to produce the act of creation, to give life to a plastic or visual creature that possessed a body, a name, and a face that were always different and unique. From this perspective growth cannot be regular and repetitive, only significant and diversified. Each object or item of furnishing, work of architecture or product will therefore be an indication of this mystery — de Chirico again — and serve to conjure up a visual and environmental enigma, that cannot be confused with other forms of creation. His work on the terror of the imaginary has evidently caused distress. The continual diversity and ambiguity are disturbing because they are not defined by the categories of the usual and the ordinary. They are discordant because they are too primitive. But it is on just this force inherent in the primitive and the primary that Ponti drew to render his design disquieting, and therefore problematical and experimental.

Germano Celant

Gio Ponti, 1923.

Portrait

This book is, in spite of everything, a «Pontian» book. It does not deal with its subjects separately and it is mainly concerned with the «form» of the «architectural objects» that it presents. It is also Pontian, perhaps, in the way that it combines the testimony of a daughter, the opinion of an art critic, and the elegance of an «English» layout.

It is still a «homage» to Gio Ponti. Homage is critical analysis «forgotten by heart,»[1] and with him this comes naturally. It is the process he used himself.

Gio Ponti worked «by admiration.» Admiration immediately translated into «promotion.» Promoting is an aspect of designing, deriving from the same concern for the present. Do you admire this artist? Buy his paintings. Do you admire this poet? Publish his poems. Do you admire this architect? Make it possible for him to build. This was the way Gio Ponti worked, and his two magazines, *Domus* and *Stile*, consisted of recommendations and invitations, to anyone who was listening — backed up solely by his own vision and experience. Driven by hope about the possible. Hope is ingenious.

His magazines were born out of love, as a game, by chance (and then turned into business ventures, but for other people). He never ceased to look on them as a diary. They were, along with the exhibitions, the place where he most liked to be. I have experienced his way of running/not running a magazine, as a «teacher/non-teacher.»[2] Edoardo Persico said in 1933 that «Gio Ponti is the isolated inventor, for whom the history of art is not a progression but a succession of diversities.» («We proceed, we don't progress,» Gio Ponti used to say.)

Ponti always declared himself «illuminated» by Persico. Perhaps it was a two-way process. «Drama» (Persico) recognized the value of «detachment» (Ponti). This was the form in which their «encounter» took place.

Gio Ponti worked «by encounters.» Encounters and coincidences, not debates or battles between groups. Far away from Utopia and from revolution. For the «heroes» of modern architecture, younger than himself, he felt reverence. For the «movements,» indifference.

He always referred to Palladio as his first master. Who are pop's teachers? «Serlio, Palladio, Vitruvius,» we kids had to answer, amused and uncomprehending. He pretended to have teachers in the same way as he pretended to explain his works, inventing the reasons in the same way as he had invented the building.

Whom did he like?

At times his «reverence» was a cover for a secret detachment, based on difference. In the end, the only things by the revered Le Corbusier that he really liked were Ronchamp, Chandigarh, and Ahmedabad. His Le Corbusier was the «lyrical» and «liberated» one, as well as the one who could say «je m'en fiche du Modulor» («I couldn't care less about Modulor»). Through mental affinity, he liked the self-contained architects of his time, Aalto, Saarinen and Niemeyer, whether he mentioned them or not.

In the closing years of his life Gio Ponti roamed through his own past, discovering it with amusement and even admiration. His attitude of wonder toward reality embraced his own work too. His beloved maxim, «in culture everything is contemporary,» applied to him as well. Now we are roaming too, in this book, picking up coincidences and echoes. But there is an «arrow of time,» and a final attainment, a summit reached at the very end, beyond all precedent, that needs to be described at the outset. Like the state of happiness he attained toward the end of his life, when the grace, clarity and detachment found in his work extended beyond the work itself (was it work?). Taranto Cathedral resembles Gio Ponti: architecture that tends to vanish in spectacular fashion, rising into the sky. Likewise in his last interiors everything but the spectacle tends to disappear.

There were sixty hours in Gio Ponti's day. During the first ten hours (between 5 and 6 in the morning) he would draw/write thirty letters (he was not allowed to use the phone). These were the letters that went to his friends — and his collaborators — his way of waking them up; they would find out that the project had changed overnight, that another one had emerged, along with at least eight or nine cute variants, requiring urgent attention. Only a few doors and steps (the way home from the studio) separated his nighttime and daytime designs. Over the following forty hours (from 7 in the morning to 8 in the evening) Gio Ponti was in his barn of a studio, a huge former garage where (in the early days) the draftsmen could drive their scooters right up to their tables. There were more tables than walls beneath the vaults, and the little room in the center, intended for secret talks, was open and empty. Here Gio Ponti used to work on his projects until the evening: from three o'clock on, his hands were black with graphite and ink. He did not even wash them for meals — hurried feasts of colors and shapes, rather than of flavors, followed by a little drop of concentrated sleep, 5 or 10 minutes long. Then came the night. The beautiful night in his sleeping but brightly lit house. And he used to draw in silence, with other lighted windows in other houses for company. Even when, later on in life, he no longer went down to the studio, and was left to himself in the now empty house, he went on designing, day and night, just for himself.

He traveled a lot, but he was never away. From the airplane he wrote, on thin sheets of Alitalia or TWA airmail paper, his «multiple» letters to his office: on every sheet, a line for each person (five sheets, fifty people). On arrival, the letters were cut into strips and distributed. In the car he drew, with a light board on his knees: his beloved Citroën DS gave him the soft ride he needed. When his eyes began to fail him, he exchanged the DS for a twelve-seater Fiat minibus. In this way he hoped to transform the journey into a multiple conversation. (He did not succeed.)
His last trips, though, were little processions, even if there was only one vehicle — he and his dear assistant Neri in the front, daughters and collaborators in the back. They were pilgrimages of art: to Paris, to take a look on the way at a little cathedral that Le Corbusier liked, to rediscover La Tourette on the way back, to see Paris itself (and the Bouilhets). Traveling was almost the only way he had of coming into contact — through the car window — with the great outdoors, with the stirring sky, or just of sitting for a moment on a grassy bank before going back to architecture.

It is now possible for us to perceive the breadth and length of his career. Sixty years of work, buildings in thirteen countries, lectures in twenty-four, twenty-five years of teaching, fifty years of editing, articles in every one of the five hundred and sixty issues of his magazines, two thousand five hundred letters dictated, two thousand letters drawn, designs for a hundred and twenty enterprises, one thousand architectural sketches . . . . It is a great deal, and all from one man.

He worked without a pause. Without hurry. Without effort. Without a computer. Without delegating. In solitude, as artists tend to do. He involved other people, but he proceeded alone, arriving on the spot — early, late — by his own devices.

Perhaps it was because he was so independent in his own work, in his own design of objects and buildings, in his «designing everything,» that he did not «design» his magazines, *Domus* and *Stile* (Persico and Pagano did «design» their magazine, *Casabella*). Perhaps his magazines were his area of hospitality. An open field. This, then, was his «magazine project.» And this is why *Domus* and *Stile* are the revealing archives they are today, in all their lively disorder. In *Domus*, from 1928 to 1940, there is a tension between neoclassical excellence and the emergence of the «new,» coming out of another level of thinking. In *Stile*, from 1941 to 1947, the tension is between the uniqueness of art and creativity at the service of mass production, as was required by postwar reconstruction. In *Domus*, from 1948 to 1979, the field was thrown open to distinctive talents from all over the world.
Ponti's magazines are an expression of his idea of «information.» He was not concerned with monopoly, did not care about priority, sometimes did not even bother to sign his work. What mattered to him was that information should be made immediately available to everyone, and that the magazine's pages should be put at the disposal of its contributors, so that they could give free expression to their own creativity in them. Gio Ponti allowed people to use his magazines to fight their duels. Those who called him a «mediator» missed the point. He was not interested in conciliation. Conciliation is a word used by people who see the mediator as a humble figure, caught up in the heroic battles of the opposing parties. But Gio Ponti was not an advocate of the «happy medium.» He wanted to bring different talents to people's attention. And his enthusiasm was of a demanding kind, although candid in its expression.

It was the same when he mentioned Italy. He talked about Italy when everyone did, when no-one did any longer, and when the word was on everyone's lips again. He neither noticed nor cared whether he was alone or one of many.
«Italy» was his way of saying «hurrah,» of saying «let's do it,» of saying «beautiful,» of saying «we should» — and even of saying «why, why on earth?» («Me duele España,» [«Spain hurts me»], an expression used by his great Spanish friend José Antonio Coderch, was close to his heart.) *La casa all'italiana*, his first book, is a

Gio Ponti, Caracas, 1954.

pamphlet dedicated to Italy and, inseparably, to art. A pamphlet even though it is a collection of articles (taken from *Domus*, 1928—33), since it carries on his battle over taste as an index of morality. Here already the word «civilization» appears, next to «art.» «Civilization» is the use made of art by history. Gio Ponti was in love with «Italy the artist» (as he called it), the exciting Italy of unpredictable artists, from every age (he devoted a book to it, with the title «Mad about Italy,» a book that was never published). At the same time he was in love with a «civilized» Italy, made up — or rather, still to be made up — of «beautiful» houses, schools, churches, airports, stations, villages, objects, newspapers, machines, exhibitions . . . . In the crucial years of *Stile* (1941—47), the years in which Italy had «nothing but its civilization to save its civilization,» Gio Ponti just asked, and went on asking, «does it help Italy?» with regard to every plan (for reconstruction) and every reform (in the teaching of architecture, for instance).

He was overjoyed, in the fifties, when he came across something said by Gropius, an unexpected ally: «Perhaps Italy is destined to make clear what are the factors in modern life on which we must rely in order to recover our lost sense of beauty and to promote, in the industrial era, a new cultural unity.» (For Gio Ponti, however, «beauty» came before «unity.») Gio Ponti repeated Gropius's «Italian prediction» so many times that all of us around him lost track of its meaning. He was alone when he spoke with feeling of Italy and of «honoring Italy,» or when he grew sad for Italy. We had not understood that out of this love for Italy grew his love for all the countries of the world, shaped by hope.

He never ceased to hope (the concept of «unresigned Italy» pleased him), that is, to place his hopes in architecture. He saw architecture, and the house, as a place of potential happiness, or of a «lessening of unhappiness» for human beings. As something that could still offer freedom, fun, and surprise — as well as something in which the worst forms of common idiocy were expressed. So he never ceased to design, even when alone. First he searched directly for answers and then, in the end, he designed out of hope alone. Rather than a project, what Gio Ponti proposed was a method. «De l'Italie arrive l'annonce de l'essentiel.» His «essential,» his striving to attain freedom, to create a liberating space, was in the end a happy failure. But «nothing came to pass without being dreamed of first,» and in his last years he was subject to «fits of happiness.»

(«I am happy to talk to you, for I am always alone and when I am lying down I feel that my thoughts lie down too, but it is better for thoughts to sit up and hold a conversation with us.» Gio Ponti, spring 1979.)

Even the words he used were «encounters,» that met with success or rejection. They were not many, his words, but they were irreplaceable.

«Invention» first of all, a word he took from Palladio. Then, and forever, «expression»: this was the word that encapsulated his thinking, a perfect word that made no distinction between architecture and art, and between art and the applied arts, but which could be used to distinguish between individual artists.

Espressione di Gio Ponti, a book that came out in 1954, is Ponti's autobiography, composed solely of «images» and «definitions.» The chapters have headings like «Academy,» «Machines,» «Interval,» and «Experiences,» for Gio Ponti was unable to use words ending in «ism.» He selected from his own history only those works that showed «the development and the continuity of an individual expression.» This is what makes history. And in this book, containing few plans and few dates, half the pages are devoted to projects that were never realized but which were ahead of their time: the mental forerunner of the Pirelli skyscraper was the horizontal design for the Faculty of Physics at the University of São Paulo, with its «closed form.»

«Academy» is the negative and elegant word that Gio Ponti used, at a certain time, to define his own beginnings. Later he changed it, more playfully, into «architecture d'après l'architecture,» in the manner of Cocteau. Finally, and more exactly, it became «classical education,» a term that admitted something perennial, and never repudiated, in his style, above and beyond formal references. He never said «neoclassical» because that was what he was.

«Perfect,» a much-loved and immobile word. Gio Ponti tended toward immobility of «definition»: definition leads thought into a crystalized state, and «architecture is a crystal.» But in the end he also tended to emerge from the crystal and the definition. The last of his statements on architecture, «architecture is made to be looked at,» is not a definition. It is an appeal, and one that brings everything into play, the observer, the work, the architect.

As the years went by and his thought developed in solitude, he began to coin his own words, like «lightscraping» for his architectural works that «captured» the light. And he used «proceeding» instead of «progressing» to describe a mysterious forward movement in time.

«Prodigy» is the last word. Gio Ponti did not live to see

Gio Ponti in the Taranto Cathedral yard, 1970.

the eighties but he foresaw the «invasion of images» as an alarming «prodigy.» The prodigy of the century, which for him coincided with the «prodigy» of his own approaching end. «La vida es sueño, y los sueños sueños son.» («Life is a dream, and dreams are dreams.»)

He was not afraid of books, if it was a question of writing them, rather than reading them. He had a godfather who took care of his reading, his great friend Ugo Ritter who introduced him to Cendrars, Valéry, and Cocteau — we kids were to grow up cheerfully amidst *les Eugènes* and *la Chose* — but he did not want to do his reading alone: if he liked a book we all had to read it.
He published books, his own and other people's, he imitated books (imitating Scheiwiller), and he invented books. He had no reverence for books, but wanted to produce them: books were, like newspapers and magazines, a means of communication. And they were, like *Amate l'architettura*, the only way to take a stroll with him, listening to him beating the drum about art: «... The pyramids disturb me: the big ones are heroic, the little ones ridiculous; anyone can design a pyramid, there is no need for an architect, just a pharaoh.... Many people say: I don't know how to judge modern architecture. Why not, I ask them, judge it in the same way as ancient architecture? Admiring Philip Johnson's pavilion I can say that its beauty is *Attic*.... The floor is a theorem. The obelisk is an enigma.... Fantasy is hallucination. Clear and precise as a dream. When de Chirico knew how to dream, he painted very precise manikins.... Architecture should be designed to be lived in, and judged empty....»
Amate l'architettura, 1940 and 1957, is an invented book: a paperback on cheap paper, with pages in different colors to match the different «families» of thoughts. Its image already declares: «thinking is the discovery of constellations» and «publishing is nothing but a putting of ideas into circulation.»
There are traces of another book among Ponti's last papers: «This book is not intended as a reminder of me to others, but of others to me, the others to whom I owe everything.» The book was never written but was about to take the form of an exhibition — at the Museu de Arte in São Paulo, directed by Ponti's friend Bardi — where Gio Ponti wanted to put «his» others on show, the «others» of his life.

But these «others», how can we mention them all in one book, as Gio Ponti would have liked? If we were to invite them to a party, as Ponti would have done, it would be a party as big as a city carnival (and Ponti would have immediately invited yet other «others,» whom no-one had ever seen before). For these «others» of his were not just his beloved artists, poets and comedians (to whom he wished to express his gratitude). They were the people.

He talked to everyone in the same way. He was unable to adjust his manner of speech. Someone said that he used to seduce those in «power,» like the artists of old. But for him power was in the hands of everyone, of anyone who wanted something from him.
Out of this arose his special relationship with his clients. Pleased to have met them, he dedicated his work to them, increased his efforts threefold for them, for the sake of beauty. But he did not listen to them. They ended up happy, if they entered the land of Gio Ponti. Some of them wanted to stay outside, in the name of non-design as a form of freedom.
We grew up in beautiful houses entirely designed by him. We lived in them in the Ponti style — in rooms without doors, amidst his pictures and books — in total enchantment. And only his Giulia broke down the beautiful design with her beautiful disorder. She glued family photographs on the walls, ignoring his «organized panels.» She introduced odd plates into Ponti's perfect table settings. She used to sleep in the daytime as well, during the hours when everyone else was full of zeal. She never turned on any of the «self-illuminating» pieces of furniture, so that the shadows grew in the evening, allowing her to think. In the last months of his life Gio Ponti imitated her.

Many friends acknowledged Gio Ponti's generosity. Only a few, but an extraordinary few, were generous and demanding with him — like Daria Guarnati and Mollino. And even, toward the end, the anti-Pontian Zevi, who reproached him.
Mollino: Ponti brought him «the esteem of the world» (as Mollino used to say). Ponti gave him a lot of space in *Stile* (and later in *Domus*) and Mollino gave him great works. And not just works but the best of his thoughts, with his enthusiasm for «unification,» the dream of *Stile* in 1944, and above all his criticism of Ponti himself — Mollino protested loudly about how *Stile* was produced and about some of Ponti's own works. Mollino's criticism of *Coro*, a booklet by Ponti, in a letter written in 1944, is an example of sharpness of eye and mind: here criticism was made keener by friendship, not blunted. Mollino's expression, «let it be said with admiration» (at the beginning of any criticism), was adopted by Ponti, who repeated it for years.

It was difficult to duel with Gio Ponti, who did not duel. Zevi tried. He wanted from Ponti, seriously and in jest, the «masterpiece» of his old age; not a masterpiece of youth, but one of senility, even a small one, maybe just a chair (and yet neither he nor Gio Ponti realized what a «little masterpiece» was the chair designed in 1971, nor did Zevi notice Taranto Cathedral). What Zevi wanted from Ponti was a small but «difficult» masterpiece, something that Ponti was unable to produce.

Zevi even seemed to regret an ideal encounter between the intellects of those generations. For Ponti, however, encounters were only a «recognition» that did not lead to a modification. They could lead to friendship (as one did between Ponti and Rogers, toward the end of their lives — the Elysian Fields), or to a total detachment, of the sort Ponti always felt with regard to his «so-called enemies.»

A detachment, because the real battle over design was the one that he waged with himself. He did not regret his many works of architecture that were never built («architectural scores,» Mollino said) as much as a mistake in one that was built (he used to turn his head away when passing one of them). He did not suffer much if one of his buildings was scheduled for destruction (there was talk of demolishing the Tower in the Park, years ago) or if one of them showed the effects of the passing of time (indeed, he hated the idea of restoration, which was based on a lack of confidence in the new, and even on a lack of trust in chance). He thought in a different way. He knew what his gifts were. And it was not enough to be grateful. He had to respond — with his fine profession, that of architect.

[1] Vincenzo Agnetti.
[2] Alessandro Mendini.

Lisa Licitra Ponti
Milan, Fall 1989

Gio Ponti receives the Laurea Honoris Causa at the Royal College of Art, London, 1968.

Richard-Ginori factory, Doccia, 1923—25: blue and gold porcelain plate, diam. 23 cm.

The twenties: «the classical conversation»

Gio Ponti was an architect who started out with ceramics. It should be said straightaway: being an architect was not one aspect of his versatility, versatility was one aspect of his being an architect, owing to the all-encompassing sense that he gave to architecture («In each different thing there is always the same process and the same hand»).[1]

Right from the start, he got involved in both design and promotion. He was not afraid of luxury or of mass production. For quality lies in form, and it can be spread around. Indeed, it has to be. And at once. These were the roots of both his enthusiasm and his detachment.

This can be seen in his first major assignment: from 1923 to 1930 the young Ponti was art director of the Richard-Ginori factory, and he made a complete change in its output. The famous «Grand Pieces,» as well as the minor ones, of the «Ponti period» at Richard-Ginori were all inspired by the idea of quality in industrial production. («Industry is the *style* of the 20th century, its mode of creation» wrote Ponti in the catalog of the Paris Expo, 1925, where his porcelain won the Grand Prix.)

Thus the «luxury furniture» that Ponti designed in these years was paralleled by his low-cost furniture for the department store La Rinascente (the «Domus Nova»[2] series, 1927). And he would show both kinds (his own pieces and those of other designers) at the great exhibitions of the time (the Biennali and Triennali in Monza, the Venice Biennale).

Industry, mass production, distribution, advertising, exhibitions, magazines. An exciting sequence, at that time. Ponti brought the «art industries» into contact with each other (Christofle with Venini). He got architects and manufacturers to go into partnership (in «Il Labirinto,»[3] 1927). He presented designers and designs in the exhibitions he staged. He published them in the magazine he founded.

The magazine was *Domus*. It was born, in 1928, at the suggestion of the great journalist Ugo Ojetti,[4] the Florentine patron of the young Ponti in those years (later they would courteously drift apart). It was set up almost as a joke, as a «Milanese improvisation» (and was to remain such). It was, at the outset, a vehicle for Italian neoclassical «domestic» culture, and Ponti used it to fight his battles: «almost won, against the fake antique» and «still to be won, against the ugly modern.»[5] The publisher was Gianni Mazzocchi, even younger than Ponti — they were to work together for years.

Ponti met the «applied arts» first, before architecture. His first house in Milan, the one on Via Randaccio, dates from 1925. It was immediately followed by his first construction abroad, the Villa Bouilhet at Garches, Paris. They are his two most typical works of architecture:[6] the roots of their design are neoclassical, their layout innovative.

We say «neoclassical» today. Ponti would say «of classical inspiration, owing to the enormous impression made on me by living, while resting from the front during the war, in buildings by Palladio, and seeing as many of them as I could.»[7] It was a «non-programmatic starting point» which was never to disappear, even though the forms did vanish.

During these years, from 1926 to 1933, Ponti was in partnership with the architect Emilio Lancia.

Gio Ponti in Milan, 1922.

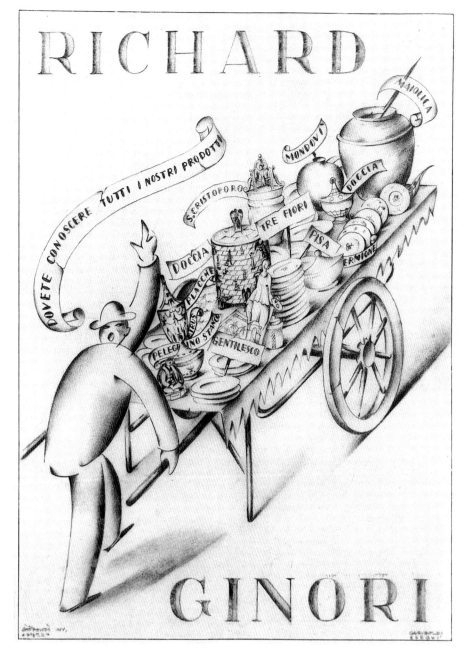

Richard-Ginori advertisement in *Domus*, 1928.

Porcelain and pottery for Richard-Ginori, 1923—30

When the Richard-Ginori company won the Grand Prix at the Paris Expo of 1925 («Exposition Internationale des Arts Décoratifs et Industriels Modernes»),[1] the young Ponti had been «artistic director» for two years and had revolutionized the firm's entire output. (There were two Italian high spots at this Expo, Ponti's small neoclassical room and Prampolini's futurist room: both made a great impression on the French critics, while ignoring one another.)[2]

There were two sides to the «Ponti period» in the modern history of Richard-Ginori. At the Richard-Ginori factory in Doccia, Ponti not only designed (for the «skillful hands» of that time) the famous «Great Pieces of Art for Museums and Collections» but also organized its whole output into «families of pieces» (from the large to the very small), pushing it in the direction of mass production. In the same spirit Ponti brought out the first complete catalog of «Richard-Ginori Modern Art Ceramics» (with texts

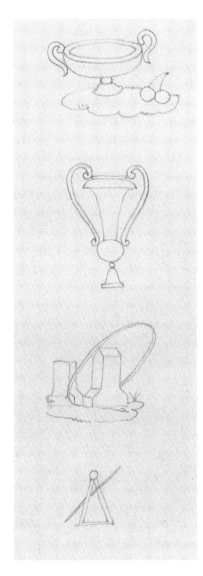

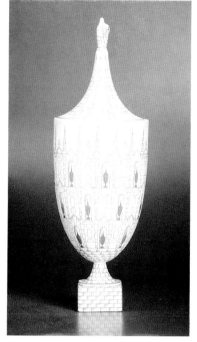

Richard-Ginori factory, Doccia, porcelain, 1923—25, and drawings. *Above, from the top:* «Serliana» urn, *h* 50 cm, «Triumphus Amori» urn, *h* 50 cm. *Center, from the top:* «Sfida» plate, diam. 23 cm, «La passeggiata archeologica» plate, diam. 35.5 cm. *Left, from the top:* «Documenta,» pencil drawings, 1924 (A.G.P.), and sketch for Richard-Ginori.

in Italian and English),[3] designed the advertisements for Richard-Ginori products in Domus in 1928, promoted Richard-Ginori's participation in the great exhibitions of the time, and created opportunities for the use of ceramics in major works of «interior decoration.» This was Ponti's approach to collaboration with industry, and it was to remain this way for the whole of his life. He brought to it both enthusiasm and detachment. (In the same way his «neoclassicism» concealed a secret joke: angels carried golf bags through his mazes.[4])

Carlo Zerbi and Luigi Tazzini, managers of the Doccia factory when Ponti joined the company, were the first people to receive the urgent «written/drawn letters» that were to shower onto all his future collaborators (they are his finest letters, free of deference and sentiment). They contained such instructions as «let the execution be expressive, and perfect and beautiful» and, for the vases, «let the architecture graze the clouds a little, it doesn't look bad: all the rest is fine.» Or «copies should be made at once,» «reproductions of the pieces sold in Paris have to be very faithful and accurate: it is for the honor of our firm,» and «have all the new pieces photographed: we will send the pictures to Ojetti, to Paris and Monza: it is worth keeping a series or two for Maraini, who might write some articles for English and American magazines: have you read today's Corriere»?[5]

Among the collections of the Museo delle Porcellane di Doccia in Sesto Fiorentino are four hundred pieces from the «Ponti period,» part of the fifth period in the history of the factory. Ponti was to renew his collaboration later on during the thirties (when he was still able to rely on the «skillful hands» of Elena Diana) and again in the forties and fifties.

Right, «L'angelo giuocante,» 1930 (designed for a golf tournament at the Villa Reale in Monza, during the 4th Milan Triennale).
Below, Richard-Ginori porcelain, 1923–25: «Le sirene» plates, diam. 23.5 cm, and ashtrays, diam. 8 cm.

Left and below, two of the Richard-Ginori «grand pieces,» 1923—30, at the Doccia factory: «La conversazione classica,» porcelain vase, *h* 57 cm, and «La casa degli efebi,» majolica vase, *h* 81 cm. *Bottom*, «Alato» and «Celesio,» porcelain goblets, *h* 19 cm, and «Le quattro stagioni,» porcelain plates, diam. 23 cm.

Above and right, a one-off piece of Richard-Ginori pottery from 1922: a teapot for Ugo and Friquette Ritter (it has two bases, and can be placed in two positions). *Below*, Richard-Ginori porcelain, 1923–30: *in the first row*, five vases «con piume,» *h* 29.5 cm in white, blue and gold, and two plates «con rovine,» diam. 23 cm, in white, gold, violet, and gray; *in the second row*, three «Venatoria» plates, diam. 31 cm, in white, blue and gold, and two «Carmen» plates, diam. 23 cm.

Richard-Ginori factory, Doccia: «Prospettica,» majolica vase, *h* 52 cm.

House at no. 9, Via Randaccio, Milan, 1925

The house on Via Randaccio was Gio Ponti's first house in Milan, and it was also the first of the four houses that he «designed and lived in.» A small «Palladian» monument, the house has a fan-shaped plan, a concave facade «with obelisks,» suites of rooms almost «without corridors,» and an out-of-scale staircase, designed to be viewed from below as well.

Right, side view, from Via Randaccio, in a photograph taken in 1925, and scketch of the facade. *Below*, plans of ground floor and second floor. From the ground floor apartment there is an exit into the front garden.

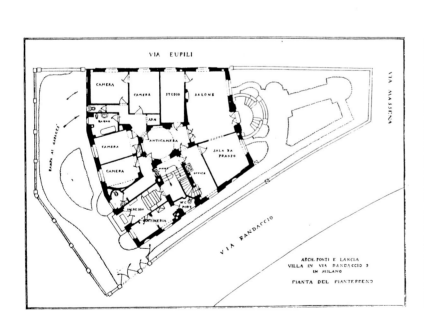

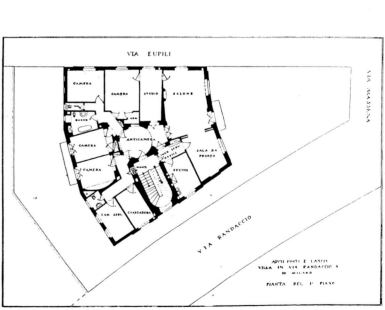

The concave facade, overlooking the front garden, in a photograph taken in 1925.

The entrance hall.

INGRESSO PRINCIPALE

❖ *CASA IN VIA RANDACCIO 9 · MILANO* ❖

❖ *USCITA CON TERRAZZO SUL GIARDINO* ❖

House at no. 9, via Randaccio. *In the drawings*, the entrance from the back garden, and the exit into the front garden. *In the photographs*, the obelisks on the facade; the profile of the steps of the grand staircase.

Villa Bouilhet, Garches (Paris), 1926

«L'Ange Volant» was the name that Ponti gave (after the initial one of «La Saint-Cloudienne») to the «Italian» villa he designed for Tony Bouilhet[1] and built at Garches, outside Paris in the vicinity of Saint-Cloud's Golf Club (a place that seemed to stimulate architectural events in those years: from Le Corbusier's villa for «the four Americans in Paris» — Gertrude, Leo, Michael, and Sarah Stein — to Perret's villa for Numar Bey).
This villa was the first house that Gio Ponti built abroad. The central hall is two stories high and contains the stairs (a motif that Ponti would return to over the years). Its painted ceiling (designed by Ponti) is a sort of «large colored tent» suspended over the room.

The facade overlooking the garden, in a photograph taken in 1926 and, *right*, a sketch.

36

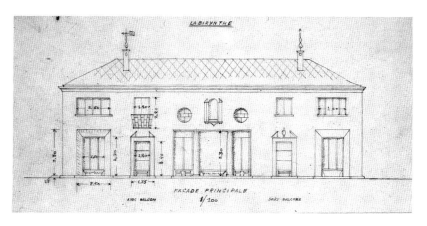
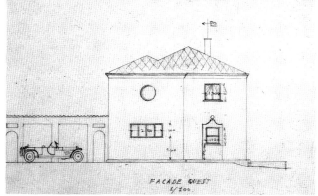

Front and side elevation with garages.

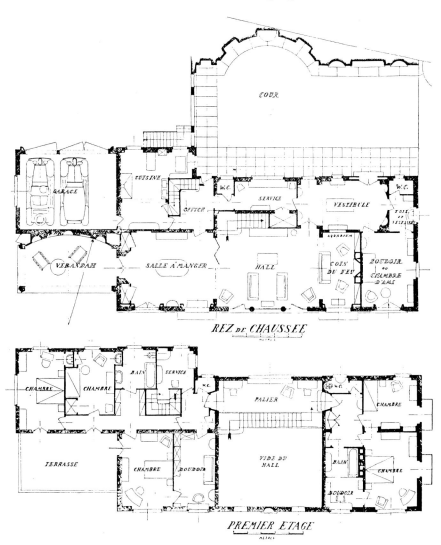

Plans of ground floor and second floor: the hall is two stories high.

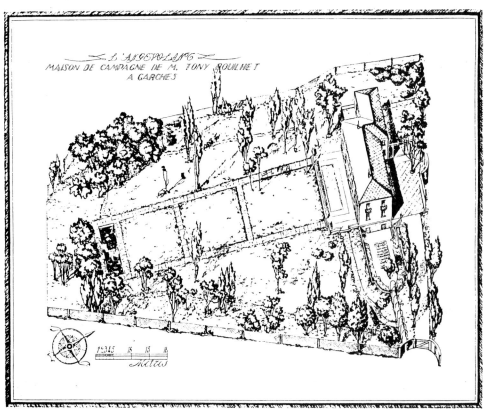

«L'Ange Volant,» country house for M. Tony H. Bouilhet at Garches, Paris. The facade has a long view over the formal garden, concluding in a swimming pool (see general plan).

Sketch by Gio Ponti for the staircase in the hall, and, *below left*, detail of the painted ceiling, over the hall. *Below*, the entrance hall.

39

Richard-Ginori stand at the Milan Trade Fair, 1928, and pavilion of the Printing Industries at the Milan Trade Fair, 1927, with Emilio Lancia. Immediately published in the magazine *Architettura e Arti Decorative*.

Large, «highly ornate» table made of aluminum presented at the 4th Monza Triennale, 1930 («The Montecatini company has promoted this splendid presentation of aluminum to demonstrate, as well as its well-known properties of lightness and strength, the great esthetic possibilities it offers»). Execution: Volontè, Milan.

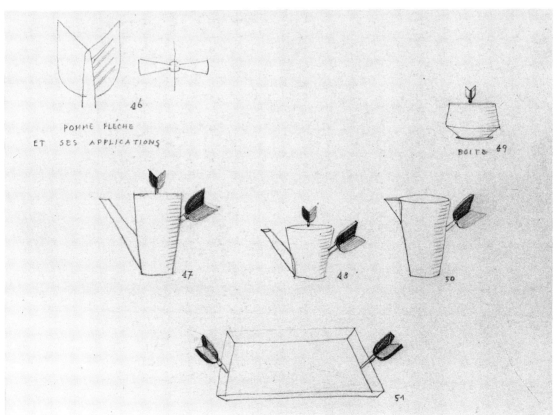

Top, «Mirrors and arrows,» Venini and Christofle pieces at the 16th Venice Biennale, 1928.
Above, designs for Christofle, 1926 (A.G.P.).

DIS. 8.

Drawing of facade for a bank, 1926 (A.G.P.).

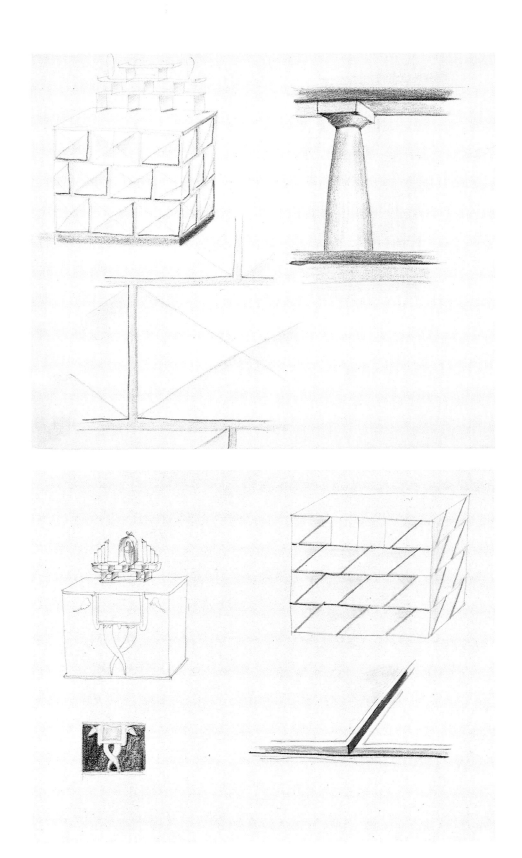

Furniture designs, 1926 (A.G.P.).

Furniture in walnut for the Schejola apartment, Milan, 1929.

Preliminary sketch for the Rotunda in the central pavilion at the
16th Venice Biennale, 1928.

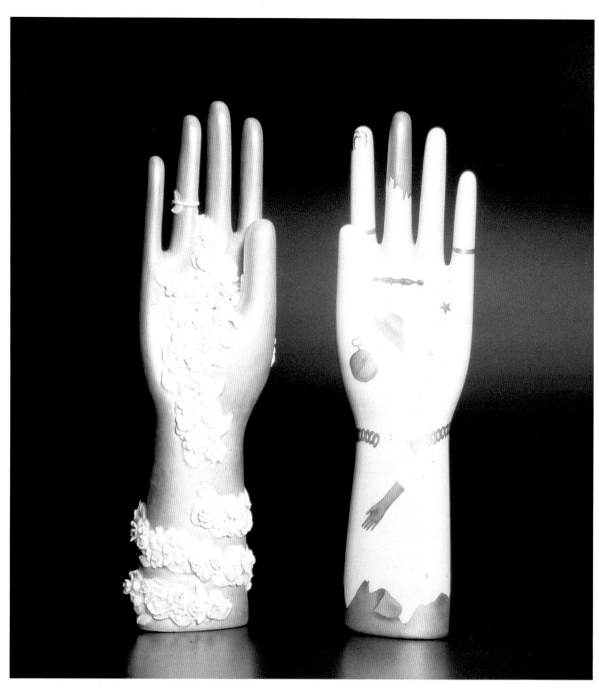

Richard-Ginori factory, Doccia, 1925—35: «Mani,» *h* 34 cm.

The thirties: the great themes

At the 4th Triennial Exhibition in Monza, in 1930, it was the «Palladian» Gio Ponti who promoted the «Electric House» designed by the young rationalists Figini and Pollini,[1] while he himself was represented by the «neoclassical» Vacation House.[2] That was how Gio Ponti worked.

During this great and controversial decade for Italian architecture, the young Ponti went straight into the eye of the storm, with *Domus* and the Triennali (the 5th Triennial Exhibition, in 1933, was «his»). His design was innovative but he stayed on the sidelines of the theoretical and political debate (perhaps this is where his innate neoclassicism lies). His admiration was for the «individual artists» (from Terragni to de Chirico) and his interest lay, at the same time, in «custom.» This is how it would always be. He himself appeared to be, in these years, a multiplicity of individual artists, proceeding (he would say) «by ramblings and by chance occurrences» as well. He worked in Milan, Rome, Padua and Vienna. Milan provided him with great private opportunities: from «domestic» architecture (the «Typical houses» or «Domus,» 1931—36) to designing «for industry» (first Montecatini Building, 1936, building and fittings) to a case of industrial design on an architectural scale like the steel tower in the park (Torre Littoria), 1933. Rome provided him with great public occasions: the first major competitions lost («Palazzo del Littorio» or Fascist Headquarters, 1936, Foreign Ministry, 1939), commissions that came to nothing (a preliminary master plan for Addis Ababa, with Vaccaro and Del Debbio, 1936, a «House of Italy» in Buenos Aires, 1937) and two successes (the School of Mathematics at the new university campus, 1934, and the Exhibition of the Catholic Press in the Vatican, 1936). Padua gave him the opportunity to build the memorable «atrium» of the Liviano (the seat of the Faculty of Letters at the University of Padua) in 1937, a space he devised for Campigli's vast fresco and Martini's huge sculpture, in accordance with the idea of «grand decoration.» Vienna brought him back to domesticity (with the furnishings for the Fürstenberg Palace) and seemed to teach him, through its architects, the value of «architecture without an architect.» With the Austrian architect Bernard Rudofsky, Ponti developed his «Mediterranean» design in these years.

From 1933 to 1945 Gio Ponti was in partnership with the engineers Antonio Fornaroli and Eugenio Soncini.

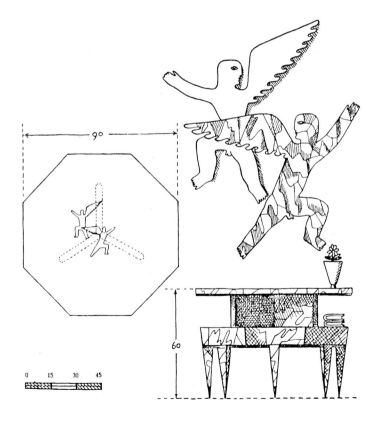

Design for a small table in walnut and bronze with inlaid work, 1930.

Furniture and objects for the Fontana firm, Milan, from 1930

For Gio Ponti crystal was the material for objects of «great luxury.» («Luxury» puts the designer's skills to no less of a test than the «economic.»)

In 1930 Gio Ponti designed for Fontana the large table with black crystal top and cut crystal legs that was presented at the 4th Triennial Exhibition in Monza.[1] In 1931 Ponti began to design for Fontana a series of pieces of furniture topped with mirrors, «exceptional furniture,»[2] together with the first totally transparent ones made «entirely of glass.»[3] In the spring of 1933 Ponti took over, along with Pietro Chiesa, the artistic direction of «Fontana Arte,» a branch of the Fontana firm. And the Fontana Arte output began to expand (as had happened with Richard-Ginori), producing a multitude of large and small objects, from paperweights to lamps. At the same time he gave Fontana Arte the opportunity (again as with Richard-Ginori) to produce «major works,» such as the stained-glass walls he designed for the Faculty of Mathematics at Rome University, 1934, and for the Exhibition of the Catholic Press in the Vatican, 1936.[4]

Above left, large cup in black crystal with polygonal base of engraved mirrors, 1930.
Above, dressing-table for Margherita Sarfatti, in curved and colored crystal with mirror finish, mountings in nickel silver, 1932.

Lamp with crystal disks, and two wall mirrors, 1933, for Fontana Arte.

Drawing of furniture for the Contini-Bonacossi apartment, Florence, 1931.

«The Agreement,» a 1933 drawing.
Below, «Amazon,» oil, 1931.

51

Borletti Chapel in the Cimitero Monumentale, Milan, 1931

This is a small work, one of Ponti's favorites. He described it as his first step away from an «architecture d'après l'architecture.»[1] He liked the two angels on the facade, a high-relief by Libero Andreotti. The building is faced, inside and out, with marble; bronze doors, travertine altar, gold mosaic ceiling.

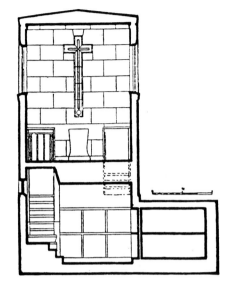

Below left the two angel s by Libero Andreotti, in white marble, above the doors of bronze with a green patina. The Crystal cross is by Pietro Chiesa. The outer facing is of gray marble. *Below right*, the crypt, in travertine.

House at no. 1, Via Domenichino, Milan, 1930

This is the first of Ponti's strongly colored facades, typical of his Milanese houses of the thirties (the «Domuses,» 1931—33, Casa Marmont, 1934). Ponti's favorite colors: red, ocher, green, yellow. There's always an interplay between the colored and the white parts of the facade. Here the plaster is red, with white horizontal fascias. The gazebo on top of the building is red and white. The building has a travertine socle.
The project was by Gio Ponti and Emilio Lancia.

In the plan, the ground floor. *Left*, the gazebo.

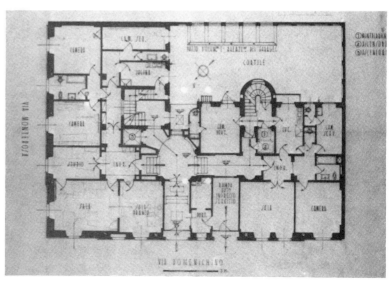

Embroidered silk fabrics, for Vittorio Ferrari, Milan, 1930 and 1933 (A.G.P.).

Project for «an apartment house in town,» 1931

Ponti: «when the plot of land is deep, and the street front narrow, each apartment can be laid out on two floors.» Here each apartment has the living- and dining-rooms and the parents' bedroom on one floor (with higher ceilings), and the children's rooms and services on the other (with lower ceilings). There are separate entrances, one for each floor, and large front windows with verandas.»

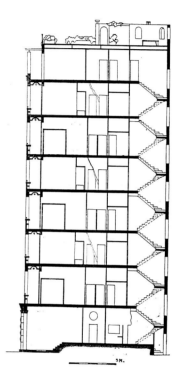

In the section, the difference in height between the two floors of each apartment is evident. *In the plans,* the high-ceilinged floor of the living-rooms and the low-ceilinged floor of the bedrooms. The facade is in red plaster, with socle and doorway in stone, verandahs in white plaster, yellow drapes.

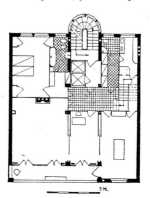 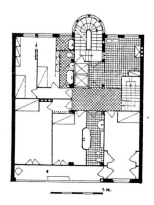

55

«Domuses,» or «Typical houses,» Milan, 1931—36

These consist of ten apartment houses, each of which has a name: Domus Julia, Domus Carola, Domus Fausta, Domus Serena, Domus Aurelia, Domus Onoria, Domus Livia, Domus Flavia, Domus Adele, and Domus Alba. The «Domuses» of Via De Togni (Julia, Carola, Fausta), like the «Domuses» of Via Letizia (Livia, Serena, Onoria, Aurelia) were designed to create, when lined up, a unitary «road scene,» a stretch of street, colored «in the Italian manner» (ocher, green, yellow and red facades). And the apartments have innovative layouts (concentration of service areas «to increase living space;» built-in closets and facilities, to «free the space from furniture»). These innovations were intended for use in ordinary housing: elements to be adopted «in the building of a happy city of the future.» This was the whole point.

Ponti indicated other «elements to be adopted» in other Milanese houses that he designed (the Rasini, Marmont and Laporte houses): roof terraces, loggias on the facade, and, above all, an «out-of-scale» room in every apartment: «a man wants to have, in at least one room of the house, a wall five or six meters away from him and, if possible, a ceiling at least four meters high....»[1]

Gio Ponti always thought in terms of repeatability; in his designs for housing he never envisaged a scale for others that he would not have desired for himself. His Existenz-minimum *demanded space, even if only visual, rather than objects.*

The apartments he was to design in the future grew ever smaller but increasingly spacious in visual terms: apartments with sliding partitions (opening up perspectives), with furniture on castors (that rolled away out of sight) and with more books than pieces of furniture, in any case. «The true luxury in the home, the one for which it is worth making the greatest sacrifices, and the one that is a true measure of our sensitivity and intelligence, is the work of art. Those who don't have the feeling for it, should leave their walls blank.»[2]

Details of the «Domuses»: a balcony and a facade of two Domuses on Via Letizia.

56

The fronts of three «Domuses» on Via Letizia, in a photograph taken in 1937. Colors: ocher, white, red.

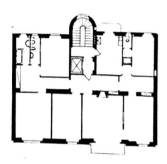

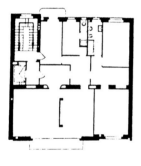

The «Domuses,» or «Typical houses» in Milan, 1931—36. The fronts on Via De Togni, in two photographs taken in 1933. Colors: green, red, yellow. *In the plans*, a typical floor of the Domus Carola (seven rooms) and a typical floor of the Domus Fausta (six rooms).

Interiors of the «Domuses» on Via De Togni: the dining and living areas.

Ceramic panels for the Ferrario Tavern, Milan, 1932

An all-over ceramic facing, in this restaurant. Red and gold figurations on an ivory background (ceramic tiles by the Richard-Ginori factory, San Cristoforo). Ponti was a promoter of the «incorruptible»[1] ceramic facing. In fact, these wall panels, however mutilated, are what still remains of the once famous «Ferrario Tavern,» the restaurant of Milan Stock Exchange (the building, by Paolo Mezzanotte, is now under restoration). Note also the light fittings (red and white glass pipes).
In the same year Ponti also designed the colored ceramic walls of the entrance-hall in the Ministero delle Corporazioni (by Piacentini) in Rome.

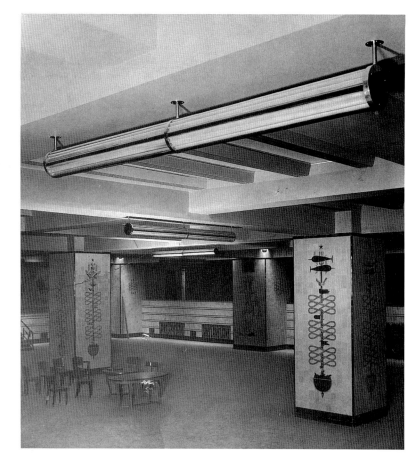

Breda electric train ETR 200, 1933

A prototype of the new, very fast, Breda electric train (ETR 200) was presented at the 5th Triennale in 1933. For the first time in Italy, two architects had been involved in a train's design. They were Pagano and Ponti. Pagano was responsible for the exterior: the engineer's cab, with its triangular front, has a perfectly streamlined shape. Ponti designed the interior: coaches without compartments, high adjustable seats with head rests, like in aircraft, bright colors (first class was green).[1] This first design led to another one later on,[2] in 1935: this time the designers were Gio Ponti and Paolo Masera and their contribution was more limited. They proposed using linoleum on the walls: why not have trains with totally colored interiors (the first class green, the second blue, the third Havana-brown, or the first red and the second green)?[3]

Torre Littoria in the park, Milan, 1933

The little masterpiece of the «Torre Littoria,» erected in 1933 in the record time of two and a half months, has been out of commission since 1972, and is now «restructured.» The Torre Littoria — which Persico immediately categorized as «architecture»[1] — was erected in the Parco Sempione for the 5th Triennale, close to the six great temporary arches designed by Sironi. It is a tall prism, 108.60 meters high, with almost no tapering («an arrow thrust into the ground from above»), built, by Dalmine, entirely out of steel tubing (instead of the customary section irons) joined together by electric welding.

At the base, the hexagon formed by the six tubular uprights of the main structure has sides six meters in length. At a height of 100 meters, the sides are still 4.45 meters long. At a height of 97 meters a platform supports the cabin of the restaurant, the upper belvedere and the lantern. A smaller hexagonal tower within the main structure (the elevator cage) supports a spiral staircase. The tower is moored in a cylindrical foundation block, six meters in depth.

Design by Gio Ponti, structural calculations by the engineers Cesare Chiodi and Ettore Ferrari.

The temporary arches by Sironi, at the
5th Milan Triennale, 1933.

Casa Rasini, Milan, 1933

After this project the two designers, Ponti and Lancia, split up. And there was already some distance between them in this building, made up of two distinct blocks: there is perhaps more of Lancia in the «tower» (except for the stepped terraces of the top floors, a typical Pontian solution) and more of Ponti in the cubic «villa.»[1]

Over the years this «group of houses,» as Ponti called it, has become a symbol of Milanese architecture in the thirties, almost a small «piece of city» in which the opposing tendencies of the time (the «novecento» and the «razionale») were brought together. In these years the magazines carried pictures[2] of the «tower» that conveyed a metaphysical image of the deserted architectural pergolas on the top floor (Savinio, 1944: «up here there is an air of the gods»[3]); but Ponti wanted them populated in the Mediterranean fashion — with awnings, parasols, trees, flowers — in short, happily lived in.

The terraces at the top of the tower. *Far left*, a complete view, with the main block in white marble and the brick tower.

«Lighter-than-air» room at the Aeronautics Exhibition, Milan, 1934

A large number of Italian architects took part in the memorable «Mostra dell'Aeronautica» in Milan, organized by Pagano and Felice at the Palazzo dell'Arte (site of the Triennale). Gio Ponti designed the «lighter-than-air» room: nothing standing on the ground, walls lined with silvered canvas for airships, hanging models.

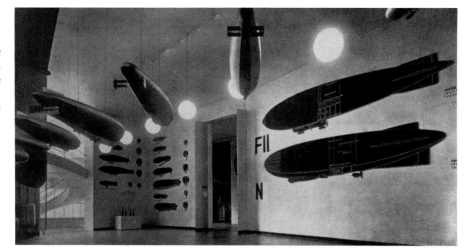

«Italcima» Factory, Milan, 1935

Luciano Baldessari and Gio Ponti collaborated on this small building, immediately singled out (in Casabella[1]) as a «very fine example» of what can happen when architects are entrusted with the design of industrial buildings.

In the drawing, the block at the back. *Below*, one of the entrances to the building.

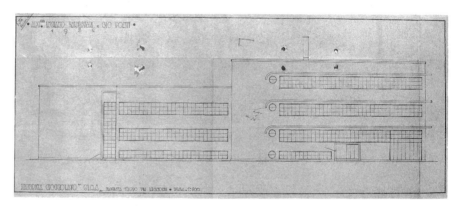

Casa Marmont, Milan, 1934

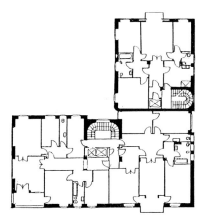

All the houses designed by Gio Ponti in Milan in these years were intended as «demonstrations» — demonstrations of the possibility of a «pleasant» urban architecture (unpleasant buildings are the result of a moral shortcoming, not an economic one: they derive from a lack of thought). For this reason Ponti liked to present his projects himself, when they were published (in Domus), so that he could point out the «aims» achieved (he never spoke of «form»).

About this house, the one he liked best, he said: look at the plans, look at the basements, look at the porter's lodge, look above all at the top two floors, treated as if they were a single terraced «villa» («today the privileged floor is the top floor... it is necessary for more dwellings to reach the roof...»).[1]

The facade is in red plaster with white bands. *In the plan*, a typical floor.

School of Mathematics at the new university campus, Rome, 1934

At the invitation of Piacentini,[1] some of «the best young architects from every region of Italy» contributed to the plans for the new University of Rome, designed to provide facilities for twelve thousand students and inaugurated on 31 October 1935. Ponti was one of the young architects invited. The feature of his non-monumental project that he liked to draw attention to was the use of separate blocks: a rectangular block for Pure Mathematics, with a library and lecture halls, two curved wings for the two technical drawing rooms, and a tower for the three lecture theaters. Above all he liked the tower, in which the profile of the three superimposed windows was the same as that of the theaters. The engineer Zadra collaborated on the structure.[2]

Aerial view of the School of Mathematics, at one end of the university campus, Rome: in the foreground, the curved tower block containing the lecture theaters. *Top and on opposite page*: views of the tower block.

67

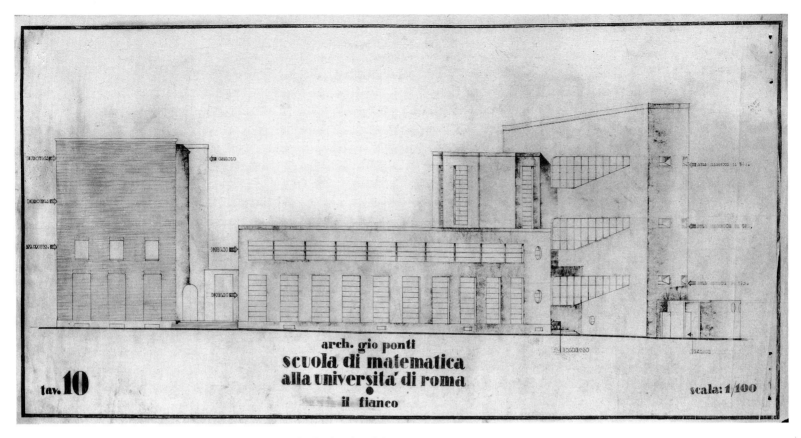

arch. gio ponti
**scuola di matematica
alla università di roma**
il fianco

tav. **10**

scala: 1/100

School of Mathematics at the university campus, Rome, 1934. In the drawings *below*,
plan of the reinforced concrete piling, and structural scheme of the tower block.

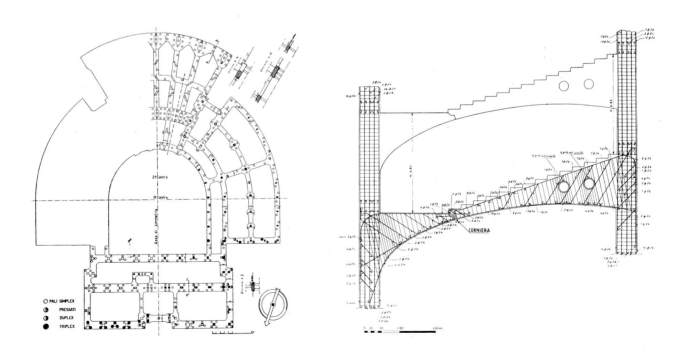

In the library, linoleum floorings, iron shelves painted red and white. The stained-glass window is to a design by Gio Ponti, executed by Fontana Arte. *Bottom*, the internal court.

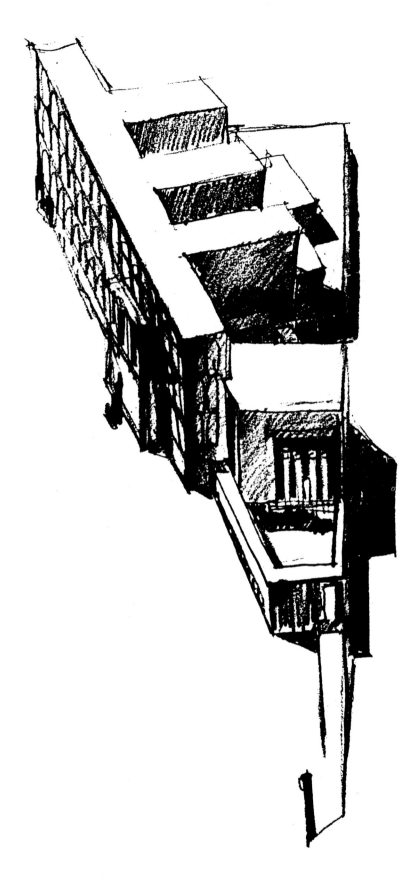

Competition project for the «Palazzo del Littorio,» Rome, 1934

The idea: «not just another sort of ministry,» «not a monumental facade with clerks behind its windows, but a group of buildings, each with its own function.» Almost «a small city, an island of buildings, separated from the city traffic by ramparts and grassy areas: within the island the two traffic systems, for pedestrians and automobiles, are independent... the high-rise office blocks are set on top of porticos, allowing the public free movement in all directions on the level.»[1] The idea Ponti used for this «Palazzo del Littorio» seems to anticipate some of his much later projects (Anton Bruckner Cultural Center in Linz, 1961,[2] Administrative Center in Munich, 1970): break down the whole into its different constituent elements, make them into separate buildings, each of them immediately recognizable («each element is displayed in its true and unique form»[2]) and set them on a platform that isolates them from the conditions, dimensions and influences of the surroundings. (In this project, the separate buildings are: the office block, the block of the «Exhibition of the Revolution,» the block of the «Domus Lictoria.») It was a solution that «liberated» Ponti from the influence of the site (the Forum) — an influence that hampered Pagano[3] and inspired Terragni.[4] In spite of its theme, Ponti's was not a stately design, and was unconcerned with the intense ideological debate of that time.

Left, distribution of masses, in a variant.

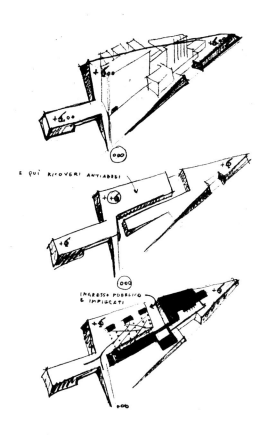

E PUI RICOVERI ANTIAEREI

INGRESSO PUBBLICO E IMPIEGATI

In the schemes *above*, the basic principles of the project: «isolating the plot» (by raising its level), «traversing the plot» (the roads descend across a sloping plaza onto Via dell'Impero), and «lifting the office blocks» (on porticos, for pedestrian traffic). *Right*, sketch of the Domus Lictoria. *Below*, plans of the ground floor level.

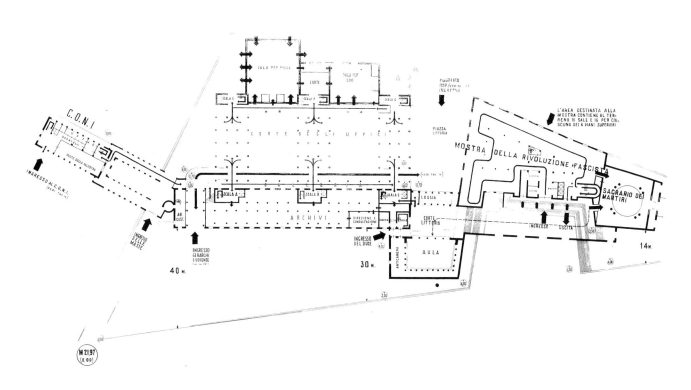

Standard for the Ospedale Maggiore in Milan, 1935

Just as he did with ceramics, Gio Ponti designed for the «skillful hands»[1] of embroideresses. This «monumental embroidery» (produced by the Bertarelli workshop in Milan) is a large standard made of red and silver silk, embroidered with gold thread in high-relief, and studded with gems. The red side bears the image of the Annunciation (symbol of the Hospital), the silver side the coats of arms of the charitable institutions of the Hospital and of Cardinals, Popes, and the Knights of the Holy Sepulchre (who had the privilege of carrying the standard, on two silver staffs, at grand ceremonies).

This standard later prompted another «monumental embroidery» in gold on silk, the standard presented to the University of Trieste by the University of Padua in 1938. The work was carried out by the embroideresses of Pia di Valmarana.

The Knights of the Holy Sepulchre holding up the Standard: the names of donors are engraved on the silver staffs.

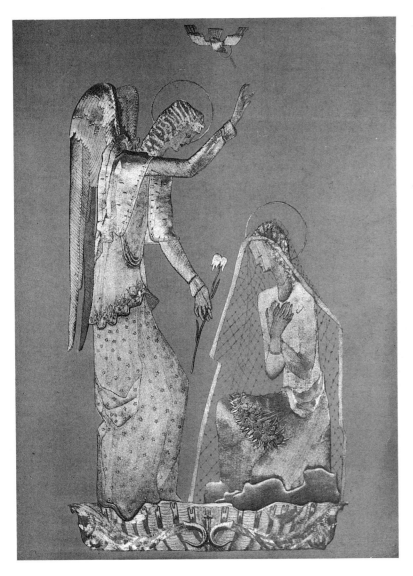

72

Richard-Ginori factory, Doccia, «Dafne si sente divenir pianta» porcelain plate, 1930.

Richard-Ginori factory, 1929—30. *Above*, pottery flower vases from San Cristoforo.
Top, porcelain ashtrays from Doccia.

Stainless-steel flatware for Krupp Italiana, Milan, 1936, at the 6th Milan Triennale.

Office of the chairman of the Ferrania company, Rome, 1936.

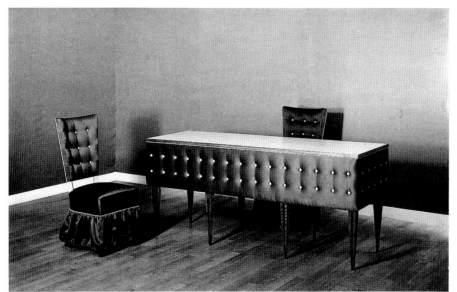

Interiors of the Fürstenberg Palace, Vienna, 1936

In arranging the interiors of the Fürstenberg Palace in Vienna (for the Italian Cultural Institute) Ponti chose his own way of commenting, in a light and detached manner, on the old architecture of the building.

But his ties with Vienna amounted to more than that. There was a kind of affinity, an affinity that lay more in a way of thinking than in form. His love for domestic architecture and for the «applied arts» was a trait he held in common with the Viennese. Working in Vienna in those years and coming into contact with Hoffmann, Frank, Wlach, Strnad, and Haerdtl, he was most strongly impressed by the Kunstgewerbeschule, the famous school of applied arts, as he had earlier been by the Wiener Werkstätte: he dreamed of having such a school in Italy as well. «I got to know the Vienna of the Secession, of Klimt, Loos,[1] Max Reinhardt.... I owe to these examples of modern perfection of expression my first feeling of a European motherland.»[2] A motherland that he found again (after the Second World War) in what he perceived as the splendid «fragility» of Viennese culture, «ennobled by the presence of a lofty nostalgia and that touch of melancholy that makes things human» (this is what Europe was for him, «sacred to civilization» and equally fragile).[3]

Details of the interiors. *Below*, a chair.

Universal Exhibition of the Catholic Press, Vatican City, 1936

«I have worked at Court.» This is how Ponti described the experience of staging the Universal Exhibition of the Catholic Press in the Vatican. It was Ponti's first work for the Church, the first major Exhibition he was entrusted with, and his first encounter with the Monument.

The Monument (the walls of Julius II, Bramante's great niche of the Pigna, Maderna's seventeenth-century fountain, the colonnade of the Chiaramonti wing) was approached, and in places included, «with detachment»: the ancient surroundings only influenced the «scale.»

The Exhibition was seen as «a work of art whose observer is in movement»: its means of expression were the routes, the through-views and the counterpoint of light and dark. The Church is what prompted Ponti to say (discussing the exhibition in Domus*): «... severe and pure, as if the exhibition were the house 'of a monastic order', the order of the Catholic Press.»[1]*

The heart of the display was the «Salone Maggiore,» or Throne Room, with its tapestries designed by Raphael, flooring of white linoleum and red canopies (Ponti red). And then there were the «devices» that Ponti was to use again later, such as the staircase with the tops of the steps in white marble and their fronts in colored marble (making it white when viewed from above, brightly colored when viewed from below),[2] the sequence of screens like «giant» written pages, and the «perspective with a rising floor.»[3]

(Piacentini said about this exhibition: «here there is everything of Ponti, the dreamer and the mathematician.»[4])

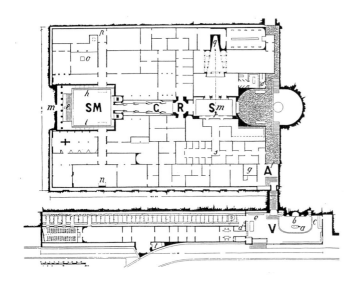

In the plan: SM (main hall, with the Pope's throne); G, central perspective gallery (see photograph, *right*).

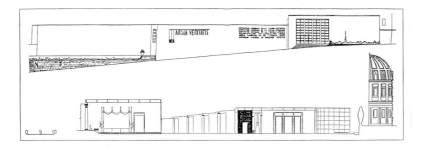

In the main hall, the throne of Pius XI, in gold and white morocco leather, and Raphael's tapestries.

Casa Laporte, Milan, 1936

One of the most significant of Gio Ponti's houses during these years was the one he lived in from 1936 to 1943, Casa Laporte at no. 12, Via Benedetto Brin.

«I go along with Cocteau when he says that the new does not lie in the new form used to express something but in the new way of conceiving it.»[1] Here the new way of conceiving the house (and, at the same time, of preserving the house, that is the pleasure of living in it) is primarily expressed in the large central room two stories in height, onto which faces the winter-garden (a game played with views: seen from above «the human figure is framed in a pleasing manner»[2]). It is expressed in the analogous large terrace on the roof, a «room with the sky for a ceiling,» enclosed by walls and used for many hours a day and many days of the year (and the dress, footwear and habits of the people living in the house are determined by the long time spent on this «patio,» in sandals and bathing costumes). It is expressed in the idea of having bookcases in each room, «built-in» bookcases, and in the use of «beautiful» but inexpensive materials, linoleum, hemp, wood, wicker, and cotton. The Mediterranean and Vienna. «I have learned from Wlach»[3] (the idea for the «very low dining-table» may have come from Oscar Wlach).

The apartment that Gio Ponti and his family lived in was part of a «three-apartment town house.» Facing the road the house has a flat closed front. On the garden side it has an open front with pergolas and terraces.

The roof terrace (see plan), enclosed by walls and covered by retractable awnings, has a small swimming-pool, an expanse of sand, and a small vegetable garden. *Top*, the front on the street.

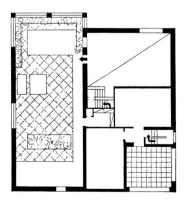

The winter garden, on the level of the roof terrace, opens onto the two-story-high living-room.

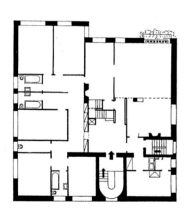

Ponti's apartment on Via Benedetto Brin, Milan, 1936. Two details of the living-room viewed from above. The dining area is visible, *right*: on the wall, a portrait of the Ponti family by Campigli, 1934. *Opposite page*, drawings of the Casa Laporte on Via Brin.

At the 6th Milan Triennale, 1936, Gio Ponti presented in a «demonstrative dwelling», *left*, the principles of which his home on Via Benedetto Brin was a «living demonstration.» This was his method.

Project for a day nursery at Bruzzano, Milan, 1934

Within a rectangular perimeter, «open/covered» spaces, on both levels, counterbalance the «closed» volumes.

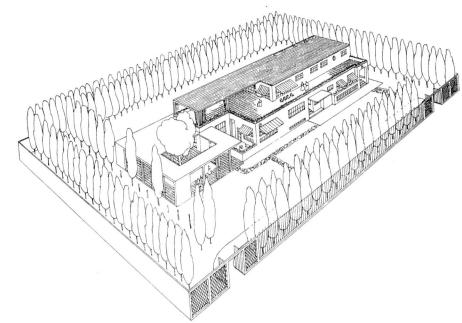

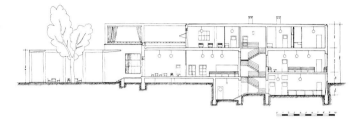

Project for the Villa Marzotto, Valdagno, 1936

A beloved unexecuted project, belonging to the never denied and often re-emerging «neoclassic academicism» of Ponti's design. Villa Marzotto reveals Ponti's «instinctive tension to simplification.»[1] The villa stands between two landscaped gardens: the «garden of the games» and the «garden of the arts.»
The project was by Gio Ponti and Francesco Bonfanti.

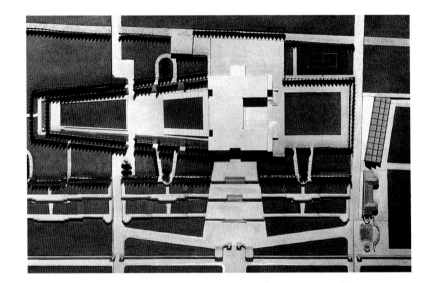

Below, the front overlooking the «garden of arts.»

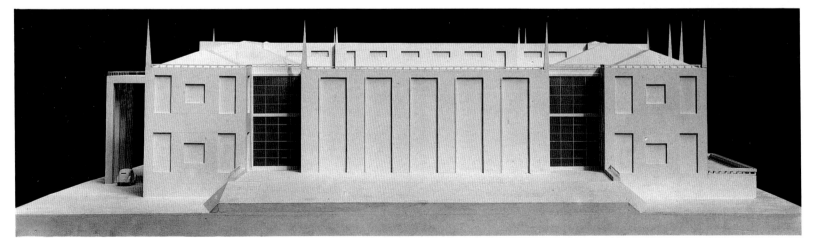

Vanzetti furnishings, Milan, 1938

Some leitmotifs of Ponti's interior design appear in this early work: the slanting cantilevered glass racks (for magazines) and the «organized wall,» as Ponti would call it: the wooden wall of the library includes the bar-desk, the bookshelves....

Below, the bar-library.

First Montecatini Building, Milan, 1936

«The history of modern architecture owes a particular debt to the captains of industry» (Pagano's first comment about this work, 1939).[1] «Industry» is expressed by the building itself: unitary in its module, advanced in its building techniques, pioneering in its installations. The H-shaped plan, suggested by the (difficult) site, expresses the functioning of the building: the managers' offices in the high central block are connected to the employees' offices in the two side blocks (a representation of hierarchy which would not be found in the Pirelli building) and are served by the car-park in the open court at the front. The module on which the building is based (axes of 4.20 m) derives from the uniform size of the steel desks. This permits the use of movable partitions. The module is revealed to the observer by the pattern of windows on the facades.

For the young Ponti the first Montecatini Building was a special opportunity, one that put his brain and his studio (reinforced by two engineers) to the test in a case of «total design» at a high technical level and on a large scale. The intense (and stormy) collaboration between the architect and the client (Guido Donegani, founder and president of the Montecatini company)[2] raised the sights of both, and the building turned out not only to be efficient but to have an image that achieved immediate popularity. The Montecatini «image» is not created by the solemn front (set back, on a minor road) but by the long side wall on the main street. Perfectly level, with frames and windows set flush with the surface, this «impenetrable» wall appears «without thickness» (and already, in the Pontian manner, a sheet reflecting the sky), and the «repetition» in the openings seems, significantly, to be «weightless.»[3] Aligned with the massive facade of the old Montecatini building, this airy wall (Malaparte[4] and Savinio[5] liked it) is an expression of the complete detachment of the two works of architecture. (It is a green and silver wall, made of marble and aluminum, Montecatini materials. About the marble Ponti said «I have had the blocks cross-cut, and I have invented a new kind of marble.» He gave it the name «Tempest.»[6]

The first Montecatini building was described in full by Casabella (130 pages were devoted to it, in 1939).[7]

Record-breaking speed of construction: twenty-three months, from November 1936 to September 1938. Exemplary installations, from the air-conditioning (rare in Italy in those days) to the advanced elevator and telephone systems — and Ponti did not want to «conceal» the «beautiful» plants, but to make them visible and visitable.

Experimental use of aluminum alloys (in the window frames and roofing) and of mosaic grès facings (on the facades around the court). Appliances and fittings all «revised, with enthusiasm»[8] by the designers, or designed by them for the purpose (and destined later for mass production, such as the SVAO sanitary appliances, designed by Ponti). For Ponti, the encounter with Montecatini also meant the beginning of a study of prefabrication: see the Montecatini «ready-made staircases» (designed by Libera, Ponti, Soncini, and Vaccaro).

In the photograph, from the left: first and second Montecatini buildings, 1936 and 1951.

As for the architecture of the building, Gio Ponti expressed doubts about it, years later: to what extent can this building, which relies for its image on a rhythmically «endless» wall, and to which another story was easily added after the war,[9] be called architecture, if architecture is (as in the Pirelli building) «finite form?» The building was subject to the dimensional «constraints» of the site and the building regulations («we should look forward to a kind of city planning in which buildings, independent of frontal alignments, can be unitary, rational, correctly oriented, free from distortions....»[10]

There were two images of this building that were particularly symbolic for Ponti: the foreshortened view of the airy side wall and the interlacing of the colored tubes of the pneumatic dispatch system («my Léger»[11]).

The design of the building was the work of Ponti and the engineers Antonio Fornaroli and Eugenio Soncini (Studio Ponti Fornaroli Soncini), with the collaboration of engineer Pier Giulio Bosisio.

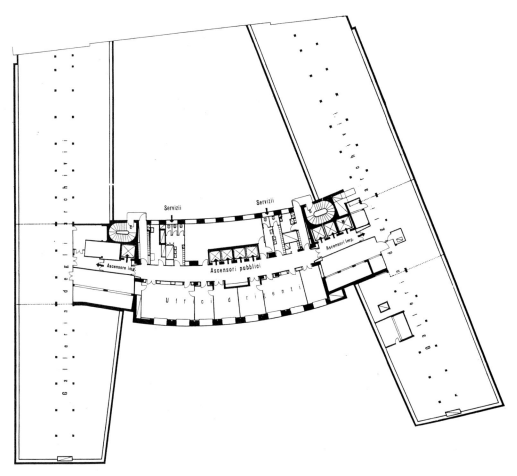

First Montecatini building, 1936. Plan of the eighth floor.

Above, drawing of the aluminum window frames. *Left*, foreshortened view of the side on Via Turati (formerly Via Principe Umberto).

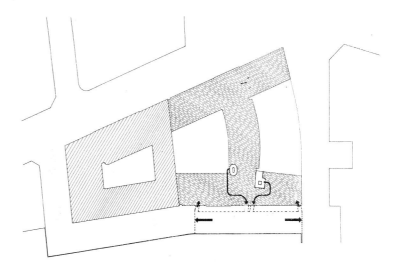

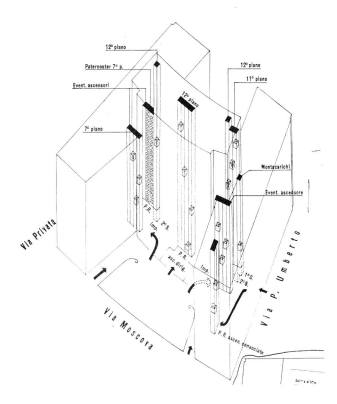

First Montecatini building, 1936. *Above*, scheme of the elevator system. *Below*, sink and faucets designed by Gio Ponti for SVAO; the pneumatic post central; the internal store. *Top right*, the entrance hall; *right*, the aluminum roofing. Photographs taken in 1938.

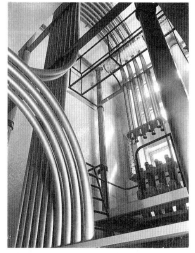

First Montecatini building, 1936: view of the central block.

The Liviano, Padua, 1937

Today in Padua one can see frescoes by Giotto, Mantegna, Altichiero, Menabuoi, Campigli (and Ponti).

«It is part of my expression as an architect to have wanted, with Carlo Anti, Rector of the University of Padua, this great fresco by Campigli»:[1] the atrium of the Liviano (now the seat of the Faculty of Letters at Padua University) was designed by Ponti for this fresco — a fresco that covers two hundred and fifty square meters, an image of «antiquity as excavation» (both the ground and the underground level are populated). It took five months to execute (Campigli would have preferred three years).[2] A work of sculpture by Martini, his Livy Alone with History, *is also located in the atrium.*

The atrium is in a central position in the building of the Liviano; it substitutes for the portico (or the court) as a place for students to meet. A combination of flights of stairs and balconies replaces the usual «grand staircase»: as crowded as Campigli's fresco, on different levels, this atrium transforms ceremonies into spectacles.

The front and ground floor of the Liviano, in the competition plans. *Top*, view of the front.

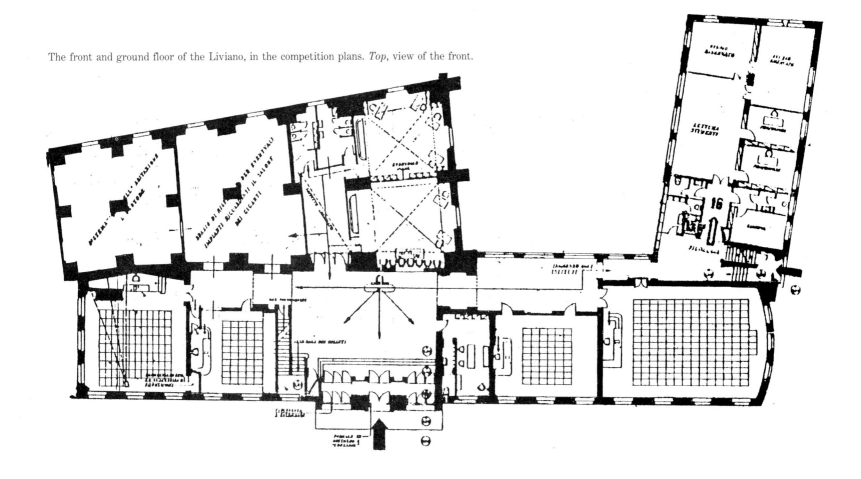

In the atrium of the Liviano, the large fresco by Massimo Campigli and Arturo Martini's sculpture «Livy alone with history.»

Pozzi apartment, Milan, 1933: couch and picture frames in red and white oilcloth, floor in black cloth.

Villa Marchesano, Bordighera, 1938

One of the first «small houses by the sea» designed by Ponti. White walls, internal and external floors in ceramic tiling. An outside staircase, from the patio to the roof.

Project for a «hotel in the wood,» on Capri, 1938

«The Mediterranean taught Rudofsky, Rudofsky taught me:»[1] this is how Gio Ponti described his collaboration with Bernard Rudofsky in the forties. Rudofsky had just designed, together with Luigi Cosenza, the most beautiful Mediterranean architecture in Italy (before the house on Capri designed for Malaparte by Libera), the Villa Oro in Posillipo, in 1936.[2]

Ponti's and Rudofsky's ideas come together in the project for the San Michele hotel on Capri: a «spontaneous hotel,» made up of separate houses/rooms scattered through a wood, each with its own patio and name; from the rooms many paths/corridors converge on a tiny «village,» the heart of the hotel and residence of the manager (or rather, «the gentleman who manages the place»[3]).

Rudofsky's Mediterranean is white, Ponti's colored. The names of the rooms («room of the angels,» «room of the doves,» «room of the sirens») are Ponti's. The idea of the bath basin sunk in the floor, surrounded by walls, a «cool watery grotto inside the house,» is Rudofsky's; and so is the idea of the masonry stairs with colored ceramic risers,[2] and the idea that guests, on arrival, should leave all their clothing in a closet and use sandals, hats, and umbrellas designed by the architects[4] (a Japanese idea: Rudofsky discovered Japan, still in a pure state, before the contemporary Japanese).

Ponti and Rudofsky designed a great deal together, but none of the designs was built. They were linked by the idea of «architecture without an architect.» Rudofsky was to develop it further in his travel books (journeys through countries, journeys through museums), his «primers for Americans.» (In the fifties and sixties, messengers/interpreters of other people's cultures, like Steinberg, Eames, Wirkkala, Sottsass, and William Klein, would also travel in this way, taking photographs, making drawings, and writing — and the pages of Domus were to reflect all this. Gio Ponti traveled only in the country of Gio Ponti, under construction.)

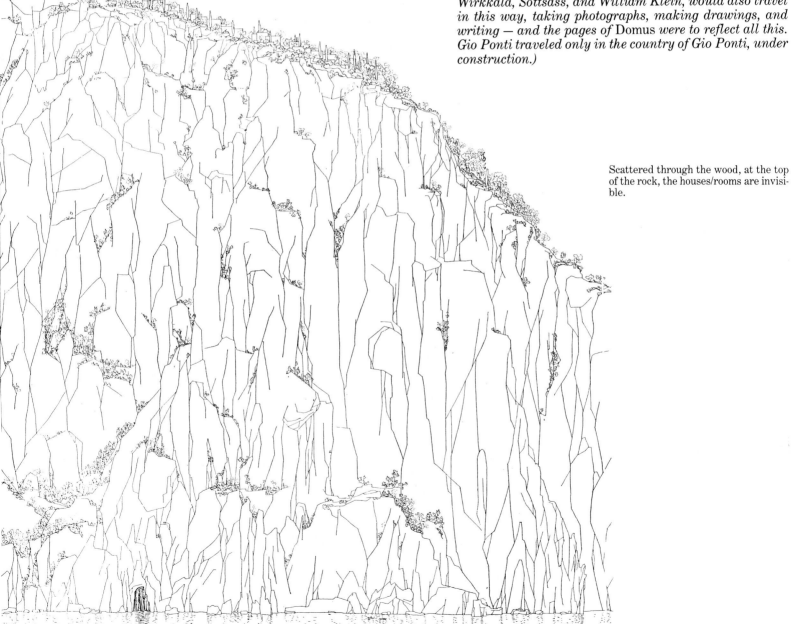

Scattered through the wood, at the top of the rock, the houses/rooms are invisible.

Some of the houses/rooms: «the room with a black wall,» «the room of the doves.» The rooms, scattered through the wood are reached by paths leading from the (small) central building.

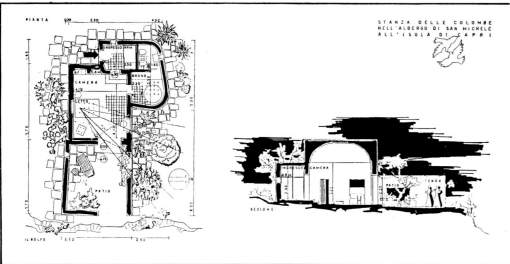

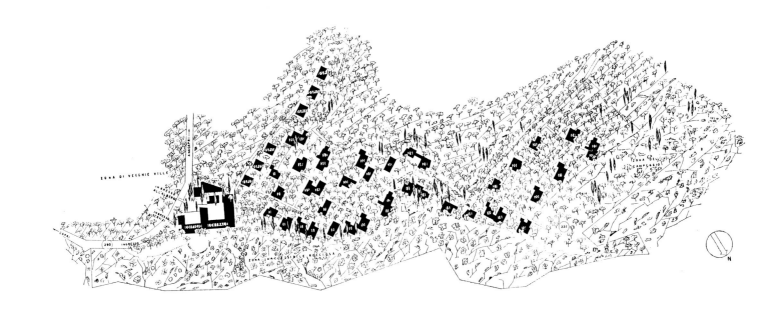

Hotel project for the Adriatic coast, 1938

The main innovation: at the top, two-story-high duplex rooms, provided with solaria. And then the garden that «penetrates» through the arcade of the restaurant and the veranda, raised so that they have a view of the sea. The hotel is conceived as a complete organism — provided not only with stores, but also with gyms and facilities for physiotherapy.
The project is by Gio Ponti and Guglielmo Ulrich.

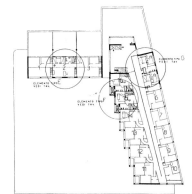

Plan of the top floor and terraces.

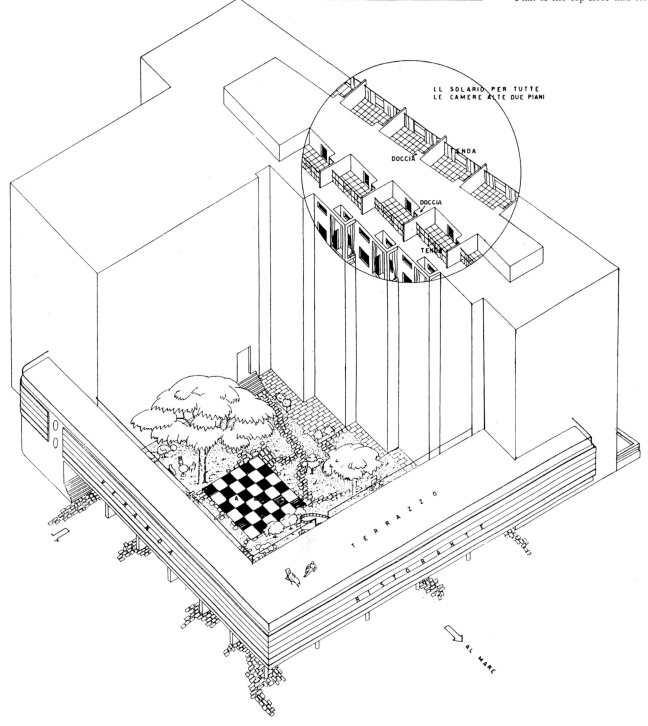

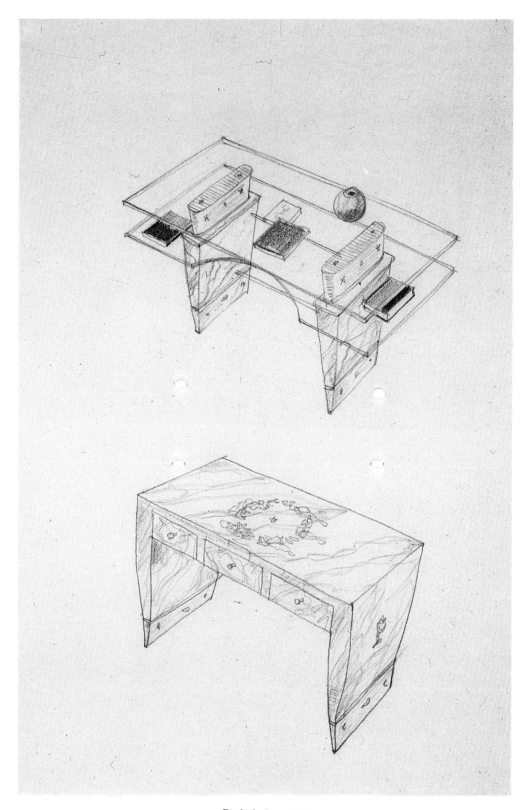

Desk designs, 1930.

Project for the master plan of Addis Ababa, 1936

Charged with producing the preliminary master plan of
Addis Ababa, shortly after its conquest, the architects Gio
Ponti, Giuseppe Vaccaro and Enrico Del Debbio, together
with the engineers Cesare Valle and Ignazio Guidi, saw
this native town as a spontaneous garden city, to be developed as such: «The whole city is a thick wood of tall euca-
lyptuses, with green glades; the new city as well....»[1]
Their plan was dictated by the courses of two streams (em-
banked and lined with trees) which naturally divided the
areas set aside for the natives and Italians. Their road
system was laid out in such a way as not to disturb the
existing, spontaneous one.[1]
They even suggested the use of lightweight local materials
and techniques, in low buildings. There were only two
strongly «Italian» features: a «Torre Littoria» (Tower of
Fascism) and a large bridge (a single 120 meter span over
the valley of the Gamelé stream).
This non-stately plan came to nothing.

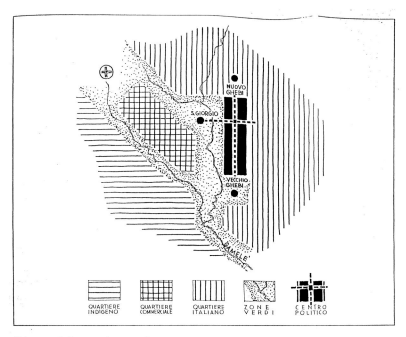

Scheme of the new layout of quarters.

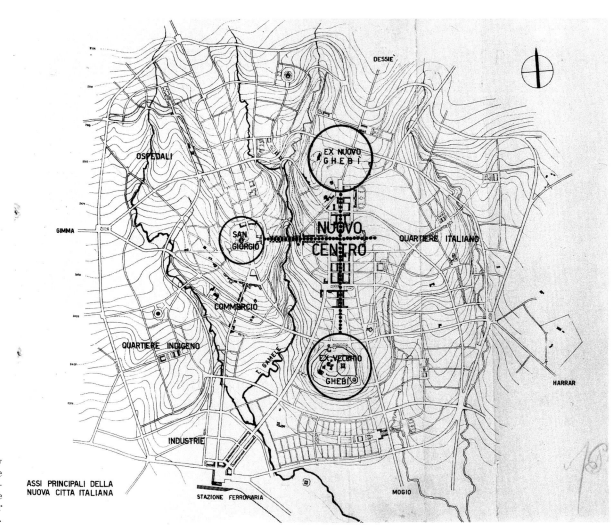

Addis Ababa: the main axes of the new
Italian city. In the zone between the
two streams (Gamelé and Curtumì) —
the commercial center. The native
quarter to the west, the Italian quarter
(including the new center) to the east.

100

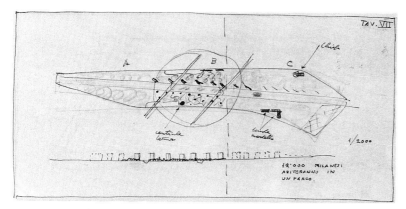

Urban development scheme for the area of the former Sempione station, Milan, 1937—48

As early as 1937,[1] Ponti proposed a «unitary» project for this large free area (300,000 m²) wholly owned by the municipality, almost in the center of the city: an exceptional «unit» not to be broken up by an ordinary network of streets.[2] He proposed a long «perspective spine,» an avenue 1500 meters in length, that would traverse the entire area and graft it onto the axis of Corso Sempione and the solemn neoclassical «scale» of the Foro Bonaparte, «the only recognizable urban layout in Milan.»

It was not intended to be the usual garden district, but to provide the «magnificent spectacle» of a broad (and perhaps elevated) avenue set in a park, and in the park «tall enchanting houses,» with terraces and hanging gardens: isolated towers, with grass at their feet (and alongside the towers, in Ponti's sketches, also appeared Vaccaro's «hill shaped» houses, from 1937).[3] This was Ponti's view of a happy city.

When, ten years later (and still in vain), Ponti again proposed (with the Studio Mazzocchi-Minoletti[4]) a unitary solution,[5] the towers were still higher (twenty stories), the park area had increased (the «perspective spine» was no longer an avenue, but a «river of grass» with «islands» of sports facilities), the traffic was shifted further away (it no longer cut through the area but went round it, with underground links). The idea of «mixing» the society of inhabitants, within this «green island,» had also gained ground: «here the dwellings are distinguished only by capacity, that is by the number of rooms, and not by use.»[6]

Above, sketches for the layout of the tower blocks. *Below*, a view of the projected «green spine» traversing the entire area.

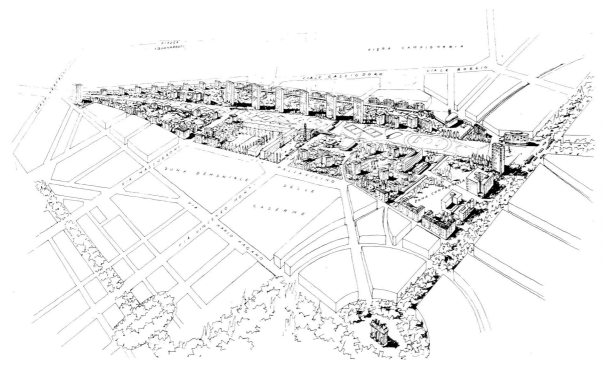

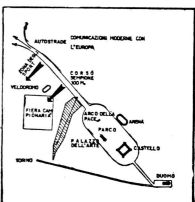

Below, the plots of land formerly occupied by the station (hatched) are connected to Foro Bonaparte, «the main urban structure of the city.»

Competition project for the Foreign Ministry, Rome, 1939

A project founded on the idea of the «grand spectacular decoration,» a recurrent idea in Ponti's work.
«The location does not permit frontal views, hence an architecture that exploits the effects and surprises of foreshortened views.»[1] Inside this «citadel of political thought,» the project functions on two distinct levels or registers: first, the «register of honor» (portal of honor, court of honor, staircase of honor, hall of honor, and there is even an elevator of honor) so that «visitors from all over the world will pass through the monumental halls, as happens in the Vatican and in ancient palaces;» and the «register of service.»
There are many «inventions» (amusement suited Ponti better than the monument) in the honor suite: the portal of honor, taking up the whole height of the building, is set back from the facade (it comes as a surprise); the hall of honor has a marble-inlay floor, an immense, colored carpet of marble, and visitors gaze down upon it from a white marble step around the edge; the court of honor has a «colonnade in perspective» consisting of eighty-four columns (each made of a different kind of marble) in diverging rows that «descend» toward the garden; in the garden, enclosed by the Aurelian walls, spectacular displays of water and light are staged in the ancient «Italian» manner. The artists invited to provide frescoes and sculptures were Funi and Martini.
The «register of service» has dictated the layout: there is also a shelter, where the Ministry can carry on its functions underground, a small but perfect sunken ministry; here too, the plants are a spectacular complex, accessible to the public.

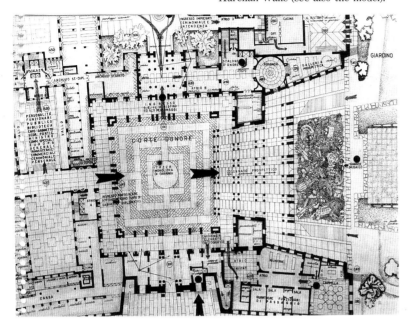

In the plan, a detail of the ground floor, with the «court of honor» and the «perspective» colonnade, sloping downward to the garden, which is bounded by the Aurelian Walls (see also the model).

The project lost the competition. Gio Ponti entered it with his Studio (then the Studio Ponti Soncini), the Studio Ulrich and the Studio De Carli Angeli Olivieri. Piero Fornasetti and Enrico Ciuti collaborated on the decorations.

Left and bottom, the «portal of honor,» stretching from ground to roof, set back from the front of the building. *Below*, the «court of honor.»

Villa Tataru, Cluj, Romania, 1939

A quiet, asymmetrical villa, designed, as a duet, by Gio Ponti and Elsie Lazar, the young pupil of Oscar Strnad.

The villa, surrounded by a garden, stands on a hill, with views to the south, east, and west. *In the drawing,* south elevation, with the major openings. *In the plan,* the ground floor.

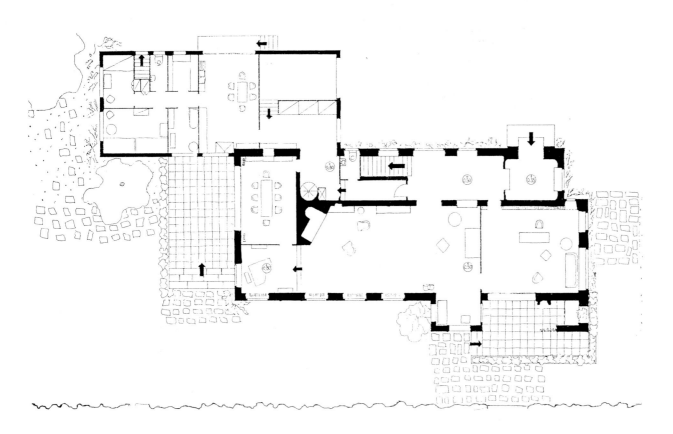

«An ideal small house,» 1939

Gio Ponti produced many designs for «small houses by the sea» during these years, publishing them in Domus *(and later in* Stile*): little theaters for the «human figures» that roam about; the white walls are «wings,» the colored tile flooring is the scenery.[1]*

«Mediterranean law: everything, by the sea, must be colored» (G.P., 1949).

Project for the Palazzo Marzotto, Milan, 1939

Facing onto Piazza San Babila, in Milan, are the large «palazzi» designed by Ponti together with the architects De Min, Rimini and Casalis in 1939.[1] But the one that Ponti cared about most (he published its model time and time again) is not there. It would have allowed him to try out two of his favorite ideas: the necessity, in every architectural unit, for «out-of-scale» rooms and the need to make them visible on the facade.

We are speaking of the project, never put into effect, for the Palazzo Marzotto, drawn up in collaboration with Francesco Bonfanti: in each of its three fronts the pattern of ordinary windows belonging to the ordinary rooms is «broken» by the special windows of the special, two-story-high rooms. «Composite architecture.» Ponti proposed another «out-of-scale» feature for the central front: a large work of sculpture, projecting from the facade and supported on corbels. It might have been an «airy» piece by Arturo Martini, 17 meters high, 10 meters wide, cast in aluminum and illuminated at night.[2]

Below, model of the Marzotto building, never built. Below left, model of the building on San Babila, actually constructed.

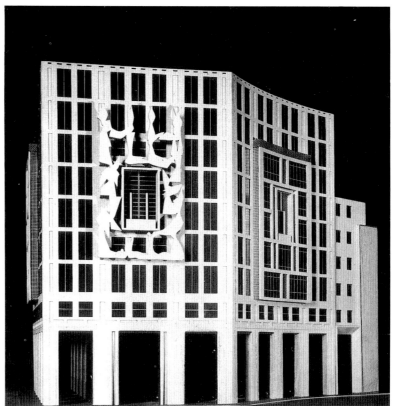

EIAR Building, now RAI Building, Milan, 1939

In 1939 — the year of Milanese «palazzi» for Gio Ponti (from the ones in San Babila to the Palazzo Ferrania in Corso Matteotti) — this building, the new headquarters of the Italian Broadcasting Corporation, the EIAR (later renamed the RAI), was the result of a competition that had been won by the Studio Ponti Fornaroli Soncini, in collaboration with the engineer Nino Bertolaia. The idea (a Pontian one) was that the three sections of which the building was composed (offices, broadcasts, theater) should be separate and individually recognizable. There should have been a luminous gap between «offices» and «broadcasts,» the transparent block containing the elevators and stairs. In practice, and over the course of time, the building has been extensively modified. A few parts remain (the portico and the doors onto the road) that maintain the original discourse on proportions.

Competition project for the Palace of Water and Light at the «E42» Exhibition, Rome, 1939

For the great imaginary event of «E42,» the 1942 Universal Exhibition of Rome that was never staged, a competition was announced for this «fantastic» building. No prize was awarded and the palace was not built.
What Ponti's project proposed,[1] grasping the spectacular nature of the theme, was a non-building: a very high and slender «screen,» made up of two parallel glass walls, through the transparent ends of which the luminous trajectories of moving elevators could be seen (an idea that Ponti revived, thirty years later, in his competition project for the Plateau Beaubourg); in front of the «screen,» a display of flowing water; the back of the «screen» was (in one version) a sort of huge heraldic «folio,» bearing the coats of arms of all the nations, almost a «curtain» behind which the spectacle of the exhibition was prepared. It was the concept of a building as a curtain, a pure theatrical structure, that led to the project's rejection.[2]

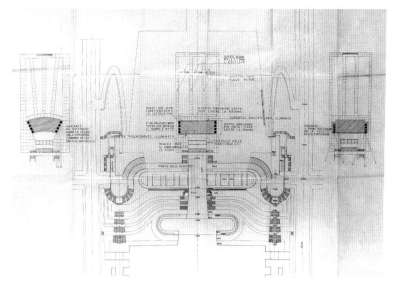

General plan, the palace (with two variants). *In the sketch*, the elevators, with a view of the «E42,» are a spectacular sight behind the luminous glass.

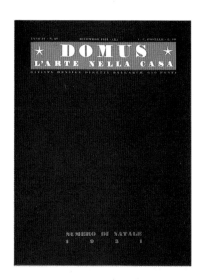
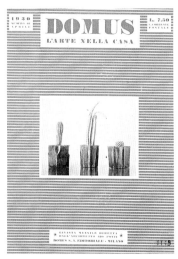
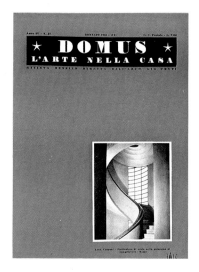
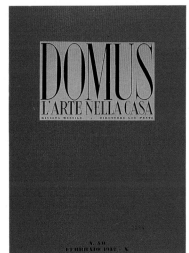

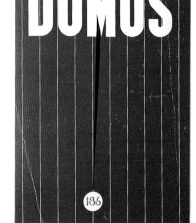

Covers of *Domus* in the thirties.

Domus 1928—40

Like Gio Ponti himself, Domus *always contained everything, its before and its after, so long as Gio Ponti was there.*

In the early period of Domus *(1928—40), all that we find later on had already commenced, for good or ill. There was, in the first place,* Domus' *reliance on «intelligent amateurs» (it was a young woman, Carmela Haerdtl, who sent the first news about Strnad, Neutra, and Sobotka from Vienna in 1931 — and it would again be her who, in 1965, first drew attention, from Vienna, to the young Heinz Frank and Hans Hollein, and who, in 1971 and 1973, made the first trips to Russia for* Domus*). Then there was the «giving away of plans» (very many of them) for a «charming house» to be built «without an architect.» At the same time, there was the «promotion of competitions» to encourage the development of a link between architects and the world of manufacturing. As with the big exhibitions, many talented architects entered these competitions.*

Domus*: a contradictory, living complexity, which did not achieve definition in the «graphics» (*Domus *redeemed itself mainly by its covers) but one that was valid as such. There was a peak of intensity, in the early thirties, when the neoclassical* Domus *gave space to the «new,» with reservations, doubts, and affinities, careful not to lose sight of «quality» in the «new.» In a fine contribution Michelucci pointed out, in 1932, the «points of contact» between Giotto's architecture and that of Libera and Ridolfi.[1] Albini published in* Domus *the beautiful lace[2] he designed in those years. For Ponti, Albini was «one of the young architects (along with Figini, Pollini, and Bottoni) who prefer the skeleton to the solid.» (The dressing-table for Margherita Sarfatti, a luxury piece that Ponti designed and published in 1932, was a «solid.»[3])*

Domus *published Lucio Fontana immediately, although without giving his work pride of place at first.[4] Persico's most daring article, «Punto e da capo per l'architettura» («A new start for architecture»), was given pride of place in* Domus *in 1934,[5] but it was «a new start» that never occurred in* Domus *(or in Gio Ponti).* Domus *published Ponti's work rapidly, but just an indication of it (though a repeated one). Or the magazine disseminated it, sometimes anonymously, in its pages of advertising (the Montecatini building of 1936 was given this treatment). For Ponti* Domus *was a living journal, to be kept alive.*

Pages from *Domus* in the thirties.

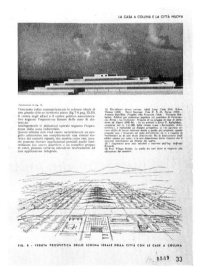

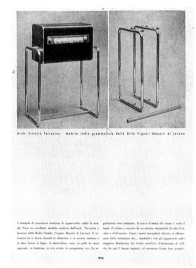

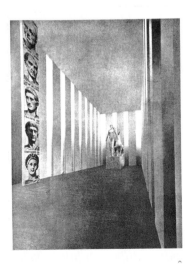

Gio Ponti in Padua, 1940.

The forties: writing, painting and projecting

«Italy has nothing but its civilization to save its civilization.» This motto appeared, in 1943, on the cover of *Stile* nos. 32—34, an issue that appeared miraculously after the bombing of the offices of its publisher (Garzanti).

In this decade, spanning the war and the early postwar period, the word that counted, for Gio Ponti, was still «Italy,» and his most important work, alongside painting, was *Stile*, the magazine that for years (from 1941 to 1947) lived through the war and its aftermath with style.

The Italy that Ponti upheld was (as always) the one whose preeminence lay in art (including architecture) and the applied arts — an Italy that was also to find expression, at the end of the forties, in the boom in «art ceramics» and in the decorative ingenuity of Gio Ponti himself. But it was the other Italy too, the bombed-out Italy to be rebuilt with the help of «standards of excellence,» the «charter of the home,» and the «texts for reconstruction» which Ponti (and others with him) impetuously published in *Stile*, in the newspapers, in pamphlets (*Cifre Parlanti*, 1944[1]), and in *cahiers* (*Verso la casa esatta*, 1944[2]) which involved both designers and industry. This Italy has not been spoken of since.

Ponti himself was to emerge, in the end, from this impassioned solitude, also made up of books (soliloquies like *Il Coro*, 1944, and *L'architettura è un cristallo*, 1945), of painting (allegorical: the frescoes in the Palazzo del Bo, the seat of the Rector of Padua University, 1940), and of work for the theater (scenes and costumes for Stravinsky's *Pulcinella* at the Teatro della Triennale, 1940, and Gluck's *Orpheus* at La Scala, 1947 — but Ponti dreamt of being a director).

It was when he came back to *Domus*, in 1948, that he encountered the first stimulating comparisons with the outside world, and he resumed his travels (he went to Barcelona in 1949). In the last two years of the decade, which for good or evil were an anticipation of the fifties, Ponti's architecture (at the time more planned than built) reached a mature definition that was to find full expression in the coming decade.

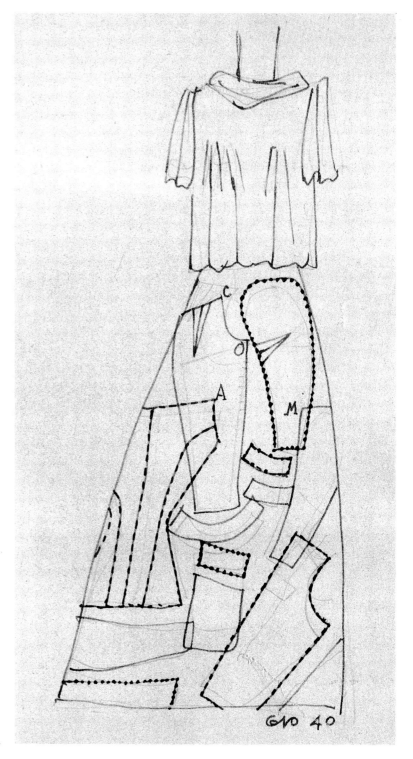

Drawing, ink on paper, 1940 (A.G.P.).

Scenes and costumes: for Stravinsky's «Pulcinella» at the Teatro della Triennale, Milan 1940, and for Gluck's «Orpheus» at La Scala, 1947

These were Gio Ponti's two principal encounters with the theater,[1] taking place within the same decade and centered on La Scala: «I have worked at La Scala»[2] (see also pp. 122—23). Scenes and costumes: but Ponti would have liked to be the director and not just «dress the characters and dress the stage.» He had felt this way ever since he had fallen in love with the Russian ballets of Diaghilev at first sight,[3] and then with Appia's theater.[4]

Gio Ponti's architecture was itself almost a theater, a «stage» for the moving «figures» that appeared and disappeared from its staircases, balustrades, balconies, and perspectives. And the clothes that he loved to design[5] were already «costumes.» Like the ones for his theater: costumes that looked as if they were cut out of paper, that one «slipped into» to make them dance: total costumes, in which the wearer disappeared; the hands vanished (always gloved), and so did the hair (always under a hat). Simplified costumes, made to be viewed from afar, with nothing «material,» and still less «historical,» about them. So were his scenes, which had to look like mere enlargements of rapid sketches. That is to say, they were intended to allude to scenes, not to be them. To simulate the theater. This is why Ponti wrote on his sketches, «do it badly.» What he loved about theatrical costume makers was their extraordinary capacity for improvisation. What he feared, and detested, were attempts at theatrical realism. It could be said that «his» kind of performance was the ballet, and «his» kind of character was Harlequin,[6] an acrobat of grace and detachment — even if (see his theater script Il Coro[7]) he sometimes lapsed into solemnity.

Scenes and costumes for Stravinsky's «Pulcinella» at the Teatro della Triennale, 1940 (A.G.P.).

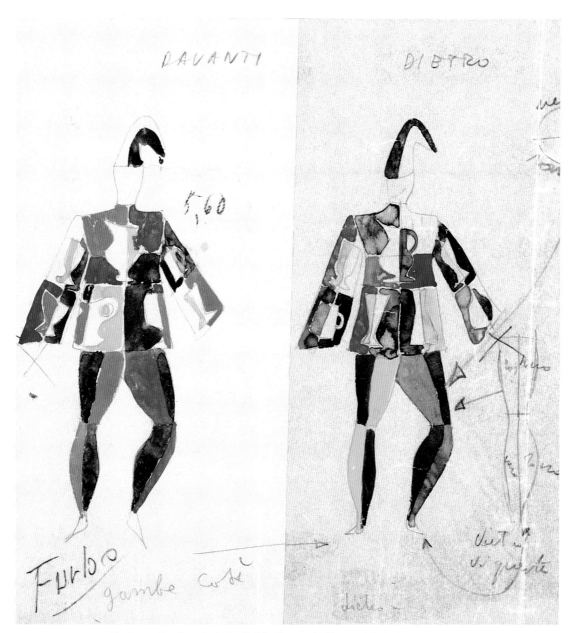

Costumes for Stravinsky's «Pulcinella» at the Teatro della Triennale, 1940.

Villa Donegani in Bordighera, 1940

White walls under the sun. A pattern of planes designed for the play of light. The central living-room is two stories high and contains the staircase (a favorite motif of Ponti's). The patio at the front is two stories high, and contains the volume of the dining-room (one story high), covered by a solarium with masonry beds.
The apertures all look like «cuts in the wall» (the window panes have no frame). The doors are all sliding ones. White walls, and a white tiled roof.

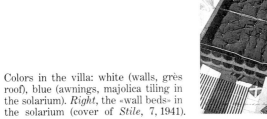

Colors in the villa: white (walls, grès roof), blue (awnings, majolica tiling in the solarium). *Right*, the «wall beds» in the solarium (cover of *Stile*, 7, 1941).

Villa Donegani in Bordighera. Every window has a window-box filled with flowers.

Grand frescoed staircase in Palazzo del Bo, Padua, 1940

In the entrance to Palazzo del Bo, the ancient building housing the university Rectorate, one can find this large fresco by Gio Ponti, surrounding the grand staircase.
The high curved wall, cut in half by the flight of stairs, is transformed by the fresco into a sort of large «sheet,» on which the painted figures are set against a void. The steps of the staircase (white when seen from above, colored when viewed from below) are part of the effect of lightness. The painted sheet unfolds around Arturo Martini's «Palinurus» in white marble — his last statue.
Gio Ponti executed the fresco with the assistance of the painter Fulvio Pendini and of his own daughter Lisa.

Opposite, the fresco along the staircase. «In the upper part I painted,» explains Ponti in *Stile*, 13, 1942, «the university disciplines, inventing their symbology.... Below I depicted the primeval chaos, and the powers of evil that perpetuate chaos in time... and the Angel, that comes and calls man....» *Below*, Arturo Martini's «Palinuro,» and a detail of «The Sciences.» *Right*, the Basilica, hall of the columns, on the second floor of the Palazzo del Bo. (In the Palazzo del Bo, Ponti was also responsible for the layout and decoration of the Aula Magna, the Basilica, and the Rectorate; the Rector at that time was Carlo Anti.)

117

Columbus Clinic, Milan, 1940—48

A building designed before the war, and constructed afterward.

Ponti had an ideal scheme for a clinic already in mind, born out of conversations with a famous surgeon, Mario Donati («Architecture is a matter of mental lucidity and the capacity for coordination. Therefore we can learn from architects and non-architects»[1]). And he also had a basic principle in mind: a clinic should never look like a clinic, but like a house. «Leaving the clinic, the patient will express his gratitude to the doctors and nurses, and to the architect too, who has thought about him as a human being.»[2]

When the opportunity arose, with the Columbus Clinic, the ideal scheme was realized (rooms facing south, vertical communications and floor control at the heart, operating theaters to the north, connected directly to the heart). The principle of a «non-clinical» appearance was also applied: the rooms in the Columbus Clinic were each painted in a different color, and had wooden, not metal

Right, the medicine and surgery wing, with the balconies facing the garden. *Below*, the entrance gallery with walls and pillars in glossy green plaster.

furniture. *In the maternity wing, each room had a balcony and a pergola. And in this case it was the architect who had to express his own gratitude to the client, the Missionary Sisters of the Sacred Heart.*

(The legendary founder of the order, the Blessed Cabrini, Mother Cabrini as she was called in the hospitals she founded in New York, inspired Ponti to write a book in 1946 with the title Ringrazio Iddio che le cose non vanno a modo mio *(«I thank God that things do not go my way,» a saying of hers[3]).*

It was to be another order of nuns, the Discalced Carmelites, that would give Ponti the opportunity to build, in 1958, his beloved Convent of Bonmoschetto in San Remo.

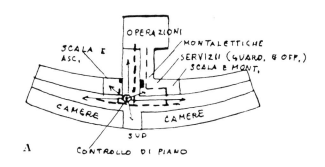

At the top, a sketch for the plan, and the balconies with flowers, in the maternity wing. *Left,* a room, with all wooden furniture.

119

«The Miser,» cartoon for the fresco, 1940 (A.G.P.).

Frescoes in the «Popolo d'Italia» building, Milan, 1940

Ponti painted frescoes not only in Padua but also in Milan, in some rooms of the «Popolo d'Italia» building. In these frescoes the painted figures are not set against a void (as in the Padua frescoes) but framed by painted doors — a play of doors, which would reappear in Ponti's «surprise furniture» of these years.

«Henry IV,» idea for a film, 1940

The idea was to use the script of Luigi Pirandello's «Henry IV» for a movie made up entirely of «close ups» of talking faces and talking hands, with no background. Ponti dedicated this «screenplay» to Jouvet and Anton Giulio Bragaglia.

The scroll of the script.

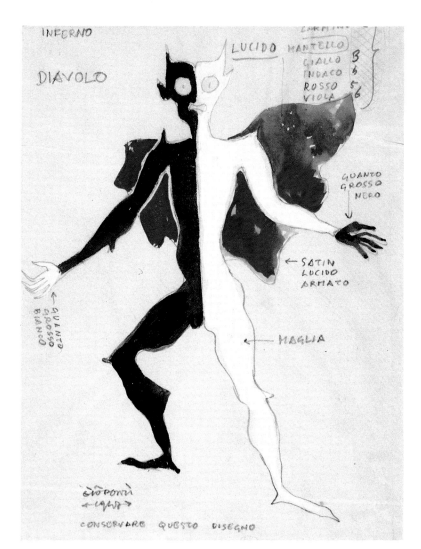

INFERNO

DIAVOLO

LUCIDO MANTELLO
GIALLO 3
INDACO 6
ROSSO 5 6
VIOLA 6

GUANTO GROSSO NERO

GUANTO GROSSO BIANCO

SATIN LUCIDO ARMATO

MAGLIA

CONSERVARE QUESTO DISEGNO

INFERNO

(1) NERO - BIANCO (2)

VERDE - MARRONE

GIALLO - NERO

ROSSO - BIANCO

INDACO - ORO

MAGLIA

CORO : BASSI E TENORI AMMANTELLATI

SOTTO MANICHE E GUANTI BIANCHI

ALTRE VARIANTI
VERDE E BRUNO

DANNATA

BIANCA CON ORRENDE MACCHIE ROSSE

o VERDI
o MARRONE

SEMPRE VISTA DI SCHIENA APPOGGIATA ALLE ROCCIE.

Costumes for Gluck's «Orpheus» at
La Scala, Milan, 1947.

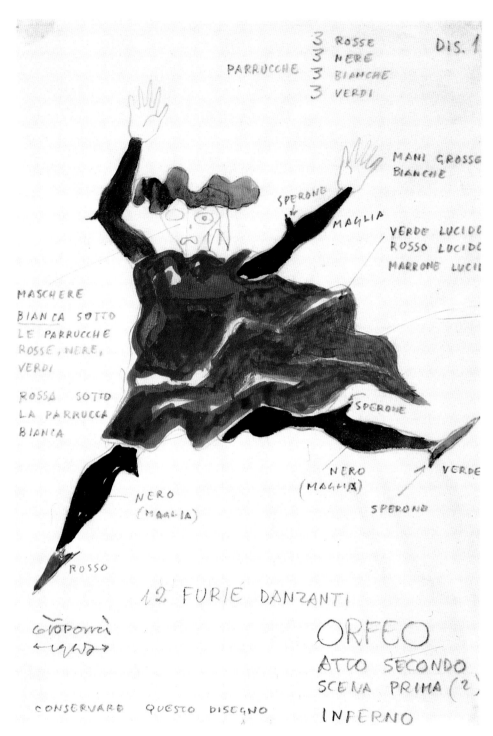

Costume for Gluck's «Orpheus» at La Scala, Milan, 1947.

Costumes for the ballet «Mondo Tondo,» at La Scala, never performed, 1945.

«Bellezza» 1941—43, fashion, women

Bellezza *was the Italian fashion magazine to which Ponti contributed from 1941 to 1943,[1] fighting «for art» in its pages as well. He saw couture and fashion as forms of art. And when, in* Bellezza *as in* Stile, *Gio Ponti addressed himself to women («You, O women»), he did it «on behalf of art.»*

*From his women — even when he drew them, in the manner of Campigli, as women/angels — he asked a great deal. He wanted them to be the «creators» of their own homes, free from «unfavorable preconceptions.» Women who would teach him the «living» house (even though in reality the houses he dedicated to them were already designed in all their details). Women who loved books, books they would scatter all over the house. Women for whom the house was a place to «stay» (*stanza, *the beautiful Italian word for room, derives from* stare, *to stay). Women who liked to be given works of art for the house («a noble expenditure»), works by Scipione, Severini, Sironi, Martini («a genius»), Carrà, Tosi, and De Pisis. Women who ought to buy the (just published)* Apocalisse *illustrated by de Chirico,[2] and read the (just published)* Anthology of Frank Lloyd Wright *(«architecture is part of everybody's life»[3]).*

But why did these women have Vogue, Harper's Bazaar, Life, *and* Plaisir de France *in their rooms, and not Longanesi's* L'Italiano, *Maccari's* Il Selvaggio, *and* Omnibus? *Gio Ponti laid siege to the impregnable fortress of snobbery, and almost won. He grasped the identical nature of house and clothing (as for «his» clothing, the clothing he designed in these years, it was a sort of colored costume, like a ceramic object, in which the body was «splendidly concealed»). He did not like fashion as fashion, that is, where it meant slavery to the fashionable and not a real change in habits (he would love Mary Quant). For him, where fashion could not be art, then the only surviving elegance was «personal dignity.»*

Below left, drawing for a magazine cover, 1943. *Below*, an image from *Stile*, 1946.

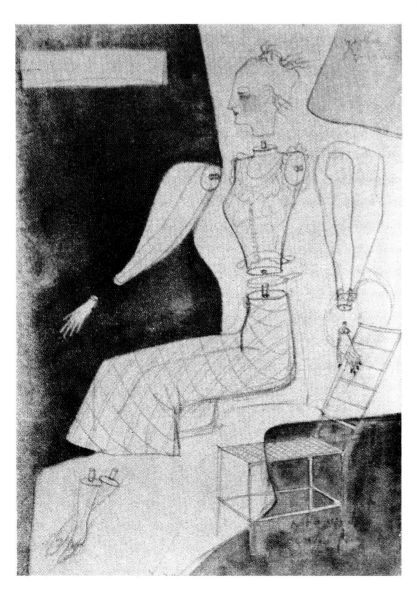

Furniture with enamel decorations by Paolo de Poli, Padua, 1941

This furniture, «which was to the liking of De Pisis and Daria Guarnati,»[1] is a high spot in the long collaboration between Gio Ponti and Paolo de Poli, the master of enamel work on copper, indeed the man who refounded this art in Italy in 1933. The collaboration commenced in 1940 with the panels designed by Gio Ponti and made by De Poli for the halls of the rectorate at the University of Padua, and continued with other panels, some of them very large, for the transatlantic liners whose interiors were designed by Ponti, from the Conte Grande to the Conte Biancamano.[2] Ponti and De Poli were to work together again in 1956.

With De Poli, Ponti, «the Italian designer of longest standing,»[3] was able to carry on with his everlasting amusement and play with «the arts.»

Sketch for the table «Labirinto,» 1941.

«Smalti azzurri» table, top 42 x 93 cm   (formerly De Pisis Coll.).

«Scacchi» small portable bar.

Top of the «Labirinto» table (formerly Guarnati Coll.).

127

Casa Ponti at Civate, Brianza, 1944

A little wartime and postwar house, lived in rather than designed. «As in evacuations and escapes, we carried the dearest and most useless objects to safety first. We heaped them up like a pile of booty, one on top of the other, concentrated as in one's memory. It is the passing of the years, or of a war, that leads us to reduce the gaps between the things precious to us, and that makes us indifferent to dividing walls and functions....»[1]

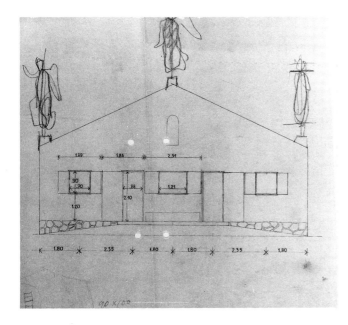

Top right, the living-room. In the foreground, «Cinghiali» (Wild Boars) by Salvatore Fancello, in ceramic and terracotta, and a large vase by Pietro Melandri. Above the fireplace, a Madonna in bronze by Ettore Calvelli, a white ceramic «tuft» by Luigi Zortea. On the wall, a pastel by Antonio Mancini. *Right*, plan, elevations, and sections. *Above*, preliminary version for the main facade.

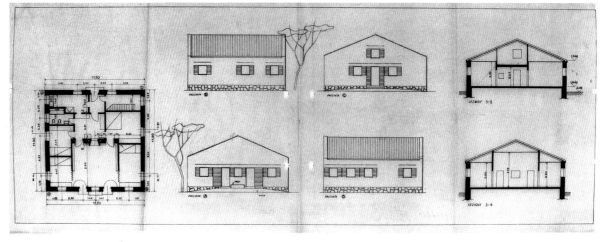

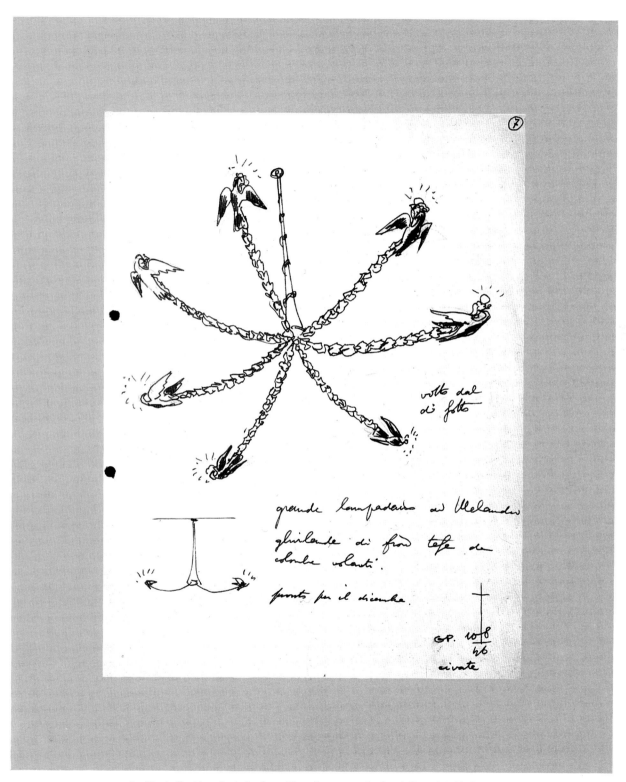

In Civate Ponti projected, *above*, ideas for a ceramic chandelier, 1946 (A.G.P.).

Designs for Venini, Murano, 1946—49

The collaboration between Gio Ponti and Paolo Venini, the founder of the modern history of Murano glass, dates right back to the twenties, when the «Labirinto» group,[1] formed around Carla Visconti di Modrone in Milan, brought the industries of art together, for the first time, with architects (at that time, the architects were Buzzi, Lancia, Marelli, and Ponti) for the Triennial Exhibitions in Monza and Milan. Ponti's admiration for Venini's modern production was a lasting one.[2] His direct involvement in its design took place in three phases, separated by long gaps of time: glass and silver objects for Venini and Christofle in 1928 (16th Venice Biennale); lamps, drinking glasses, and bottles (bottles in the shape of women) in 1946—50, playful combinations of blown glass and color; and, lastly, the «thick stained glass» of 1966.

Bottles, glasses, and a chandelier in multicolored blown glass, 1946—50.

Bottle with «crinoline,» in colored blown glass, 1949.

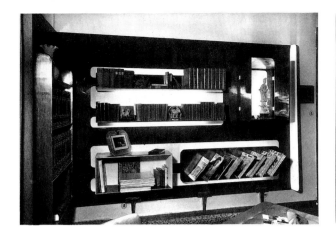

Above left, «organized wall,» in Cremaschi apartment, Milan, 1949. *Above right,* desk with «wall-panel,» for the publisher Gianni Mazzocchi, Milan, 1949.

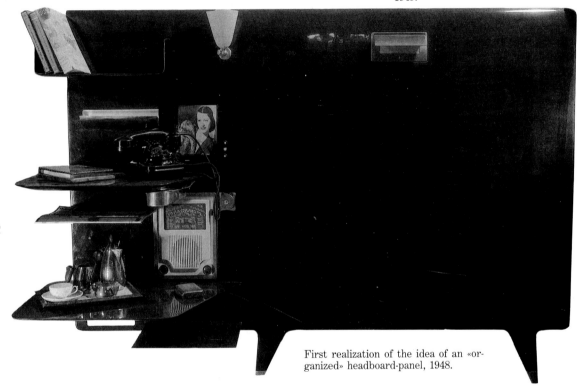

First realization of the idea of an «organized» headboard-panel, 1948.

«Assembling» and «lightening,» 1948—50

At the end of the forties Gio Ponti defined a principle that he was never to abandon in his interior design: that of the «organized wall» (as he called it), that is, the principle of assembling shelves, light fixtures, and objects within a single wall panel.[1]

Out of this came the idea (1948) of the headboard-panel for the bed:[2] a wall panel containing all the required facilities (consoles, shelves for books and the telephone, light switches, built-in radio, built-in cigarette lighter, etc.) combined with a light, mobile bed on castors. He devised a writing desk on the same lines:[3] a table clear of encumbrances, with a well-equipped panel on the wall behind it. (The idea of «assembling» and «combining» items within a definite area may also underlie the concept of the «furnished window,» 1954: a set of consoles and shelves, bearing objects, is inserted into the «empty» rectangle of the window, to be looked at «in silhouette» against the sky.[4])

In 1950 the principle of «assembling» within a panel was refined by the idea of «sharpening» the edges of the panel and shelves, in order to strip them of their visual weight. A «lightening» that was taken further by illuminating the panels «from behind.» (Ponti would apply the same criteria to architecture as well, in the fifties and sixties.[5])

He insisted on «lightness.» In fact it was a «lightening,» and a purely visual one (the tapering support, the sharpened profile).

La Pavoni coffee machine, Milan, 1948

The «legendary» Pavoni espresso coffee machine of 1948: all the intricate and protruding mechanisms of the «old» coffee machine have been eliminated or enclosed within just three volumes: casing, central body, spouts. The appliance achieves the «perfect simplicity attained, in their form, by certain wind instruments.»[1]

This is the first La Pavoni with a horizontal boiler.

133

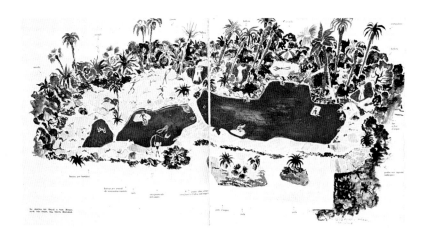

San Remo

Swimming pool at the Hotel Royal, San Remo, 1948

«I hate rectangular swimming pools. Are lakes or rivers rectangular? I want swimming pools for nymphs. And that one dives into from the top of a tree. And that have a bar in a cave, reached by swimming underwater.»[1]

The swimming-pool was designed with small islands for sunbathing («Récamier islands»), a bridge with an arch above the water and another below, jets of water from the outside, a grotto with an underwater entrance, and a water-level bar.

134

«Mediterranean law: everything, by the sea, must be colored;» detail of fabric for Jsa of Busto Arsizio, 1949—50.

«Amusement» and «disquiet of fantasy,» 1948—50

«A degree of amusement should not be excluded from interior decoration... it is an old tradition.» In these years Ponti's amusement, once secret, became explicit. The furniture he designed from 1948 to 1949 was based on spectacular complication, and «excess» turned into the «substance» of these objects, rendered acrobatically useless, although not to the eye.

He created «surprise» furniture, with one piece hidden inside another (the «fireplace in the closet,» on a sharpened support),[1] with edges cut down «to a blade so that the thickness disappears.» The material itself, wood, was pushed beyond its nature: the walnut was a special, «Ponti-style» wood, artificially «inlaid,» to intensify the cloudy effect.[2]

In this climate Ponti's collaboration with Fornasetti flourished. Fornasetti's contribution was not «added» decoration; it was a sort of «projected» decoration that cancelled the surface and that, as part of the environment, destroyed space and volumes (helped by the use made of lighting); an example of this was the Dulciora store in Milan, all in black and white (now demolished).[3]

These exploits were made possible by exceptionally skilled cabinet makers (like the Radice brothers and Giordano Chiesa in Milan). They also fell in with Ponti's idea that, with the war over, it was necessary to «foster autonomy» in order to «save the world from a pernicious unity» — and one area of autonomy, for Ponti, was that of the «Italian crafts.»[4]

The pages of Domus were filled with marvels of craftsmanship, and so was the MUSA traveling exhibition of 1950,[4] which gave the United States its first glimpse of an «Italian domestic landscape» with a lot of «art ceramics.» (Domus, 226, 1948: «Picasso will convert artists to ceramics, but we, says Lucio Fontana, had already started.» Renato Guttuso designed fabrics.)

Top, metal table: the fragment of marble is «displayed» beneath a sheet of glass; on the table, the new white majolicas by Gio Ponti and the Doccia artists, 1948. *Right*, the «fireplace in the closet,» closed and open. (All these pieces were on show at the MUSA, the first major exhibition of Italian design in the USA, 1950—53.)

Above, the Dulciora store in Milan (now demolished), 1949: Fornasetti's decoration is «projected» on Ponti's forms. *Left*, radio-phonograph on castors, with two sides covered with mirrors and folding top.

Covers of *Stile*, 1945—47, designed by Gio Ponti.

«Stile,» 1941–47

Rich at the beginning and poor at the end, the magazine Stile *dealt with two burning themes in its pages: Italy and art, architects and the war.*

At the outset Stile *was mentally akin to* Aria d'Italia, *the Italian version of* Verve,[1] *but with far more «verve.»* Verve *opened its pages, with solemnity, to the great French artists.* Aria d'Italia *(a magazine founded by Daria Guarnati, a talented Parisian in Italy) did the same for the great Italian artists, but in a less solemn fashion. And so did* Stile, *focusing on the writings of de Chirico, the poems of a painter (De Pisis), the painting of a sculptor (Martini), the writings of an engineer (Nervi), and films by architects (BBPR), while poets and columnists (Gatto, Bontempelli, De Libero, Sinisgalli, and Irene Brin) wrote on colored paper. But in* Stile *there was also the innovation (a true one) of bringing out (with Carlo Pagani and Lina Bò) a monthly art magazine with a publisher and a readership who did not belong to the art world. Gio Ponti addressed everyone, not even making a distinction between art and the crafts. His aim was to make «kinships» visible, the kinships between the «many things» that «express, adorn, or serve our lives — and homes.»*

At the beginning there was in Stile *the magical and motionless atmosphere of a war over art, «for the sake of Italy.» But the Pavilion of Italian Civilization at the «E42» in 1942 already looked like a funereal «manikin of architecture»[2] to Ponti. And soon his enthusiasm for «the perfect and total simultaneity of ancient and modern art,» and for architects as artists (Mollino, «principally an artist,» Libera «an extremely architectural artist»), and poets as artists (reading Ungaretti, reading Emilio Villa), in short his determination to indicate and preserve the «isolated units,» seemed to isolate him from history. It was from 1943 to 1945, with the magazine operating under straitened circumstances, that his sorrow over «the evils of war» changed into hope, hope about what an architect could do.*

Whole issues of Stile *were brought out on reconstruction, unification, city planning, homes for everyone, with contributions by Michelucci, Mollino, Pica, Vaccaro, Libera, Vietti, Bottoni, Sartoris, and Banfi. And plans for small houses and standard furniture were presented — to help in the construction of those «over twenty million rooms» that «are needed by Italy.»*

Even if the «assembly of architects» to whom Ponti addressed his appeal Politica dell'Architettura *(the title of a pamphlet)[3] was an imaginary one, his magazine was real. Printed on cheap paper with the minimum of means, its graphics relied on the use of black-red-black, positive-negative, and a lot of boldface type for its many slogans.* Stile *held out with style for as long as Ponti made it his obsessive diary, writing under twenty-two different pseudonyms, commenting on everything. He saw the war as «bringing the world into the world,»[8] and yet he did not foresee that new world. In the end Ponti himself grew tired of his own solitude. He emerged from* Stile *(even before he left the magazine) through the covers: from 1945 to 1947 the covers he designed were his real message.[9]*

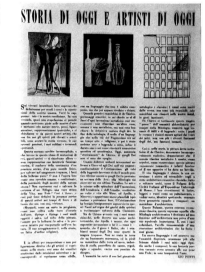
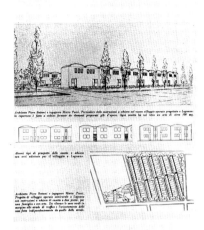

Pages from *Stile* in the forties.

Ship interiors, 1948—52

Ponti had always been interested in interior design for ships (he was an admirer of Gustavo Pulitzer and the innovative interiors that he designed for the 1931 motorship Victoria*). At the end of the forties he was involved in the postwar renovation of four Italian liners (the* Conte Grande, Conte Biancamano, Giulio Cesare, *and* Andrea Doria*), in collaboration with Nino Zoncada.*

It was still a question of «dressing» the liner, not designing it. Yet «his» ships — ships he loaded with art, as traveling heralds of Italy — had two innovations in their unalterable internal spaces: partitions and pillars lined with light sheets of aluminum (a new application of the material), and «illuminating» ceilings: the low ceilings of the ship were transformed into airy displays.

As in Ponti's interiors of the time, his decoration of these ships tended toward «excess.» And again, as in his interior decorations and in the pages of Domus, *the Italian art that Ponti put on board was mainly ceramics: ceramic sculpture by Fontana, Melotti, and Leoncillo, as well as vases by Gambone, Melandri, and Zortea, and enamels by De Poli, designed by Ponti himself. There were also paintings, like the ones by Salvatore Fiume, on a theatrical scale. They were beautiful ships, even if sailing a little late.*

Designs by Ponti, in collaboration with Nino Zoncada.

Right, top and opposite page: luminous ceilings on the *Andrea Doria*, 1952.

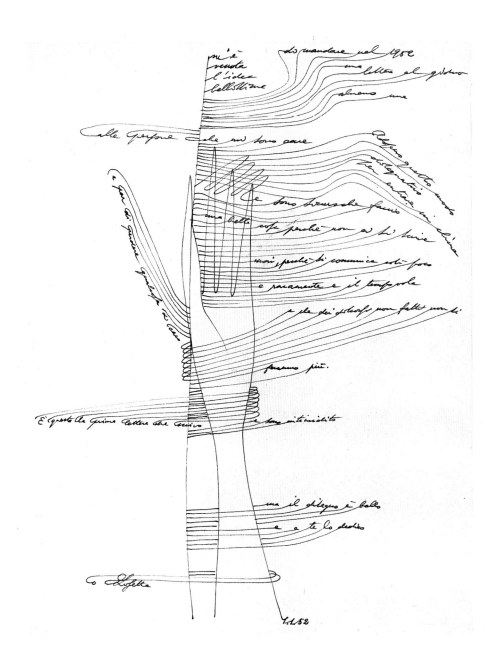

Drawn letters, 1950—79

Thought as sign, sign as thought. Speed and lightness over the surface: just like acrobats, who can never afford to make a mistake or come to a stop.

This Pontian way of «thinking by drawing» never stopped either. He turned out dozens of letters every day, for decades. (There are the letters using line and pen alone, from the fifties; the letters made up of lines and clouds, that is pen and fingertip, from the sixties; the letters of line and color, that is pen and felt-tip, from the seventies). A hundred of these letters, chosen rapidly and at random, were published in a small book and put on show in an exhibition, staged in Milan in 1987.[1] But there are hundreds of letters received (and kept) in other cities around the world — the game was an endless one.

The fifties: *the theory of the finite form*

It was in 1954 that Ponti published, with Daria Guarnati, the first book dealing with his own work, and he called it *Espressione di Gio Ponti*.[1] He had reached the point where he could take a critical look at his own history as «continuity of an individual expression.» And he did it at the moment when this expression appeared to have been unified by a «theory» about form (for the first time): the theory of the «finite form.» Ponti perceived the «form» of each of his projects in his own terms — from «essentiality» to «expressiveness,» «illusoriness,» and «structural invention» (but with him theory too was an «invention»).

In the «fabulous fifties,» very productive years for Ponti in the fields of both architecture and design — before and after the Pirelli Tower, 1956, which represented their climax, before and after his great journeys (to Brazil, Mexico, Venezuela, the USA, and the Middle East) — Ponti's works (from car bodies to skyscrapers) had a formal relationship with each other; they came from an imaginative treatment of form that evolved out of itself. In this creative and individual manner, Ponti opposed both recourse to the «existing context» and the «international style,» terms of the debate under way at that time.

Gio Ponti was in his sixties. They were years in which the masters, from Gropius to Le Corbusier, gained a new vision, as masters/non-masters,[2] on the new world scene.

During the fifties Ponti's studio in Milan and the magazine *Domus* gradually turned into «international» workshops, against a background of explosive growth in the world of both architecture and design. Ponti's book from 1945 (*L'architettura è un cristallo*), republished in 1957 became *Amate l'architettura*, his diary-cum-notebook of ideas, and was soon translated into English (*In Praise of Architecture*) and Japanese.

During these years Gio Ponti was associated with the engineer Antonio Fornaroli and the architect Alberto Rosselli, in the Studio Ponti Fornaroli Rosselli, 1952—76.

Gio Ponti: paintings «on support,» 1950.

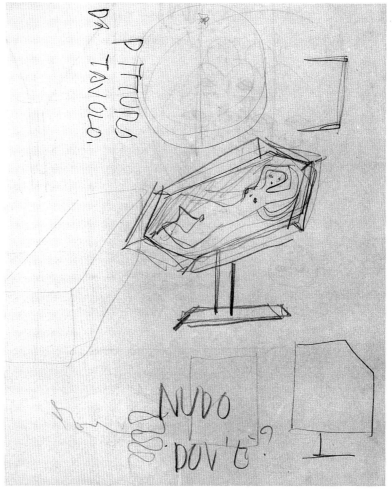

143

«Amusements» with Fornasetti in San Remo, Turin, Genoa, 1950

Ponti+Fornasetti «amusements» would flourish in the fifties in many ways. After the first black-and-white decorations (on the walls of the Dulciora shop and on the fronts of Ponti's «neoclassical» trumeaux), Fornasetti turned now to color, stamping with colored images (hundreds of them) all the surfaces of Ponti's rooms and pieces. In the Casino rooms in San Remo, designed by Ponti, Fornasetti imprinted small and giant playing-cards, hundreds of them, on sofas, armchairs, curtains, ceilings and walls (on the walls and ceilings the «flying» cards are set in luminous cavities). In the Vembi-Burroughs offices in Genoa and Turin, designed by Ponti, Fornasetti imprinted pens, pencils, sheets of paper, computers, on chairs, armchairs and sofas.

On the other hand Ponti, when publishing these works of his, pointed out, first of all, the «elegant»[1] new materials used: anodyzed aluminum, PVC lining, rubber flooring (the «Fantastico P.,» new Pirelli rubber flooring, was designed by Ponti).

Above, in the San Remo Casino, the large playing cards suspended in luminous cavities. *Below* Vembi-Burroughs offices in Turin and Genoa.

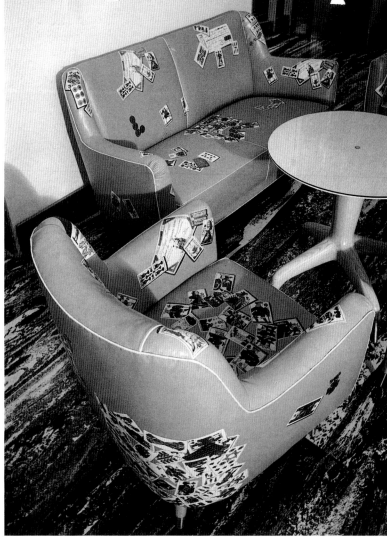

Ceccato furnishings, Milan, 1950

«A degree of amusement shouldn't be excluded from interior decoration.» Here the brass volume projecting from the wall contains a «surprise fireplace.» The walnut wall, running around the room and including the show-cases and the shelves, is an «organized wall,» as Ponti called it.

Left, the little girl's bed.

Harrar-Dessié housing development, Milan: the white and yellow house by Ponti and Gho, 1952.

Harrar-Dessié Housing Development, Milan, 1950

«For low-cost housing, inventiveness first — as in ancient times.» And the creation of «beautiful sites,» free from the complex of «inescapable equality.»[1]

The plan of this housing unit (drawn up by Luigi Figini, Gino Pollini, and Gio Ponti) is founded on a «composition of different buildings,» set in a park, not on rows of identical buildings. The larger houses (five stories high) and the smaller houses (one story high and grouped in «insulae») create a lively architectural landscape. Where, moreover, «color bursts out.»[1]

(Two houses in the development were designed by Ponti. One red and white, with duplex apartments on the top floor. One white and yellow, a typical «finite form» which he designed in collaboration with Gigi Gho.)

In those years there was a lot of concern about the «new» architectural landscape that was being constructed in Italy, as a result of the many postwar schemes and programs of low-cost housing. Ponti was determined to oppose the growing fashion for the (fake) «village,» as well as «false naturalism» in planimetric compositions.[2]

Aerial view of the development, in a photograph taken in the fifties. *Below,* general plan.

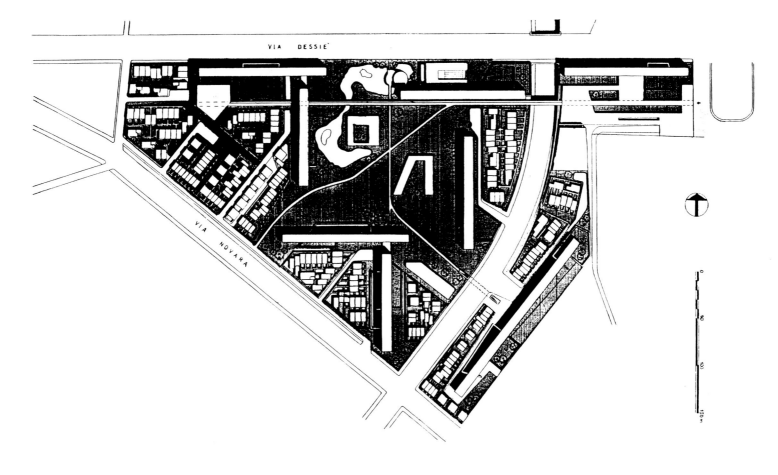

Harrar-Dessié housing development, Milan. *Right*, north end of the white and yellow house. *Below*, the white and red house, with duplex apartments on the top floor. *Bottom*, the west and east facades of the white and yellow house.

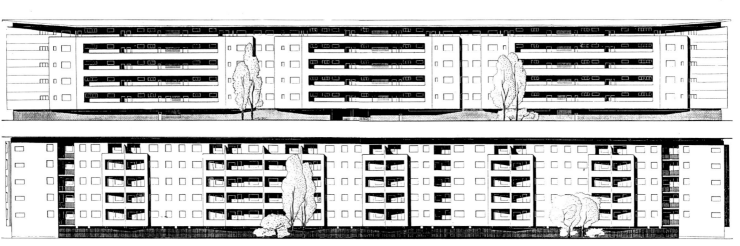

elemento d'abitazione nella unità-quartiere Dessiè, collaborazione di Gigi Gho, ingegnere

Second Montecatini building, Milan, 1951

The first and second Montecatini buildings stand side by side in the heart of the city. To the dimensional constraints imposed (on both) by the shape of the site and the building regulations, was added the «proximity» of the two works of architecture, separated by no more than a few meters and fifteen years.

Ponti used the same solution for the «wings» of the second building as he did for the first. To the front he gave a contrasting design. Since this front was only slightly taller than the wings of the neighboring building, with their strong motif, «only a slender pattern extending over the whole façade could give it a different and acceptable scale.»[1] This slender pattern changes spectacularly according to the point of view of the observer,[2] shifting from «all glass» (frontal view) to «all aluminum» (side view).[3]

Yet in the second Montecatini building, as in the first, it is not the front that grabs your attention: here it is the «back,» or rear facade, with its fine pattern of diamond-shaped surfaces.

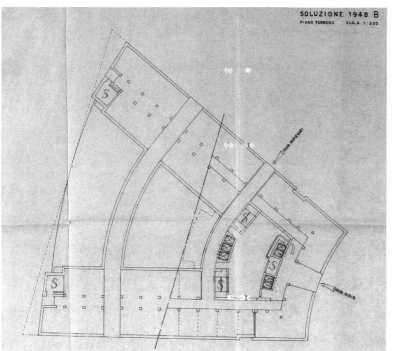

The concave front and plan of the ground floor.

Bedroom with decorations by Piero Fornasetti, at the 9th Milan Triennale, 1951.

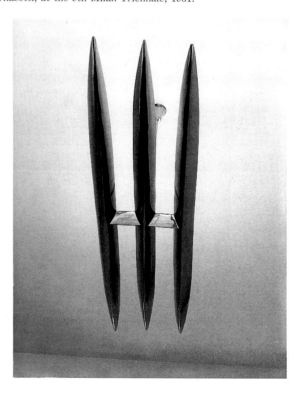

Lamp for Greco, Milan, 1951.

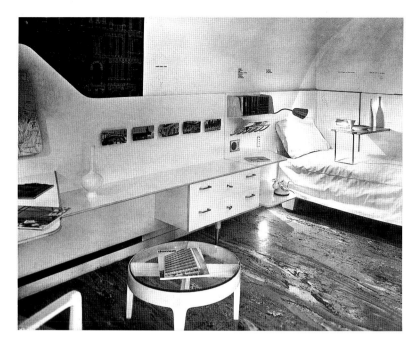

Hotel bedroom at the 9th Triennale, Milan, 1951

Intended as a «protest»[1] against the usual kind of hotel room, cluttered with furniture, this room (3 by 4 meters) has all its facilities (lamps, shelves, drawers, writing desk, etc.) located inside a single long wall panel. Note the small, folding table over the bed (it is nice to be able to eat in bed) and the «city map» over the desk (it is nice to know where you are).
(With the collaboration of Aldo De Ambrosis.)

Lucano furnishings, Milan, 1951

Details of the Milanese apartment which Ponti called «casa di fantasia»: an explosion of Fornasetti's imprinting and of Ponti's amusements (painted mirror doors, surprise through-views from one room to another...).

151

Edison power plant, Santa Giustina, 1952

Details of the Edison power plant on the river Noce at Santa Giustina, Trent: it was the first of the six Edison plants designed by Ponti's office (P.F.R.) from 1952 to 1956. It was published in Aria d'Italia ('Espressione di Gio Ponti,' VIII, 1954) in the chapter 'Experiences'.[1]

Villa Arata, Via Partenopea, Naples, 1952

This villa appears in Aria d'Italia *('Espressione di Gio Ponti,' VIII, 1954) among the few examples chosen of Ponti's «Mediterranean architecture»:*[1] *attention is drawn to the projecting loggia, as deep as a room, with its own windows, cut in the wall, and fireplace: a volume «added» to the flat front.*

The loggia with doors and windows in the side walls, and the chimney.

Gio Ponti's studio at no. 49, Via Dezza, Milan, 1952

A huge shed, formerly a garage. Gio Ponti turned it into his studio, and everyone went on calling it «the shed.»[1] In the seventies, when Ponti had begun to refer to all his designs as «forms» («form for an automobile,» «form for a museum,» «form for a cathedral»),[2] he might have called this crowded shed a «form for a studio.» This «open space» measuring 15 by 45 meters fully embodied his idea of an architectural studio (the Studio Ponti Fornaroli Rosselli) that was also a workshop, a training ground for young people (guests and students from all over the world), a place for the display of new materials and designs (indeed, furnished with just these materials and designs), and an exhibition site. For years, the shed was also where the editorial staff of Domus (two people) worked. And it was even used for family weddings and parties. It was well suited to Ponti's delight in living and working «without secrets.» His house had movable walls, his studio had no partitions.

Ponti would have liked the new premises of the Faculty of Architecture in Milan, under construction at the time, to have had a similar layout — like that of a workshop.[3]

Below, the exit of «the shed» on the garden. *Top,* inside the shed, different «new» materials on display.

154

Below, the former garage retained its central passageway running from one end to the other (from the entrance to the garden exit), flanked by the tables of the draftsmen. *Left*, the space used by the small editorial staff of *Domus*.

Project for the Lancia building, Turin, 1953

An unbuilt office building. The plan, with its closed outline and the fastigium, determines a «finite form.» The project was by Gio Ponti and Nino Rosani.

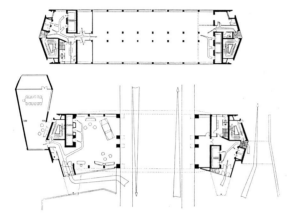

Above, plan of the typical floor and of the ground floor.

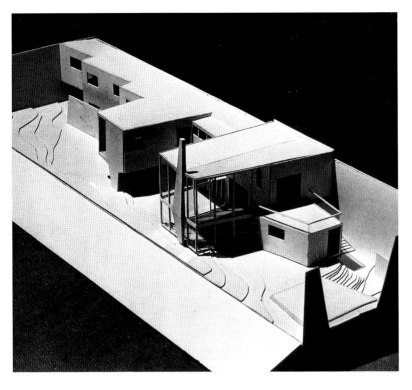

Project for the Taglianetti house, São Paulo, 1953

A Brazilian project, unexecuted. The site, long and narrow, is enclosed by an unbroken wall the same height as the house, which makes the garden a sort of hortus conclusus. *The rooms are aligned along one of the enclosing walls, and look onto the garden. An unbroken through-view crosses the garden from end to end.*

In the plan, all the rooms are aligned along the enclosing wall.

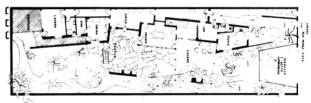

Project for the swimming pool of the Hotel Royal, Via Partenope, Naples, 1953

A swimming pool on the hotel roof. The pool and the surrounding terraces have the same lining in ceramic tiles, bearing a single, large, unbroken design that descends from the terraces, runs under the water and reappears.

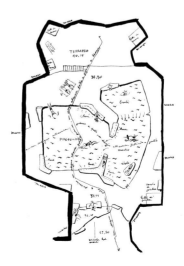

Project for the «Predio Italia» (Italo-Brazilian Center) in São Paulo, 1953

A Brazilian project that was never realized, this «vertical expression before Pirelli» was important to Ponti as a demonstration of a principle, that of the «representativeness of exteriors»: it is a multipurpose building, and it shows it.

The low block housing the Center emphasizes the special scale of the auditorium and halls. The tall blocks, with their differing patterns along their facades, make clear which areas of the building are intended for offices, for standard apartments, for duplex apartments, or for ateliers....

The project was by Gio Ponti and Luiz Contrucci.

Plan of one of the floors with apartments. *In the photographs,* the model viewed from above and from the side (main facade).

Project for the Faculty of Nuclear Physics at the University of São Paulo, 1953

The stimulating country of Brazil, which he visited in 1952, gave Ponti the opportunity to produce two projects that were never carried out but that were farsighted in their approach: the project for the «Predio Italia» (Italo-Brazilian Center) and the project for the Faculty of Nuclear Physics at São Paulo — a long horizontal building that Ponti liked to point to as the forerunner of the «finite form,» the «closed form» of the Pirelli building. The long front bends slightly in the middle, and the rear wall «turns» forward at both ends, thus «closing» the form. The walls have the appearance of «hanging screens» (another Pontian principle): the front (thin perforated surface, bent at the top to form an overhang, and bent at the bottom to give greater depth to the lecture rooms on the ground floor) does not «touch the ground;» front and sides are detached at the corner (they are two «sheets,» and their slenderness is visible); the roof overhangs at the back. Moreover — another principle — the project separates into distinct, immediately recognizable volumes, the different elements of which the building is composed: the auditorium, a volume that is «out of scale» with respect to the lecture rooms, is pulled out and set apart to form a block. Lastly, an invention: the «dedicatory wall,» along the edge of the plot. It is a long, free-standing screen on which to assemble all the «images of art» that «dedicate this building to Italy.» («This expression of dedication is the same as can be seen in the highly ornate facades of certain palaces and churches, true architectural proclamations, detached from the rest of the building.»)[1]

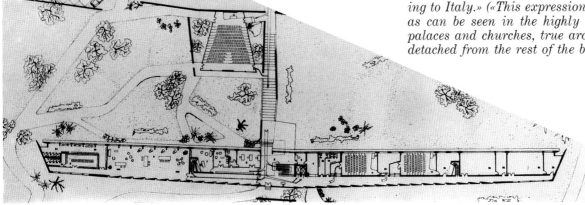

In the general plan and in the model below, the «bar» of the lecture rooms and the isolated block of the auditorium, bounded by the «dedicatory wall,» a long, external screen. *Above left*, foreshortened view of the front.

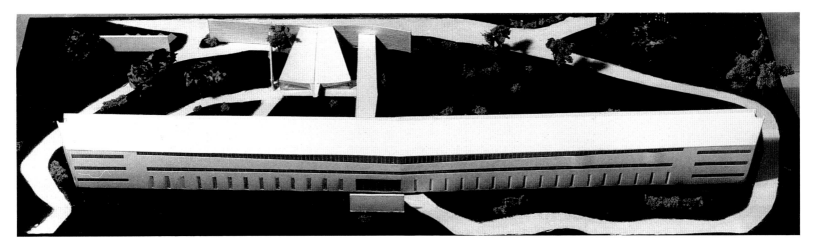

The «Distex» armchair for Cassina, Meda, 1953.

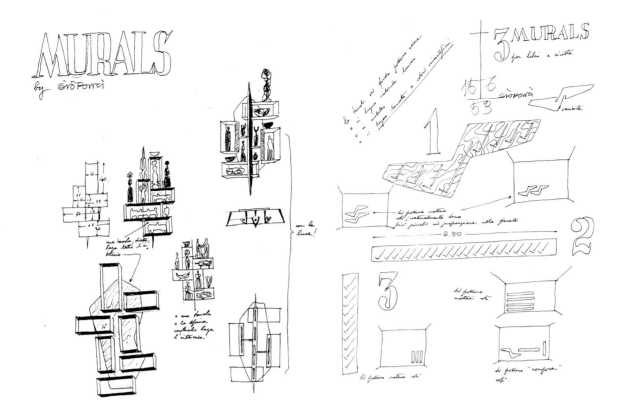

Furniture and ideas for New York, i.e. for Altamira, the New York firm that — after M. Singer and Sons and Knoll — presented the «Italian line» in the USA, in 1953 («more Italian than line,» said Ponti; «the simultaneous presence of *different* talents is Italian»). *Above,* «Murals,» some ideas for mural compositions. *Left,* an upholstered seat. *Below,* a magazine-rack.

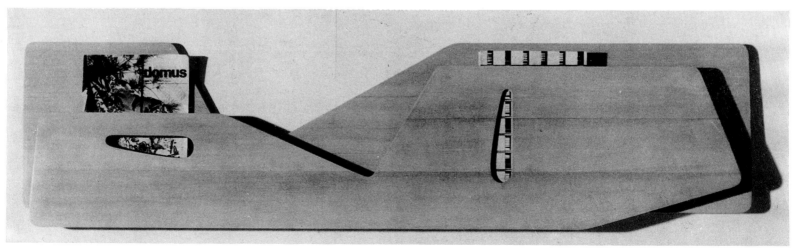

161

Ideal Standard sanitary fixtures, Milan, 1953

By taking away from the fixtures their «architectural clothing» (the «column» that pretends to support the «bowl» of the sink, the «collars» in relief that «encircle» its contours), one arrives at the «true» form, Ponti said in 1955[1] (but he had already done it in 1936, with the SVAO fixtures for Montecatini.[2]

Here the column of the sink is a simple casing (that conceals, not supports). The basin of the sink — smooth, with no projections — is trapezoidal (a shape that leaves room for the arms when washing). Ponti also designed the faucets (for Gallieni, Viganò, and Marazza): «stars» with only three points, as they are turned with just three fingers.[3]

Ponti was to design a new series of fixtures for Ideal Standard in 1966, the «Oneline» series.[4]

Ponti's collaborators: George Labalme, Giancarlo Pozzi, Alberto Rosselli.

The appliances of the «Serie P,» 1953.

DA UNA FORMA GEOMETRICA
AD UNA FORMA NATURALE

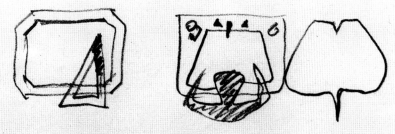

DA UNA FORMA ARCHITETTONICA
AD UNA FORMA NATURALE

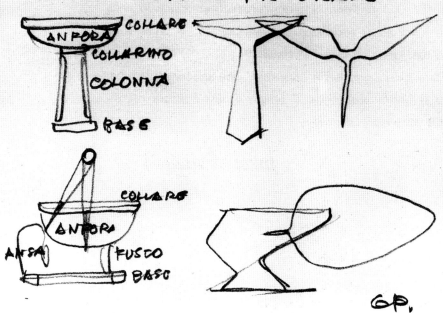

ANFORA — COLLARE
COLLARINO
COLONNA
BASE

COLLARE
ANFORA
ANSA — FUSTO
BASE

G.P.

For this series of appliances, faucets
and fittings were by Gallieni Viganò
Marazza, Milan.

163

A small table for M. Singer and Sons, the New York company that first introduced Gio Ponti's design in the USA, in 1950. Josef Singer used to promote in New York furniture by Ponti, Mollino and Parisi during the early fifties.

Below and right, furniture for Stockholm, 1953, presented by Nordiska Kompaniet, executed by G. Chiesa.

Above, the plates have the same design as the tablecloth, 1954. Prototypes, with Mucci Staglieno. *Left*, plate and tablecloth in positive-negative, 1953.

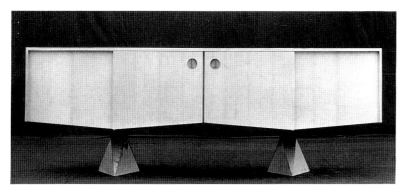

Wooden furniture for Carugati, Rovellasca, 1953.

«Furnished window,» 1954

Gio Ponti: «A room has, by nature, four walls. The room with a floor-to-ceiling glass window on the other hand has three walls and an empty space. The room with the furnished window has four walls again, of which one is transparent.»[1] And the pattern of design that is on the other three walls continues on this transparent one.

(Gio Ponti: «I have thought about Philip Johnson's house of glass again, which is just one room, with a totally transparent perimeter: it creates the same effect I was looking for in these furnished windows, as 'from inside' the outside is always seen through the foreground of the furniture, and in this lies its charm.»[1]

The «furnished window» made by Altamira, New York, 1953, and its model (*below and center*).

166

Automobile body proposal for Carrozzeria Touring, Milan, 1952—53

A «form for the automobile» designed by Gio Ponti in 1952 (for an Alfa Romeo chassis). At the time, Carrozzeria Touring did not dare to put this design for a car body into production. Twenty years later, many cars had «caught up» with it.[1]

Gio Ponti had devised this form in reaction to the cars of that time, «swollen, full of empty spaces,» («borax,» as Edgar Kaufmann used to say[2]) «with very high radiators, tiny windows, and dark interiors.»[3]

It was a form ahead of its time: the body sheets are flat, not curved (stiffened with folds and not ribs); the hood is low, the windows are very large, the back seats are adjustable (like in airplanes, as people used to say at the time), the trunk is extremely capacious (accessible from the inside and separate from the spare wheel housing); the interior is spacious, bright, and filled with «pockets.» One innovation: the bumper made of rubber (provided with spring buffers at front and rear) that runs right round the car.[4]

In the fifties this was called the «diamond line.» Another of Ponti's «diamonds.» For him it was a line that answered precisely to the requirements of the user — including that of beauty. «A car too is made to be looked at: like the gondola.»

(At the age of eighty Gio Ponti used to say: «when the Citroën DS came out, in '57, the three of us in the Studio — Fornaroli, Rosselli, Ponti — got one each: in homage to its beauty, as other cars work too. For the same reason we only use Olivetti typewriters....»[3])

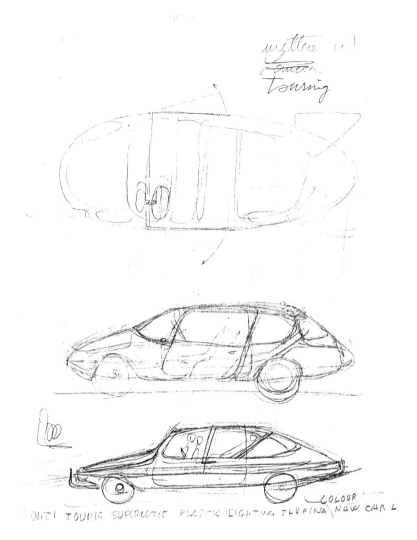

Top, genesis of the design. Left, sketch of the section. Below, the definitive form.

167

Project for the Togni system of lightweight prefabrication at the 10th Milan Triennale, 1954

The house (for four people) was designed for the Togni system of lightweight prefabrication, made out of section irons. It is made up of three rectangular cores — the bedrooms, the living room, the kitchen-dining room — linked by a corridor of irregular that variable form — a new element in design — that breaks down the rigidity of the layout. Moreover the cores are of different heights (the living room is higher than the bedrooms and kitchen): in order for the house to maintain a constant profile at roof level, the profile is variable at ground level; the difference between levels in the interior produces a pleasing effect.

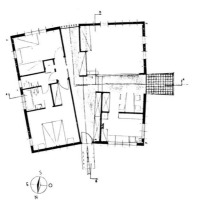

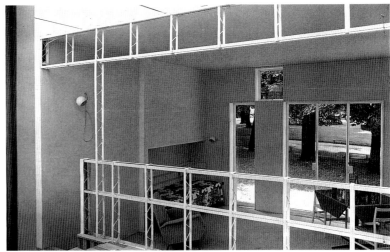

In the drawings, the north front and the plan. *Above right*, the front of the living room with ceramic grill. *In the interior photograph*, the living room.

House in the pine wood, Arenzano, Genoa, 1955

A project in the series of new «small houses»[1] by the sea that Ponti proposed in this period. Ponti only published (in Domus*) the plan and walls of this one, since the idea was contained in the walls. «Separated by the three deep wings of brickwork, each of the three bedrooms has its own loggia facing the pine wood, under the projecting roof.»*

The north front, with the entrance. The children are running toward the garage. The external wall openings are framed with blue ceramic pebbles.

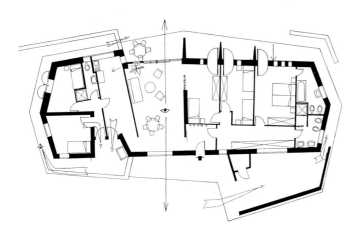

Villa Planchart, Caracas, 1955

As he was to do with the Pirelli building, Ponti published his Villa Planchart twice (both times in Domus*): first as a design[1] and then again after its construction.[2] He described the principles on which it was based and the results, for he saw the circumstance as almost ideal, and able to set a standard.*

The client was ideal, a happy client («the client, says my friend Rogers, is the person without whom one cannot produce architecture, and with whom one cannot produce it either. But here, the client has been one with whom it has been possible, to the best of our ability, to produce architecture...»[2]). The house now belongs to the Fundacion Anala y Armando Planchart, which has maintained it intact, right down to its furnishings.

And this is fortunate, for this work of architecture — «a spectacular display of spaces for whoever enters it» — has a unique combination of inventions and delights, as rich as the tropical vegetation it incorporates. (Look at the patio decorated by Melotti,[3] and the small internal windows, and the little theatrical balconies that face onto the empty space of the two-story-high living-room, and the doors and ceilings decorated by Ponti.)

The principle of this work of architecture — which is the fruit (as the Pirelli building would also be) of the «new researches» emerging out of Ponti's journeys to Latin America in 1952 and 1953 — is the «evidence of the supported surfaces»: the non-bearing external walls appear to be detached one from the other, as well as from the roof and ground. This is evident at night as well, for the plans for this work of architecture included what Ponti called a project of nocturnal «self-illumination.» Without weight or mass (and «with the slenderness that Niemeyer has revealed to us»), the construction seems to rest «graciously» on the ground, like a butterfly.

In Caracas the house was immediately dubbed «a Florentine villa.» This pleased Ponti, since Italianness was something about which he had never worried («being Italian is enough»).

Ground floor: view from the entrance (1) through to the open-air dining area (10) across the patio (11); view from the library (7) through to the dining-room (9) across the living room (8).

Second floor: cross-view from one terrace through to the opposite one (32 and 34), and from the balcony-bridge (21/22) another cross-view between the patio (11) and the living-room.

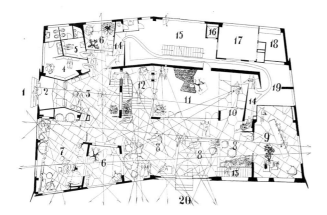

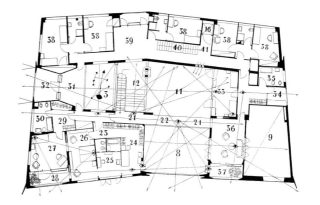

The Villa Planchart was one — together with the Villa Arreaza also in Caracas and the Villa Nemazee in Teheran[4] — of the «three villas» designed in these years in which Ponti was given full «freedom of invention.»

Villa Planchart, Caracas, 1955. The coloured and luminous ceilings by Ponti in the living room. *Below*, ceramic works by Fausto Melotti in the patio and along the stairs.

Villa Planchart in Caracas, 1955. Nighttime appearance: a strip of light runs behind the walls.

Italian Cultural Institute, Lerici Foundation, Stockholm, 1954

Ponti published (in Domus) both the model[1] and the actual construction[2] of this building, together with the modifications it had undergone. Of this building, built in a foreign country, he was pleased that people said, unexpectedly, «it is Italian.» The building is another example of Pontian «finite form,» and of his principle of isolating (not incorporating) the «out of scale» part (here, the large auditorium, with roofing designed by Nervi). Ponti's collaborator on this project was Ture Wennerholm.

Above right, the back elevation. *Right*, the stairs in the entrance hall. *Below*, the model. Original plan of the third floor.

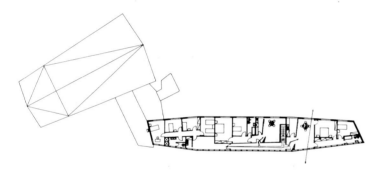

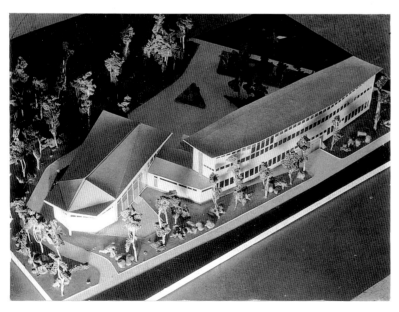

Project for the Town Hall in Cesenatico, 1959

An unexecuted project. The sky is visible through the «portholes» at the top of the front — a motif which Ponti will repeat and develop: in the seventies, with the cathedral of Taranto and its «sail,» the sky will be visible through the whole facade.

Faculty of Architecture at the Milan Polytechnic, 1956

Designed by Gio Ponti in collaboration with Giordano Forti, this new seat for the Faculty of Architecture at the Milan Polytechnic was built in the fifties. But the idea of the Faculty seat as a «teaching building»[1] and a work-shop for the students (as in a previous project by Ponti, 1954) is still unrealized.

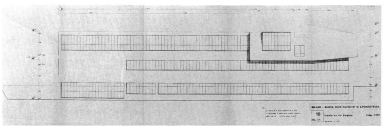

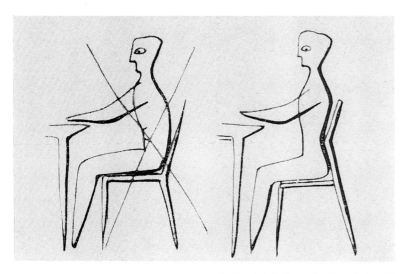

The «Superleggera» chair, for Cassina, Meda, 1957

There was a progressive lightening of the «Ponti chair» over the years. In 1949 the first chair with a bent back and pointed legs appeared.[1] In 1952 came the highly popular «Leggera» chair Ponti designed for Cassina, made of ash and very strong and light. («If you go to the Cassinas they will give you exciting demonstrations in which these chairs are hurled to dizzy heights, fall to the ground, and bounce, without ever breaking.»[2]) Finally, in 1957, came the «Superleggera» chair, that could be lifted with one finger: its struts had a triangular cross-section.[3] (Ponti produced over twenty other designs for chairs for Cassina, over the years.)

In the sketch above, the first chair with pointed legs and a bent back, 1949. *Right*, the «Leggera» of 1952. *Below*, drawing for the «Superleggera».

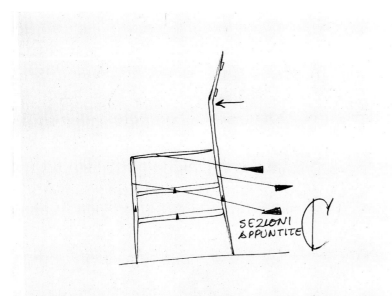

SEZIONI APPUNTITE

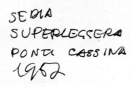

SEDIA SUPERLEGGERA PONTI CASSINA 1952

The «Superleggera» of 1957; the legs have a triangular section.

Door-painting, 1955, and printed door-painting, 1957

Ponti started out with the idea of a «painted door» («why cannot doors be as expressive as paintings, in the room?»[1]), and then came up with the idea of printing a door-sized design on fabric, and «producing it in meters and meters of fabric, for door after door.» With Jsa of Busto Arsizio.[2]

Door covered with printed fabric, 1957: the fabric, by Jsa of Busto Arsizio, is suitable for doors 70 to 90 cm in width and 200 to 240 cm in height. *Below left*, sketch for painted door, 1955.

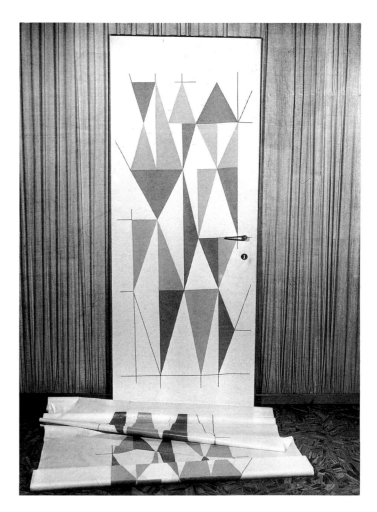

Below, Large chest of drawers: the projecting rectangular elements serve as handles. Made by Giordano Chiesa for Gio Ponti's exhibition staged by the Ferdinand Lundquist company in Göteborg, Sweden, 1955.

Above left, kaleidoscopic flooring in wooden tiles: there is only one tile and it can be laid in different patterns; executed with Maria Carla Ferrario, for Insit of Turin, 1954. *Above*, inlaid cowhide rug, made by Colombi, Milan, for Altamira, New York, 1954.

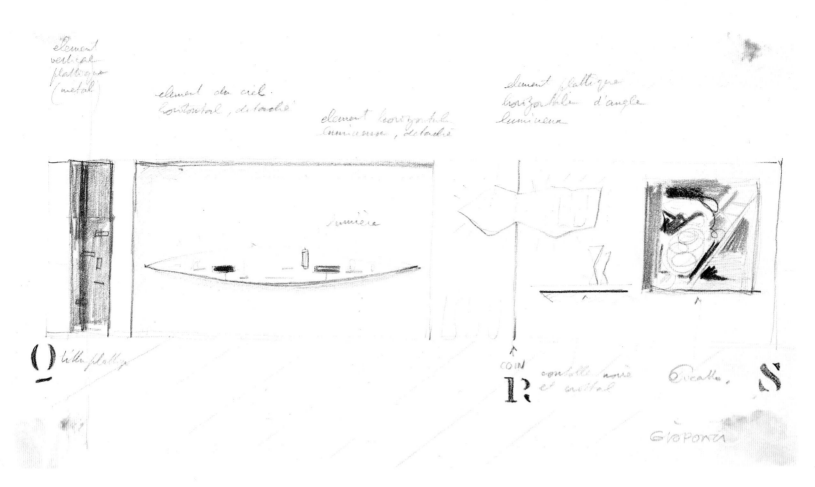

Furniture design for the Beracasa apartment, Caracas, 1956 (A.G.P.).

Alitalia offices on Fifth Avenue, New York, 1958. Ceramic works by Fausto Melotti.

Objects in enameled copper for De Poli, Padua, 1956

They are an invention, these figures of animals — cats, fish, horses, as well as water-melons and devils — «cut and folded» as if they were made of paper. Flat figures that «stand up by themselves.» They are an example of *Ponti's way of using only and always the drawing. He drew with the scissors. It was then up to Paolo De Poli, master of the art of enameling on copper, to turn these ideas into objects — with Delight and with Bravura.*

Villa Arreaza, Caracas, 1956

It stands in a park. It was immediately given the name «the diamond house» because of its facing of diamond-cut ceramic tiles. The large roof covers «groups of rooms» separated by patios: seven small patios, that bring the greenery outside into the house as well, in between the rooms.

Green is «the other color»: for walls, floors, ceilings, furniture, objects, and fabrics are all in white and blue, a playful scheme that makes these interiors still more playful.

In the model, the seven small patios. *Below*, the entrance front: the cantilevered shelter, decorated with a pattern of colored triangles, projects from beneath the roof.

Top, ceramic wall decorations, sometimes projected «by letter.» Left, the living-room, completely blue and white (walls, ceilings, floor, furniture, objects).

181

Steel flatware for Krupp Italiana, Milan, 1951

The «new way of thinking about these implements, flat-ware,» indeed their «perfect form» («adopted within twenty years by everyone»), is this, according to Ponti: a short-bladed knife with a slanted profile (we use just the point of the blade to cut), and a fork with short prongs (we use just the tip of the prongs to pick up food).[1]

Objects and flatware in nickel silver for Krupp Italiana, Milan, at the 9th Triennale, 1951.

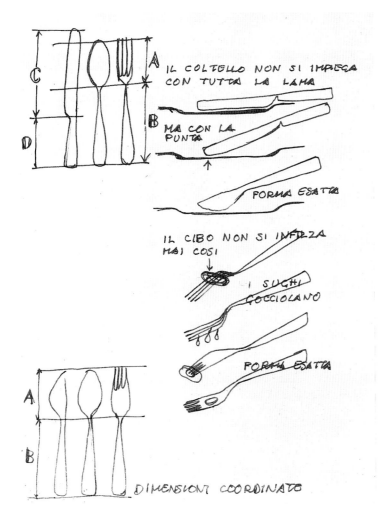

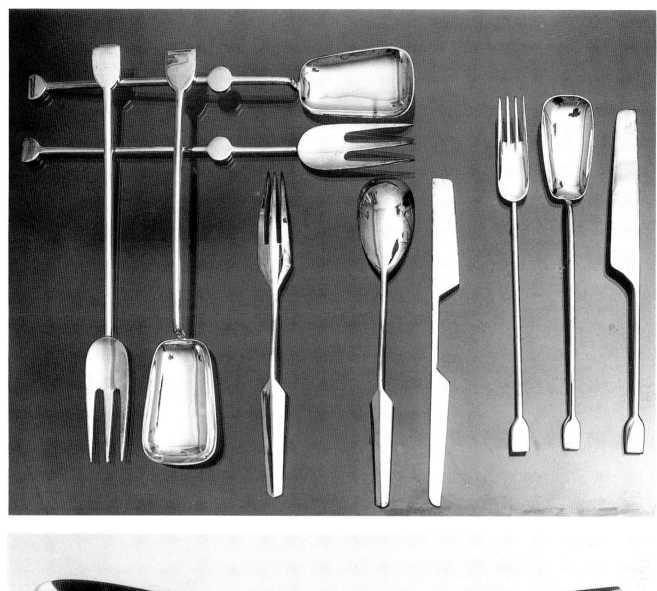

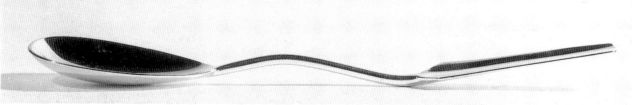

Flatware (prototypes), 1955.

Flatware for Christofle, Paris, 1955

Commencing in 1927 and lasting throughout his life, the collaboration between Gio Ponti and the Parisian Or-fèvrerie Christofle, owned by the Bouilhet family, produced new fruit in 1955 and 1956.

These were the years in which Ponti established his flexible and lively relationship with friendly industries, a relationship which permitted him to get immediate prototypes of possible series to come (his preferred collaborator,

on steel or silver prototypes, was Lino Sabattini).

In 1957, Ponti held an exhibition at the Galerie Christofle in Paris, «Formes Idées d'Italie,»[1] in which he presented, as was his habit, not only his architecture and his designs for Christofle, but also ceramics, silverware, and paintings by friends, including Melotti, Gambone, Fiume, Rui, De Poli, and Sabattini, just as he had done in Göteborg in 1955.

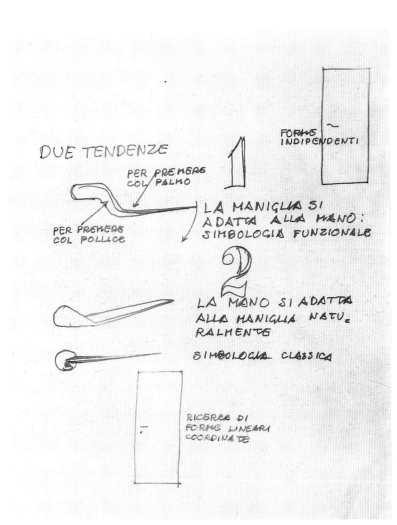

DUE TENDENZE

PER PREMERE
COL PALMO

FORME
INDIPENDENTI

PER PREMERE
COL POLLICE

LA MANIGLIA SI
ADATTA ALLA MANO:
SIMBOLOGIA FUNZIONALE

LA MANO SI ADATTA
ALLA MANIGLIA NATU-
RALMENTE

SIMBOLOGIA CLASSICA

RICERCA DI
FORME LINEARI
COORDINATE

Handles for Olivari, Borgomanero, 1956.

Flatware (prototypes) for Krupp Italiana, Milan, 1956.

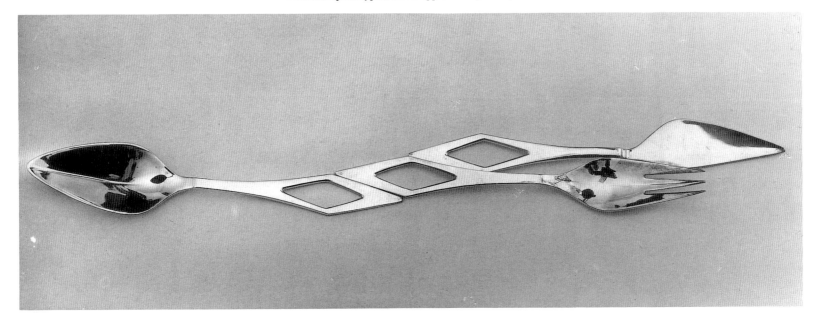

Objects for Sabattini and Christofle, Paris, 1956.

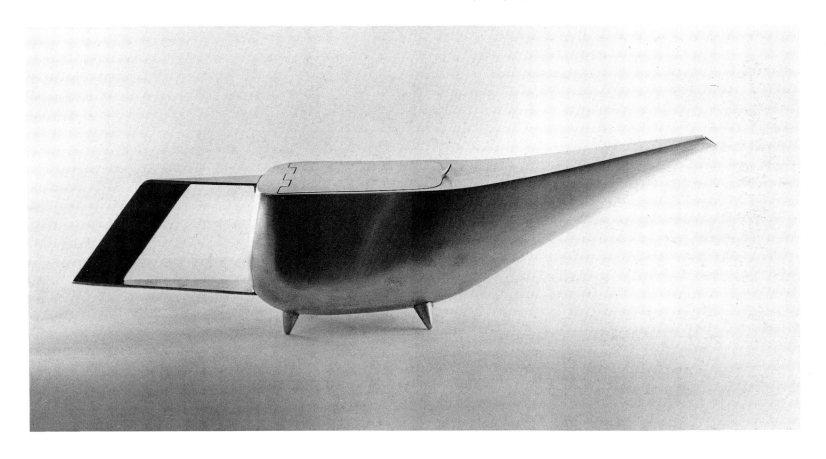

Pirelli Skyscraper, Milan, 1956

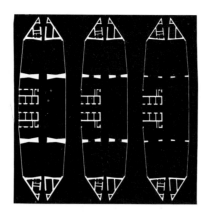

Plans of floor 2, floor 16, floor 31 (used by Ponti as a «graphic slogan» of the Pirelli Tower). *Below*, the tower, «detached» from the low blocks.

Why a skyscraper? «The high-rise building is justified when, concentrating the constructable volumes in itself, it is set back from the edges of the site and leaves room for the traffic and for parking. No more streets like trenches.»[1] Moreover, «giving up irregular space and concentrating volumes in a single building of precise shape, dictated by reason, means going back to intelligence in construction and in the end giving the buildings a shape without flaws, totally resolved.»

Ponti wrote this in 1956, that is at the time when the Pirelli building was built — this «eagerly awaited» European skyscraper,[2] a skyscraper that immediately drew bolts of lightning (from historians, both European and American, from Zevi to Banham) and by presenting itself, provocatively, with a graphic «slogan,»[3] provoked the critics to come up with slogans in turn.[4]

This «small skyscraper,» with its lean shape (127.10 m high, 18.50 m deep at the center, 70.40 m in width), does not «stand» on a basement but «emerges,» surrounded by a «void» that separates it from the low blocks around: like a missile being fired from an underground silo. Its «essential» form, perceptible from the inside as well, matches the thinness of its supporting structure, in which (as Nervi put it) «open season was declared on unnecessary weights.»

Looking at the three plans (ground floor, 16th floor, 31st floor), which make up the «graphic slogan» of the building, one can see how the central pillars taper as the load of the floors diminishes. The building cannot grow any higher just as its plan cannot expand (owing to the tapering of the axial gallery at each end, where movement within the building comes to a stop). It is a «finite form,» derived from a «structural invention» as Ponti called it.

A «structural invention» whose realization required all the skill of Nervi (responsible with Danusso for the structural calculations): stability (resistance to wind) in a building in which the ratio of width to height is so small was a problem without precedent for a reinforced concrete structure. Nervi solved it by adopting a «gravity» system, concentrated in the rigid triangles of the two «points» (pairs of hollow pillars with solid walls) and in the four equally rigid central pillars (large wall-pillars) as well as in the central tower of the elevators.[5] Tests of the structure were carried out on a special model all of eleven meters high.[6]

Typical of Ponti was the way in which he compared, in Domus,[7] the building as conceived (i.e. the «perfect» model) with the building as constructed. He drew attention to the goals achieved — structural invention, essentiality — as well as to those that, «clear in our minds, have not been attained in full» — expressiveness, illusoriness. These were the terms he used.

Expressiveness: the Pirelli building is «vertical» at the sides, but the glass facade is dominated visually by the «horizontal» strips of the opaque parapets (and yet, the very thickness of the floors had been dispensed with, by making them taper at the edges!). «We have managed to preserve a grammatical statement,» said Ponti, «by keeping the sections of glass adjoining the pillars transparent»[8] (to show that the opaque strips of the parapets have nothing to do with the structure); but, in Ponti's eyes, it proved impossible to get rid of the detested «striped pajama» effect.

The Pirelli Tower, Milan, 1956.

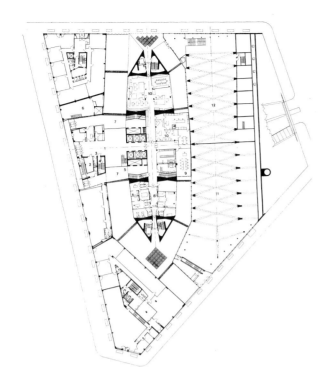

The Pirelli Tower, Milan, 1956. Plan of the ground floor and cross-section. The tower containing the offices is isolated, with its own foundations; two «bridges» connect it to the low blocks: the low block at the front (housing the auditorium), and the low block at the rear, with the staff entrance and canteen.

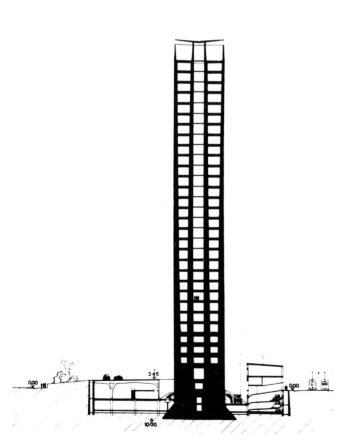

Illusoriness: another effect not achieved in full was that of the vertical cleft at each end of the skyscraper, intended to be an unbroken fissure of light. In reality it is segmented by the protruding floor slabs (those «confounded little balconies»[8]) that had to be extended for structural reasons.

Ponti, talking to himself in Domus, *lamented the fact. And he was right to do so, for with the passing of time it is only the architecture, the form, that remains, not the reasons behind it. And besides, the more intelligently it complies with them, and the more it is «made to measure,» the more, as a delicate instrument, it risks falling into disuse.*

Today, thirty years after their appearance, Milan's two «towers,» the Pirelli and Velasca buildings, antagonistic in their view of history, both belong to history. They are part of the city's «complexity and contradiction.»

«I like skyscrapers close to one another.» In this sense, and only in this sense, Gio Ponti was thinking of New York. Ponti always loved the skyscrapers of New York, the «bristling city» as Le Corbusier called it, as an «American fairy tale.» They prompted him to speak more of the sky and the city than of the architecture («penetrating into the sky with perfect building machines...,» «over the silver surfaces the sky will move, with its clouds...»).[9]

According to Ponti himself, it was not New York but his experience of Brazil (1952) that led him to the Pirelli building.[7] In Brazil (the Brazil «awakened» by Le Corbusier[10]), it was the encounter with Niemeyer[11] and with his «extraordinary formal imagination»[12] that helped Ponti to free his own «form» (the results of this would be seen in the projects for Venezuela).

There are a thousand different images of the Pirelli tower and its highly popular profile. Ponti always rejected photographs taken from below which invent a «dynamic impetus» that the building does not have. Ponti's architecture is one of subtle equilibrium, not impetus.

The Pirelli skyscraper was designed by the Studio Ponti Fornaroli Rosselli in collaboration with the Studio Valtolina-Dell'Orto; structural consultants, Arturo Danusso, Pier-Luigi Nervi.

188

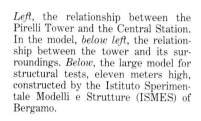

Left, the relationship between the Pirelli Tower and the Central Station. In the model, *below left*, the relationship between the tower and its surroundings. *Below*, the large model for structural tests, eleven meters high, constructed by the Istituto Sperimentale Modelli e Strutture (ISMES) of Bergamo.

The Pirelli Tower, Milan, 1956. *Right*, night view and the tower under construction. *Below*, Nervi's structure at the top of the tower. *Bottom right*, the projecting roof.

The Pirelli Tower under construction.

Casa Melandri, Milan, 1957

Gio Ponti: «In this house I played with diamond-shaped volumes, as I like to do, with the contrast of the solid, projecting volumes that rest on the empty spaces of the windows, and with the materials I love: silvery aluminum and gray, diamond-faceted tiles, very fine in their effect.»[1] The staircase is a kaleidoscopic pattern of colors, extending over five floors.

The stairs and the main front.

192

Project for the Villa Gorrondona, Caracas, 1957

The building owes its closed and elongated form to the fact that it stands on a narrow ridge. Given its location, access to the house is from below. Above the level of the covered parking lot (which also houses the portico and swimming pool), there is a level containing the living-rooms (with a two-story-high hall and library), and a level containing the bedrooms. There are two patios.

As part of the Studio Ponti Fornaroli Rosselli, Maria Carla Ferrario and Katzukj Ivabuchi collaborated on the project.

Below, plan of the floor on which the bedrooms are located.

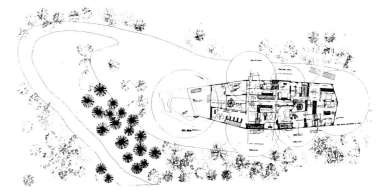

Gio Ponti's apartment in Via Dezza, Milan, 1957

The apartment in which Gio Ponti lived, with his family, from 1957 onward (his last house),[1] contains all of the Pontian «inventions» with regard to layout, walls, furniture, and objects that had appeared during the fifties, and that had originated even earlier. Here they are brought together, for the first time, in a unit and «for real»: from the open space with sliding walls to the «furnished windows,» «self-illuminating» furniture, «organized» wall panels, diagonally striped floor and ceiling, single color scheme (here, white and yellow), identical chairs and beds for the entire apartment, and paintings placed on stands (instead of hung on the walls).[2]

A «demonstration» house. And one in which everything came from the same mind and hand.[1]

And then the «demonstration» changed (as Ponti's thinking about the house progressed). This highly livable «open space» for five people turned into something else when Ponti lived there on his own: a free space in which to roam, amidst growing piles of drawings and paintings. Paintings on perspex too, an idea that Ponti came up with toward the end of his life, paintings to be looked at against the light, like stained-glass windows. At the age of eighty-six, Ponti painted twenty large «angels» on perspex,[3] and thought about making, with this «window painting» displayed on every floor, a (movable) decoration for the whole facade of the apartment building (he was always thinking in festive terms), residents permitting. The facade would have allowed this: a facade «of superimposed bands,» in which, on every floor, the residents had been allowed to choose their own «outside color,» and even their own «pattern of windows.» (Almost spontaneous architecture, Ponti used to say.)[4]

Above right, facade of the house in a «nighttime» drawing. The arrangement of openings is different on each floor. The apartment where Gio Ponti lived is on the top floor. *Right*, the living-room, with its «furnished window»: in later years the window was also decorated with «transparent» angels painted on perspex.

Above, diagonally striped ceilings and floor used all over the apartment.
Above left, view through the bed room.
Below left, view from the street facade through to the back facade.

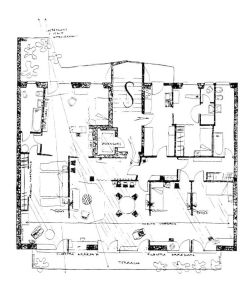

Proposals for the house at the 11th Milan Triennale, 1957

This pavilion in the park of the Triennale was not a «small house;» it was an example of integral use of new industrial products for the house, from construction to furnishings: from the Feal system of light prefabricated structure, to the roofing, the window elements, the external facings — all made out of aluminum — again by Feal, *the walls made out of colored concrete-framed glass blocks by Fidenza, ceramic «diamond-shaped» tiles by Joo, rubber floorings by Pirelli, and the two-tone folding partitions (as Ponti's new furniture for Cassina and his new lamps for Arredoluce, still prototypes, were in two colours).*

The entrance front: standard windows and external facing in aluminum strip.

196

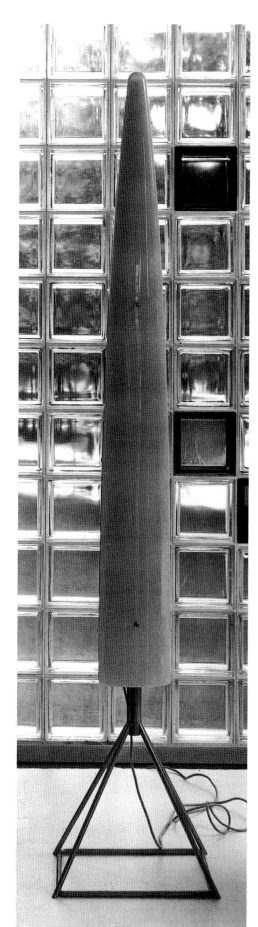

Plastic lamps for Arredoluce, 1957,
«Due foglie» couch for Cassina, 1956.

Diamond-faceted ceramic tiles for the lining of facades: the lining of tiles also becomes a «luminous» and «moving» pattern, because of the lighting effects on the relief surface; it lightens architecture. Shown, «Diamanti» and «Bugne» for Ceramica Joo, 1956.

Fabrics for the Jsa factory, Busto Arsizio, 1950—58

Gio Ponti first met Luigi Grampa, the founder of the Jsa factory, in 1950, and the relationship was a lasting one. Grampa, like Fede Cheti and like Alberto Ponis of the MITA, great friends of Ponti, was one of those innovators in the production of printed fabrics who made Italian «designer» fabrics famous in the fifties.

Gio Ponti's passion for fabrics derived from his love of printing: «is not the true, social, universal triumph of a representation to be, in the end, printed? To become image?»[1] On the page and on cloth — where, moreover, movement and repetition enter into play. And any design and sign can be «taken and printed,» turned into fabric.

«Cristalli» and «Diamanti,» fabrics for Jsa, 1957.

«Estate,» fabric for Jsa, 1957.

Carmelite Convent of Bonmoschetto, San Remo, 1958

In Gio Ponti, the sacred was expressed in joy, as it was in this convent of enclosure (contrasted in its day with Le Corbusier's monastery of La Tourette).[1]

The protagonists of this architecture are the white «walls,» in their contact with the greenery and the sky. Its heart is the chapel; transparent/non-transparent, it is set just between the «outside world» and the convent. (It does not have walls but «screens». From the outside it looks closed, from the inside, open: open to an outside world of flowers and greenery, but one that is in turn enclosed, surrounded by a wall — the parvis.) The cloister forms another heart: it is at the center of the convent, with no more transparency, and its portico has light wooden crosses as columns. The wood leads to the interiors: in the cells, the refectory, and the choir, there is nothing but wood and white walls.[2]

The three years required to carry out this work made possible a unique (and never forgotten) debate between the nuns and the architect over what is a convent and what is architecture.[3] It was the architect who said, to the «Carmelites de Saint Elie»: «bâtir un couvent n'est pas un problème d'architecture, c'est un problème de religion.» («Building a convent is not an architectural problem, but a religious one.») And it was the nuns who, on Le Corbusier's death, had a Mass celebrated for him in the chapel of their convent.[4]

The project was by Gio Ponti and Antonio Fornaroli.

Below, external walls: far left, the chapel; center, block of the cloister and cells; right, the garden wall.

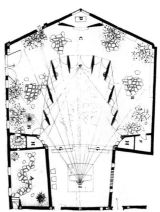

Left, the window bar is a cross. *Below*, plan of the chapel (which offers a totally transparent view onto the wall of the parvis).

Building for government offices, Baghdad, 1958

In 1955 the government of Iraq summoned to Baghdad architects like Alvar Aalto (for the city's Cultural Center), Frank Lloyd Wright (for the Opera House), Le Corbusier (for the Stadium), and subsequently Gropius (for the University) and Gio Ponti (for the Development Board building, a block of government offices).

The building is the work of «the Pirelli team» (Studio Ponti Fornarelli Rosselli, Studio Valtolina-Dell'Orto). And Ponti linked it with the Pirelli building: it was the first project «afterward».[1]

It responds, Ponti stressed, to a solely «climatic» environmental situation (the city's architectural past has been wiped out), and this was the reason for the enormous arcade that covers almost the entire area (16,000 m²), providing shelter for all the external routes, for both vehicles and pedestrians, and the car park. Out of the arcade rise the two blocks (administrative offices, executive offices) in contact with one another. The facades, clad with gray-blue ceramic tiles, have movable aluminum «brise-soleils.»

In the model, the complex viewed from above. *Above*, the complex seen from the Tigris. *In the plan*, the floor above the arcade.

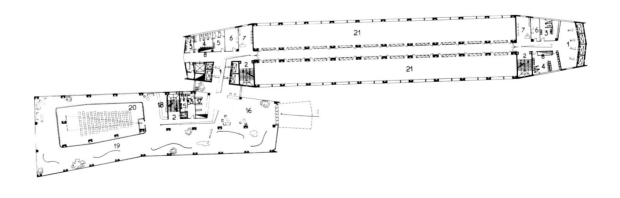

Auditorium on the eighth floor of the Time and Life Building, New York, 1959

The auditorium is a small independent building, situated on a terrace on the eighth floor of Harrison and Abramowitz's building. It is a «diamond-shaped» volume. It is not part of the skyscraper's architecture, yet it is incorporated in it through the «Pontian» pattern of its facing. Seen from above (from the upper floors or the sky), the volume, blending in with the pattern of the terrace floor (large colored triangles, blue-white, blue-gray, black) tended to disappear. (Today, as a result of the alterations carried out to the exterior, this effect too has disappeared.)

The pavilion on the terrace.

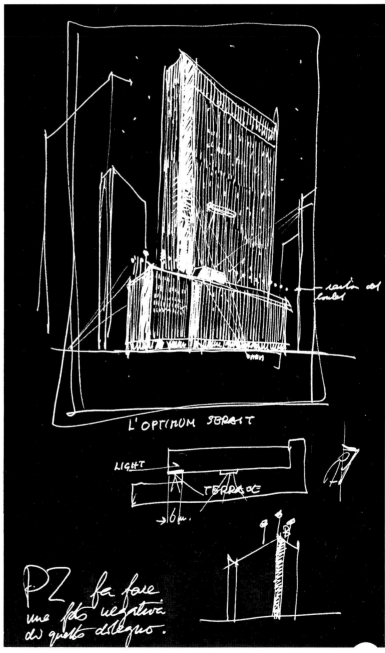

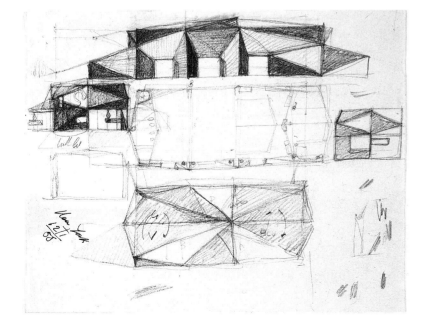

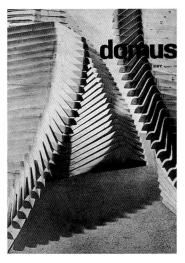

Covers of *Domus* in the fifties.

Domus in the fifties

In Italy (the key word is still «Italy») and in Domus, *the «famous fifties» started before 1950 and came to an end almost at once.*

«Industrial design,» as they called it, appeared in Domus *as early as 1948; Mollino, the first designer and last craftsman of the fifties, was there from 1948 to 1953. The fabulous ceramics of Melotti, Leoncillo, and Fontana («ceramics lend a fourth dimension to sculpture: color»[1]) were there. In 1949 came the sudden leap forward, with Fontana's «spatial art.»*

Domus *published Fontana's «nuclear forms suspended in the darkness of space and illuminated by the light of Wood» on its cover in 1949 — «the first graffito of the atomic age.»[2] It was true. It was the moment of the fantastic discovery of chaos, the discovery of forms that had no scale, as well as the discovery of the artificial (an artificial that was still elementary).*

Domus *continued to publish Campigli and Marini, as well as the Italian ships crammed with works of art, but its feeling was for Fontana who, in the void of the staircase at the Palazzo dell'Arte (9th Triennale, 1951) had «bent a bolt of lightning» with his neon; and for the Dova drawing «on the scale of a facade» that covered one of Zanuso's buildings, 1952; and for the luminous ceilings that Fontana suspended in Baldessari's cinemas, 1953 (a full collaboration, between artist and architect): «in the space age, space art, neither painting nor sculpture... we have discovered the new fantasies of art.»[3]*

«Discovery» in the world of design too — of a new, primordial idiom. It was a dawn. To make a chair, all you had to do was to bolt together two thin sheets of plywood (as Viganò did, in 1949), or bend sheet metal and screw it down (as Chessa and De Carli did, in 1950). The talk was of «making,» not «designing.» To make a lamp it was sufficient to cut it out of a sheet of metal, with a pair of scissors (as Sottsass did, in 1955). To create a room all that was needed was a bookcase and a shadow on the wall (as Tedeschi did, in 1950). It had to be possible to dismantle, reassemble, accumulate, and get rid of furniture.

These objects were invented for «mass production,» and proposed to an industry that was itself still young, rudimentary, and enthusiastic — and it did not matter if this «mass production» was more a challenge, an offering, than an industrial and political reality. It was also a desire to upset, to «shake up» means, modes and materials, in order to produce objects that did not belong to a «class.» All this appeared in Domus.

Ideas were for giving away. Just take a glance through the pages of Domus. *Ideas «for mass production» that did not even go so far as a prototype (they were just maquettes) but which it felt the need to disseminate. Industry was urged to participate as well. Fabrics? Industry took designs from artists, just as they were, and printed them. They were designs (by Fontana, Dova, Crippa, Carmi, Zuffi, Ponti, and Pomodoro) that could be used to cover furniture, walls, doors, or people. Industry immediately grasped the idea that flooring was not to be designed but «poured» (Ponti's «fantastico P.» black-and-yellow rubber flooring, 1951[4]). Or the idea that a lamp was not*

designed but «sprayed» (the Castiglionis' lamp made out of polyester plastic film, 1957). In the States, George Nelson had come up with the same idea.

Italian design immediately turned to America for comparisons — all this appeared in Domus — *rather than to the old continent — apart from France and Finland (with Prouvé and Wirkkala, respectively). And for* Domus *America was Eames, with the light reticular structure of his chairs, and Buckminster Fuller with the light reticular structure of his domes. It was Saarinen with his TWA. It was Calder with his giant «mobiles.»*

Discovery, in the early fifties, was geographical as well. Architects, even the «masters,» began to travel round the globe and develop a new vision. Le Corbusier went to Brazil in 1948 and India in 1956, and the Le Corbusier of Ronchamp, Chandigarh, and Ahmedabad, and even of the 1958 Brussels Expo, was a new one. Gropius went to India and Siam in 1956. Ponti went to Brazil, where he met Niemeyer, to Mexico, where he met Barragan, to Venezuela, where he met the new Ponti. Eames and Rudofsky discovered Japan, in 1954 and 1956. Japan took its turn on the stage with Kenzo Tange, in 1952.

All this appeared in Domus. *And* Domus *itself was, in the early fifties, a «fifties object,» in which everything was tried out and mixed together — art, crafts, design, architecture — and everyone set their hand to it.* Domus *was put together in an atelier, for that is what Gio Ponti's studio was in the early fifties, his ex-garage open to all, people and materials — the exciting «new materials.» Made in the garage,* Domus *was something unconstrained and handcrafted, but the publisher was setting up an «industrial» distribution that took it to every country — and this was its miracle, or its secret.*

And yet as early as 1954 — the year in which Domus *itself, with Ponti, prompted the setting up of* Stile Industria, *a magazine of design (founded by Rosselli), and of the «Compasso d'Oro,» an award for design — it can be seen that different activities had begun to move in separate channels. Industrial design became more and more industrial. Art went to the Biennale, the crafts went to the Triennale.* Domus *went to all the «great art exhibitions.» And so it failed to see the signs. It had no alarm system for art. It did not even notice events close at hand, like Pinot Gallizio's poetically anti-technocratic «industrial painting» in 1956, or Yves Klein's first exhibition in Milan, at the Galleria Apollinaire in 1957.*

Where the architecture of interiors was concerned, Domus *was the magazine that documented, in these years, the truly original works of Albini and Gardella, as well as the Milanese mannerism that developed out of them, and gave space to the vogue for neo-Art Nouveau. Fortunately* Domus *was protected over this period, not only by the emergence of the new talents of the sixties, but also by two personalities who were both immune to the Milanese style: the young Sottsass and Gio Ponti himself. While he gave carte-blanche to his contributors, Ponti, at the age of sixty, had set out on a new path of formal inventiveness and clarity of thinking, and this was reflected in* Domus, *a diary from which lessons could be learned.*

Church for the hospital of San Carlo, Milan, 1966.

The sixties: playing with surfaces

During the fifties and the sixties Gio Ponti's inventiveness, in architecture and in design, continued to grow, reaching a peak in the seventies. Gio Ponti's «great age» (or the «splendid age» as he called it when talking about Le Corbusier, the new Le Corbusier after Ronchamp, Chandigarh, and Ahmedabad[1]) had begun, in the happy sense of a vision that appeared (or reappeared) as he grew older. This can be seen not only in his designs, but in the way he published them (in *Domus*), in an increasingly succinct and poetic manner (even in the form of fables). And in the way he was talking more and more about form and imagination, of the «reign of Beauty» (like Van de Velde[2]), beyond the «problems.»

In this decade — a decade in which many great artists and architects died,[3] a decade of «hopes and fears» (Giedion), and of «a panorama of dawn, of revival, of new forms...»[4] — Ponti's thought and work were summed up in the maxim *«architecture is made to be looked at.»* Which is Ponti's last word, a synthesis of Vitruvius, in his own style. Ponti constructed and «proposed.» And from the Shui-Hing building in Hong Kong, 1963, to the churches of San Francesco and San Carlo in Milan, 1964 and 1966, the INA buildings in Milan's Via San Paolo, 1967, the fronts of the Bijenkorf Stores in Eindhoven, 1967, and the designs for «triangular, colored sky-scrapers,» 1967, he was playing «with surfaces,» with apertures and cladding (highly reflective, using «diamond-faceted» ceramic tiles) and with facades that were «independent» (of the structure and the plan). «Architecture is made to be looked at,» for it is also public landscape: «facades are the walls of the street, and a city is made of streets; the facades are the *visible* part of the city, they are all of the city that appears.»[5]

Top, Gio Ponti at work on designs for Ceramica D'Agostino, Salerno, 1964. *Below*, facades of the Bijenkorf department store in Eindhoven, Holland, 1967; *right*, plan of one of Ponti's «triangular skyscrapers,» 1967.

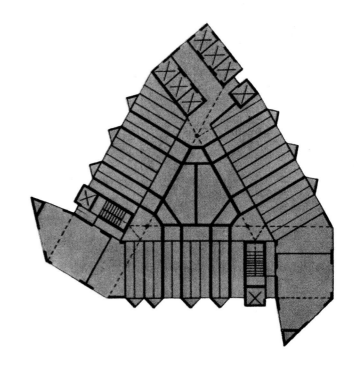

Villa Nemazee, Teheran, 1960

This is the third villa (after the Venezuelan Villa Plan-chart and Villa Arreaza) conceived for what Ponti used to call the «joie d'y vivre.»[1] Here too the inside and outside architecture, based on the large central room two floors high and on the through-views, has a theatrical appeal.

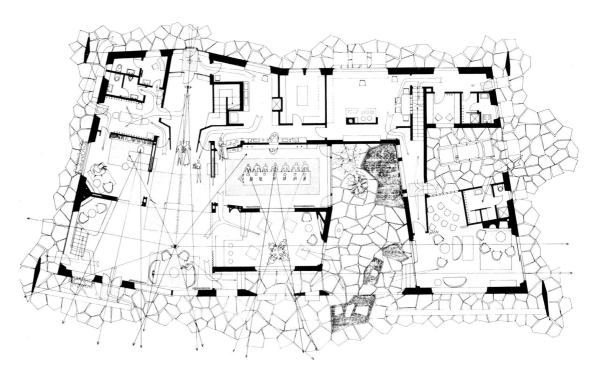

Below right, foreshortened view of the entrance front, faced with «diamond-faceted» ceramic tiles (by Joo). *Below left,* the patio with walls covered with ceramic plaques by Fausto Melotti. *In the plan,* the ground floor.

208

Office building for the RAS (Riunione Adriatica di Sicurtà), Milan, 1962

On an irregular site in the city center, a complex made up of: a large office building, a large apartment building, and a garden.

Today, at a distance of twenty-five years, this architecture stands, in its civic context, for «civility of expression» as Ponti would put it. But we know from Ponti himself that what he originally wanted was not the «introverted» design actually used (i.e. with the buildings flush with the street and the large garden located internally), but an «extroverted» one (with the larger building set back from the edge of the street, behind a raised piazza with parking facilities underneath) — a solution that «favored the city» (and instead of the present facade of red granite, he wanted bright ceramic tiles).[1]

The project was the work of the Studio Ponti Fornaroli Rosselli, in collaboration with the Studio Portaluppi.

Left, facade of the offices overlooking the internal garden. *Below left*, the chosen solution, «introverted.» *Below right*, the first proposal, «extroverted.»

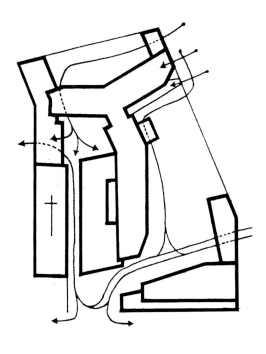

209

Hall in the Montecatini pavilion at the Milan Trade Fair, 1961

A project by Gio Ponti and Costantino Corsini, with graphics by Pino Tovaglia.
The very tall aluminum cylinders, of different diameters, that contain the showcases, look as if they are «suspended»: the conical attachment to the ceiling, made of canvas, lights up and vanishes.

The cylinders are made out of anodized aluminum in natural and blue colors; in the glass cases, models for «Montecatini in the world.»

Layout of the International Exhibition of Labor («Italia '61») in Turin, in the building designed by Nervi, 1961

A temporary collaboration between Nervi and Ponti (who had a great working relationship). For the International Exhibition of Labor, in Turin, Nervi designed the building, Ponti the internal layout.
Nervi's building is a gigantic structure, made up of independent units: 16 reinforced concrete columns of 25 meters in height, each supporting a square «umbrella,» made of steel, 40 meters along each side. In contrast, Ponti's internal layout is based on a system of thin, light partitions, that can clearly be dismantled (the «temporariness» of the exhibition within the «permanence» of the construction): but these partitions are arranged in such a way that the columns are always visible in their entirety (from four to eight columns can be seen in perspective at any one time) and from every point of the interior the spectacle of the extraordinary roof is open to view.
(With the collaboration of Giancarlo Pozzi).

210

Lamp for Lumi, Milan, 1960: a luminous panel, 40 cm sq.

Hotel Parco dei Principi, Rome, 1964

The part played by Ponti in the design of this hotel (as in its sister establishment in Sorrento)[1] was a very partial one.[2] Rather than proposing a work of architecture, Ponti just put forward some of his favorite procedures: the deceptive use of mirrors to isolate and lighten the ceilings; the insertion of slabs of white marble and ceramics (by Melotti) into the matt white finish of pillars or walls; the single and continuous flooring of white marble with inlays; the use of just one other color apart from white (here, green); the «garden motif» of green ceramic pebbles (by Joo) on the facade and even in the interiors.
The project was by Gio Ponti, in the Studio Ponti Fornaroli Rosselli, with the collaboration of Ponzio.

On the facade, and in the interiors, decorations in green ceramic pebbles, made by Ceramica Joo. In the central hall, *above right*, mirrors on the ceiling.

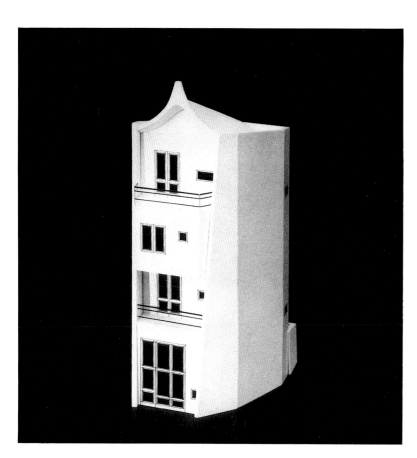

Houses at Capo Perla, Island of Elba, 1962

For a planned tourist complex at Capo Perla, Ponti designed ten types of small houses (together with a restaurant and a hotel), studied one by one in situ, to fit with the view and the site. Two of the houses were built: an «elongated house for long plots» and an «octagonal house» with a crystalline plan and views on all sides (and, note, the entrance on the corner). Among those not built, there was a «tower house for small plots,» octagonal in plan and as tall as the surrounding trees which it aims not to disturb. Walls amidst the greenery, covered with greenery.

The project was by Gio Ponti with Cesare Casati.

Left the octagonal house. *Above*, in the model and in the drawing, the «tower house.»

213

Project for the Montreal Towers, 1961

In 1961 Ponti had the following to say about the «Montreal Towers» (a project dear to him and never executed):
«If in an office building the dimension to be represented in the facade is the unique and all-embracing one of the company, in an apartment building the dimension to be represented is that of the apartment, the individual dwelling, although in the large dimensions of the whole construction, which in this way is brought back to a human scale.»[1]

In the «Montreal Towers» the individual apartments (single story or duplex) are made recognizable by the patterns of windows (standard windows, in three or four sizes) and the projections on the facade, projections that give the building the appearance of «towers standing side by side.»
So it is that, starting out from the (old) need to represent interiors on the outside, Ponti arrives at the «rhythmic» division of the front into vertical sectors, an invention that was to turn into a method.
The gardens located in front of the «Towers» have passages covered with cantilever roofs (the gardens form a green roof for the car parks and stores underneath).
The project was by Gio Ponti, in collaboration with Nathan Shapira.

Front and side of the «towers.» Ponti wrote: «the dwellings should be characterized in such a way that *anyone*, from the outside, can point out his own apartment.»

For Islamabad, the idea of a counter-facade to serve as a «brise-soleil,» 1962

Brise-soleils, *screens set on edge, usually constitute a regular pattern of individual elements on the facade. Here, according to Ponti,*[1] *the idea was to replace the* brise-soleils *with an entire, perforated «second facade,» a counter-facade that, set at a distance of eighty centimeters in front of the «inner» facade, not only kept it shady and cool but also permitted the creation of varied patterns of openings. («I had designed these facades,» Ponti explained, «with no other aim than to get a spontaneous pattern out of them, and with only a vague memory of certain rhythmic arrangements typical of the architecture of that country. But now, observing this counter-facade piece by piece, I have seen compositions emerge that would be perfect for a facade on the Grand Canal.»)*
In the Pakistan House Hotel in Islamabad, 1962, one can perhaps see an early, incomplete version of this idea.

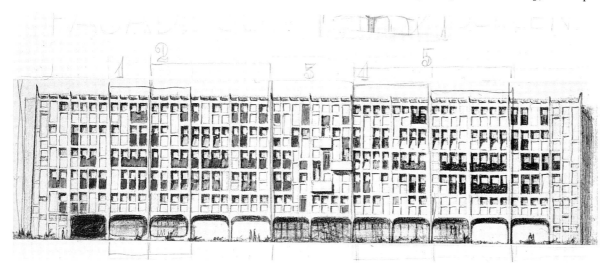

Top and bottom, the Pakistan House Hotel in Islamabad, 1963. In the drawing, *left*, the idea of a «counter-facade.»

Facade of the Shui-Hing Department Store, Hong Kong, 1963

Daniel Koo, a Chinese client dear to Ponti, gave him the chance to create a «Pontian» facade in Hong Kong. Amidst the massive buildings of Nathan Road this small, twelve-story facade, a manifesto of Ponti's principles, takes one by surprise. First of all it reveals straightaway, by differentiation, the various uses to which the interior is put (Department Store on the bottom four floors, the rest offices). It reveals the fact that it is a mere «suspended» screen (on the top floor, where the roof terrace is located, the sky can be seen through the unglazed windows of the screen — as Mollino used to say, the word «window» derives from the Saxon for «eye of the wind»[1]). It creates patterns of sunlight with its «diamond-shaped» profiles (not only are the ceramic tiles faceted like diamonds, but so are the windows with their slightly protruding glass panes, and the front itself, which is slightly bent). It is «self-illuminating» architecture (flanked by two luminous vertical slits, the facade looks at night as if it is «detached» from the building; and the building appears to be «detached» from the two adjoining constructions).

Appearance at night, in the model. Appearance during the day, in the photograph.

Villa for Daniel Koo, Hong Kong, 1963

The villa is situated in the green hilly outskirts of Hong Kong. See the south and north elevations: both front walls are pierced by windows of different forms, at different levels from the floors. In the living-room the floor «rises» towards the portholes in the back wall.

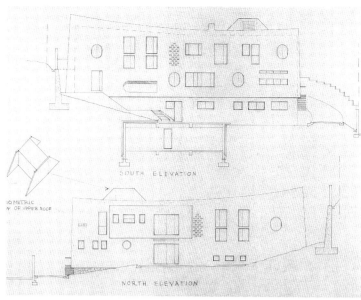

Second Ponti house in Civate (Brianza), 1960

Surrounded by fields, not by a garden, the second Ponti house rises where the first one, built in 1944, used to be. A large pitched roof, white walls.

In the large living room, with its blue ceramic floor and white walls, the isolated fireplace with its cylindrical cowl is made of black iron. The bronze sculpture is by Libero Andreotti.

Church of San Francesco, Milan, 1964

There was no choice but for the church to be located entirely «within» an old garden and to have a narrow front facing onto the road (that is, onto the parvis), sandwiched between two neighboring buildings (also for religious purposes, also designed by Ponti). The originality lay in the idea of connecting up the three facades in a single, spectacular motif that appropriates the sky: the parvis becomes the «external» heart of this church.[1]

Also worth noting in this church is the presence of a large access ramp (with a balustrade leaning outward, flared) — a feature that would appear again in the church of San Carlo, 1966 — which seems to rise up from the ground to join the body of the church. (Here the problem is how to get the building to «leave» the ground.) Inside, the altar is isolated (the congregation can arrange itself around it). The chapels have doors that can separate them from the nave (another invention).

(Over the course of time decorations accumulate inside a church, if it is a living entity. So it was with this one. Ponti, toward the end of his life, would have liked to add his own decorations: what he had in mind were very light, papier-mâché figures, hanging from wires in the transept and swinging in the air; and around the altar, aquariums set amidst the greenery and flowers.)[2]

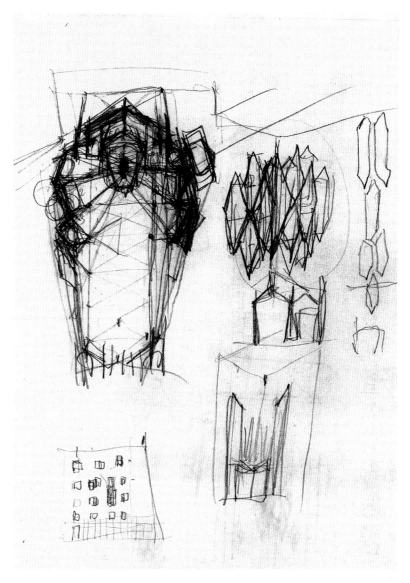

Above right, sketch for the plan and for the windows facing onto the parvis. *Below right*, detail of the parvis with the access ramp. *Opposite*, the facade.

218

The obelisks of the sixties

The Obelischi di Domus[1] were a prize thought up by Gio Ponti, «to be awarded every year, or one or more times during the year, according to inspiration.» A prize based on «admiration,» essentially. (In 1963, obelisks were awarded to Edgar Kaufmann, Ray and Charles Eames, Ralph Erskine, José Antonio Coderch, Rut and Tapio Wirkkala, and «The Architectural Review.» Afterwards they were only bestowed in people's imaginations.)

The obelisks were Gio Ponti's way of «expressing» himself in the series of exhibitions that he devised for the Ideal Standard showroom in Milan in 1964.[2] The idea: not exhibitions of art in an art gallery, but free «expressions» (of architects, artists, designers), temporary and experimental, conceived for a brief duration and a particular space — the Ideal Standard showroom — visible from the street, a spectacle for passers-by. («Expressions» were staged by figures as varied as Munari and Pistoletto, Sottsass and the Castiglionis.)

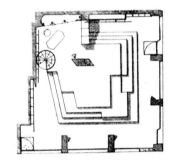

The obelisks in the exhibition «Espressioni» at Ideal Standard, Milan, 1965. *Right*, plan of the Ideal Standard area, also designed, with platforms at different levels, by Ponti.

220

Competition project for the Anton Bruckner Cultural Center, Linz, 1963

«Successful outcome of a competition lost» was how Gio Ponti described this project in 1966. It gave him the opportunity to try out, and make adjustments to, the idea of a «large raised platform» (with parking underneath) on which to assemble an «architectural landscape» of separate buildings. (Here the buildings are: large auditorium, small auditorium, cloakroom, restaurant, residence of the Director of the Center, the «Brucknerianum» or small museum, and art gallery). «Each element was revealed in its *own true and unique form, as the external shape corresponded to the internal one. Forms, forms, revealed forms; not forms crammed inside one form.»[1]*
The project was by Gio Ponti, with the collaboration of Costantino Corsini, Giorgio Wiskemann, and Emilio Giay.

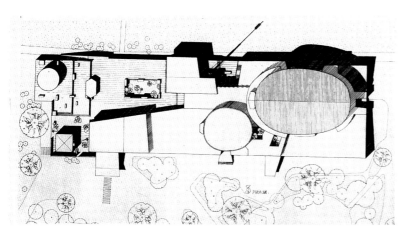

Left, the plan of the roofs. *Below*, view from the Danube. *Bottom*, view from the park.

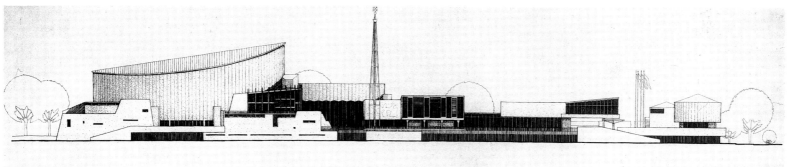

«Continuum» armchair for Bonacina, Lurago d'Erba, 1963.

Tiles for Sorrento, 1964

«I designed a hotel in Sorrento, and although there was no need I wanted each of its one hundred rooms to have a different floor. I did it out of my old love for ceramic tiles that, wherever I can use them, leads me to do more than I am asked. So, out of thirty different designs, each of which also permitted two, three or four combinations, a hundred emerged. The one reproduced here is one of those that it gave me the most pleasure to invent. And I always think of the infinite possibilities of art: give someone a twenty-by-twenty square, and even if people have been coming up with endless designs for centuries, there is always still room for a new design, for your own design. There will never be a final design....»[1]

The hundred different floors for the Parco dei Principi hotel in Sorrento are made of white, light blue and dark blue tiles (produced by the Ceramica D'Agostino, Sorrento), in accordance with Ponti's preference for décors in a single color.

Designs for Ceramica D'Agostino, Salerno.

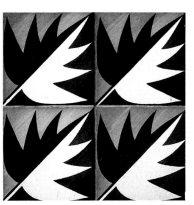

«A beetle under a leaf,» 1964

Gio Ponti gave this project away, in the pages of Domus, even publishing the executive plans on a 1:50 scale, to anyone who wanted to build it.[1] This small house, all brickwork and ceramic tiles (brickwork for the furniture, inside and outside the house; ceramic tiles for the roof, a large «leaf» that projects to form a porch) was intended as a prototype, to be reproduced, with variants. And this is just what happened. In 1970 the architect Nanda Vigo built her own version of the beetle and the leaf — an «encounter» between two architects.[2]

Plan, the brickwork furnishings in the open air, beneath the shade of the roof, are indicated. *Right*, the ceramic covering. *Bottom*, side elevation.

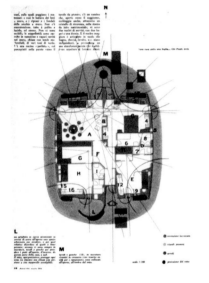

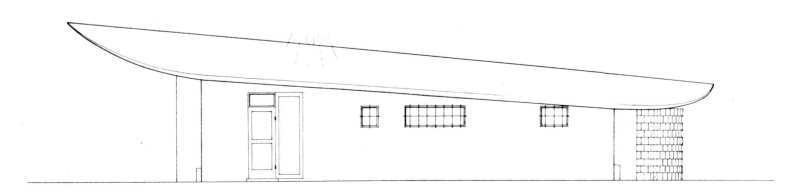

224

Ministries in Islamabad, Pakistan, 1964

In 1962 the Studio Ponti Fornaroli Rosselli was commissioned with the design of the Ministry buildings in Islamabad, the new capital of what was then West Pakistan, under construction at that time (to a city plan by Constantin Doxiadis and Robert Matthew). It was a major work to be carried out on a short time scale. A large construction site in a deserted setting.

The Ministries are conceived not as individual buildings, but as a «system» of constructed spaces, adaptable to possible changes in use. As a whole, they are on the same scale as the open landscape, but the spaces they enclose are on a smaller, human scale.

The construction, on this exceptional site, involved the combined use of prefabricated parts, made out of reinforced concrete, and parts cast on the spot. And use was made of elements of great simplicity, with very pure geometrical shapes, alternated and repeated within the system. One thousand five hundred architectural and structural drawings made it possible for the work of construction to be completed in less than two years. There were times when as many as 5000 workers were employed on the site simultaneously.

«The intention was not,» says Alberto Rosselli, in charge of the work, «to transfer an experience of Western architecture to Pakistan, but to create a new one: rejecting both the monument and functionalistic mechanics.»[1]

Structural consultants, Studio Locatelli-De Bernardinis.

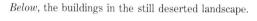

Below, the buildings in the still deserted landscape.

Church for the Hospital of San Carlo, Milan, 1966

When presenting his works of architecture in these years, Ponti was mostly concerned with pointing out their conformity with his «principles.» This church sums up many of them.

In the first place, «formal invention.» The diamond-shaped plan and the entrance set transversally to the nave are «formal inventions.» And it is an effect of «illusoriness,» another of Ponti's principles, that the building, a diamond clad in diamond-cut tiles, is made to «appear» lighter, more slender, and even larger than it actually is. In accordance with yet another Pontian principle, the subsidiary functions (baptistery, chapel, staircase) are in supplementary blocks (the small pavilions) and the church itself is nothing but the pure, simple, and expressive form of the nave. (Here there is another invention: the floor rises from the center toward the two ends of the nave; the altar, at one end, is clearly visible from the other.) Moreover, the pattern of openings in the facades of the building has been designed to be viewed at night (through «self-illumination»): large diamond-shaped apertures on the north face, thin slits on the south face. A design that plays with light, and which excludes any other «decoration.»

The pattern of openings in the facade was to be the dominant motif in Ponti's last works of architecture; to such an extent that there would eventually be more openings than facade.

Once again the design of the access ramp is interesting. With its sloping balustrades, it spans the void at the side of the building like a drawbridge. This was Ponti's solution to the recurrent problem of how to get the construction to leave the ground.

The church is connected with the Hospital by a covered walkway.

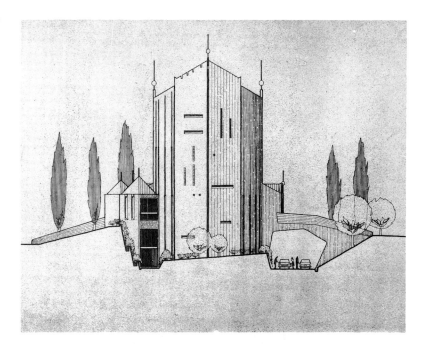

Below, the plan showing the two opposite access ramps. The ramp to the north front is a «bridge» (see also *above,* the east side). *In the model,* the back facade (south).

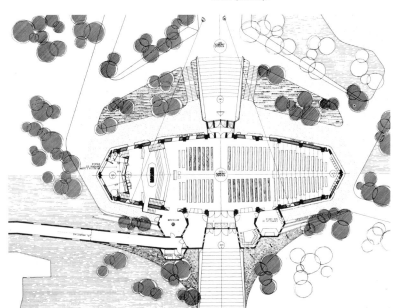

Left, the north front, with diamond-shaped windows (see also photographs, *below*). *In the photograph of the interior*, the steps to the altar.

Ciborium in the Basilica of Oropa, 1966

Ponti called his unconventional form for a ciborium (within the highly conventional and academic form of the Basilica of Oropa — a famous sanctuary) «architecture of invention.»[1]

His ciborium is a slender metal structure, sixteen meters in height, attached to the ground by only two supports. A light and empty structure (almost an acrobatic stunt «dedicated» to the deity), from which «ornaments» are hung (as if they were offerings: the oriflamme, the sphere with rays, the crown, all made out of gilded copper, as is the covering of the structure). Gio Ponti's collaborator on this work was the sculptor Mario Negri. Structural calculations were carried out by Leo Finzi.

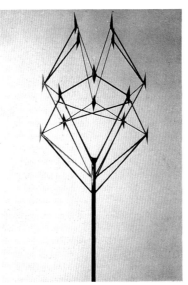

In the model *right*, side view of the ciborium. *Far right*, the ciborium in the basilica.

228

Gio Ponti at the De Nieubourg gallery, Milan, 1967

This was the time of Gio Ponti's encounter with the young Toselli, a meeting that was to lead to other meetings. In 1967 Franco Toselli opened his first gallery in Milan with an exhibition of Ponti's works. «A gallery for the man with ideas,» as Tommaso Trini put it:[1] with the idea in addition of holding «exhibitions within the exhibition.»[2] Ten years later, at the age of eighty-six, Gio Ponti received the surprise offer of another exhibition at Toselli's (drawings of the twenties and thirties), a poetic launching.

Far left, top, «Los Angeles Cathedral,» sculpture. Interpreted by some as an architectural design, it is actually a large angel, 4.20 m high, made out of 5-mm-thick sheets of stainless steel (execution by Greppi of Milano Lomagna). *Left,* gate made from a single piece of sheet iron (also by Greppi); *far left, bottom,* the «seat for three,» a prototype for Tecno, and, all around, plates for Ceramica Pozzi and lamps for Fontana Arte.

«Thick stained-glass windows» for Venini, Murano, 1966

An invention. «*Noticing a number of thick blocks of glass in the Venini kiln on Murano, I had the idea, and with it the desire, to use them to make stained-glass windows, to take advantage of the 'inner patterns' of the thick glass, which contains fractures, air bubbles, insertions of different colored pastes and various materials, immersed in its frozen depths. Stained-glass windows made out of these blocks were extremely heavy, and so the customary lead* mounting was not possible: thus I thought of inserting the blocks between vertical steel slides, without binding them together. And there was the new 'thick stained-glass,' in which not only the transparency of the colors plays a part but also the refraction of light from the inner surfaces of the blocks.*»[1] Gio Ponti produced «thick stained-glass» with Venini and with Toni Zuccheri, and put it to use in the church of the Hospital of San Carlo, Milan.*

Right, a glass block. *Below*, two windows after mounting: the individual elements within the rigid frame are always different (repetition is not possible).

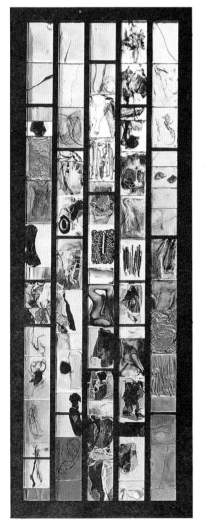
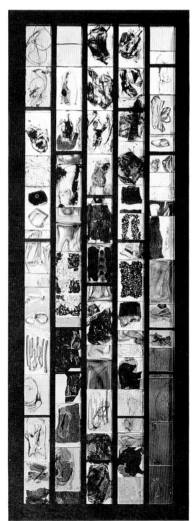
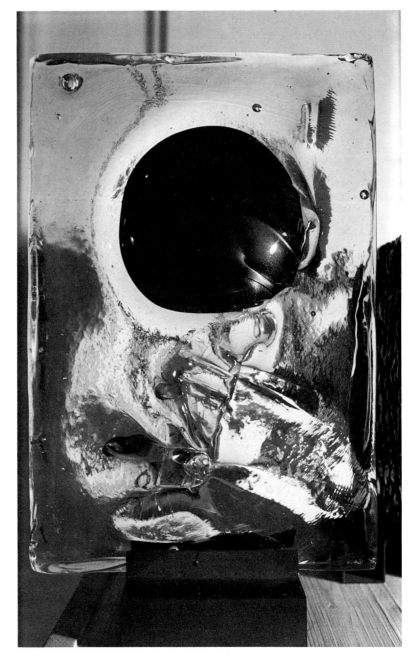

230

Dinner set for Ceramica Franco Pozzi, Gallarate, 1967

The idea is that all the plates should be the same size and shape, but each with a different decoration. On the table, surprise combinations.

Left, a service of plates ready for setting (repetition is not desired). *Below*, a later decoration (no longer a design made up of simple elements, but a «complex» one, deriving from the intersection of circles, in positive and negative).

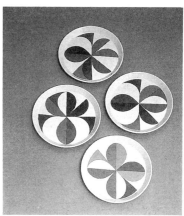

Facade of the Bijenkorf Department Store, Eindhoven, The Netherlands, 1967

Ponti designed the facade of this department store. For internal reasons of organization, the store required unbroken outside walls. So the facade will serve for its «external» function, Ponti declared, that is, for its visual relationship with the city and with passers-by.

Here the facade, clearly an «envelope,» is a long and shiny strip (made up of green, diamond-cut tiles made by Saccer of Castellamonte), divided up rhythmically into measured beats (the pattern could be repeated endlessly) and pierced by openings that are not windows but «luminous designs» intended to create the desired «nighttime spectacle.» The citizens of Eindhoven gave it a name immediately, ponskaart or punched card.

When, later, Ponti had the idea of turning an unused area next to the store into a «space for open-air performances» (and did so successfully, providing sculptures-cum-seats for the public and stands for musicians and acrobats), the citizens of Eindhoven at once christened it the piazza. Gio Ponti's collaborators on this work were the architect Theo Boosten and the sculptors Mario Negri and Frans Gaast.

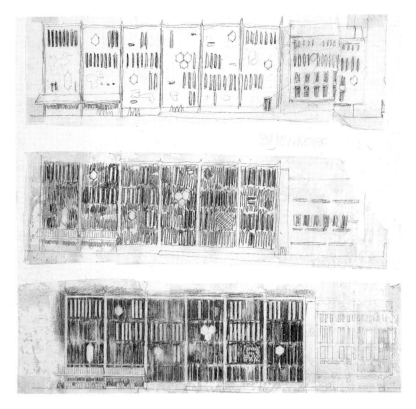

The Bijenkorf facades: in sketches, in the model, in reality.

232

The facades of the INA building at no. 7, Via San Paolo, Milan, 1967

«For smoggy cities with narrow streets, shiny facades illuminated by the sky.»[1] These were the facades that Ponti «promoted,» or suggested, for Milan. Ceramic facades (the rain washes them clean), made of «diamond-cut» tiles (that reflect the sunlight); flat facades with flush glazing (to reflect the sky, bringing it into the street); «airy» facades that «appear» to have no weight or thickness, so that the interplay is no longer between voids and solids but between reflecting and non-reflecting surfaces. And this interplay is contained within a «rhythm» (here lies its originality), a repeated pattern that subdivides the facade. And within each beat in this «rhythm» the pattern of openings is always different and always carefully considered (there is more glass in the lower, less glass in the upper parts). «Why be satisfied with lazily lining up windows that are all the same and set the same distance apart?» Facades are «the walls of the street, and the city is made of streets. They are the visible part of the city, they are all of the city that appears. Architecture also serves to be looked at .»[1]

Bottom left, in the detail, the upper part of the facade. It is faced with smooth and faceted gray tiles, by Ceramica Joo. A continuous copper «awning» runs between the juncture of the ceramic facing and the windows on the ground floor.

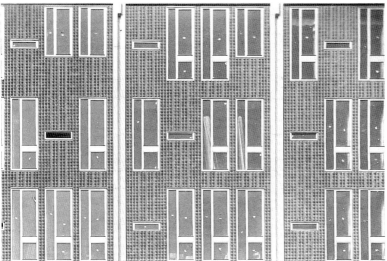

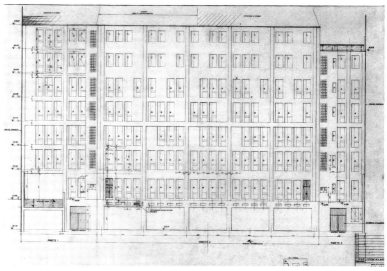

233

Couch for Arflex, Milan, 1966

A couch that converts into a bed without changing shape (in the hollow of the back there is room to «put away» bed-sheets and cushions) and that is provided with a lamp (for reading at night) and a pocket at the side (for books and magazines). It is a prototype.

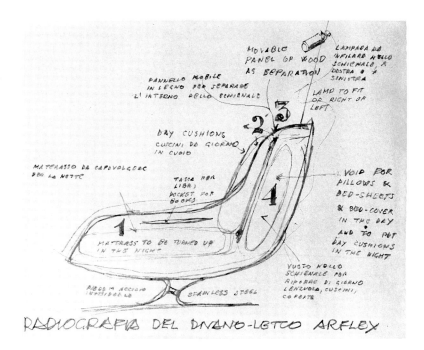

Below, the bed-settee as a couch.
Above, the bed-settee as a bed.

Lamps for Fontana Arte, Milan, 1967. Lamp for Guzzini, Macerata, 1967.

Project for a villa for Daniel Koo, Marin County, California, 1969

All that is left of this villa for a site on a hill are the sketches.[1] The idea was that of a large roof, a leaf, covering a circular building, subdivided internally by curved partitions, with surprising «minimal» passages, unexpected widenings, and convolutions in its routes (Ponti wrote on the sketches: «Palladio: let the house be like a small town, and the town like a large house»). The openings, cut at an oblique angle through the thickness of the external wall, are wide or narrow, windows or slits.

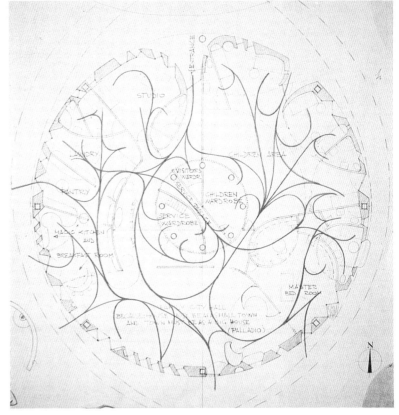

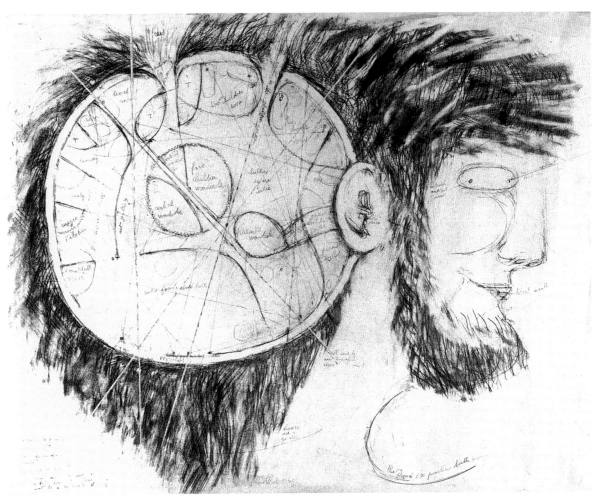

Gio Ponti, «the architect's head,» drawing, 1969.

Colored skyscrapers, on a triangular plan, 1967

«Apparitions of skyscrapers» is the title under which these models were published in Domus:[1] for «skyscrapers are also meant to be looked at,» and these skyscrapers on a triangular plan change their appearance as they are observed from different viewpoints. They are also colored (why not?), and their surfaces play with the light (they are «light-scraping»). Then «skyscrapers should not be isolated, but next to each other. If their plan is triangular, as in this case, they can be set very close together, for they do not block the view of each other, but open onto infinity from every window.»[1]

According to Ponti, these were not projects, but pure and simple «promotions,» suggestions. Imagined skyscrapers.[2] But the imagination of Ponti, an inventor rather than a visionary, was in step with his time and the possible.

Left, a forest of triangular skyscrapers (cardboard models decorated with grids of colored paper or silver foil); below, the plans: the areas of color define the different functional zones.

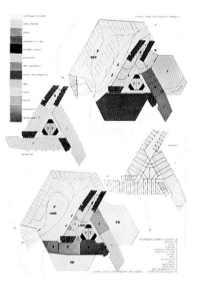

237

Coloured skyscrapers, on a triangular plan, 1967.

«Autilia,» 1968

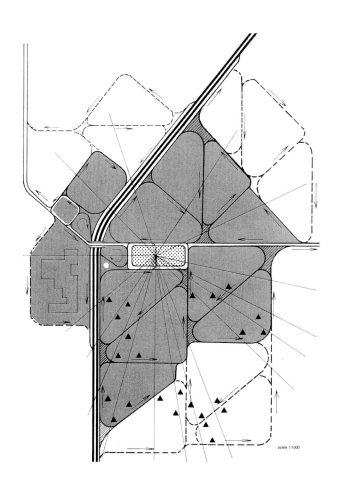

The idea: since a city is always created out of crossroads, and since nowadays all crossroads have been taken over by vehicles, for the expansion of the city an extension of the classic, non-stop, «cloverleaf intersection» could be devised that includes residential areas: that is, large «insulae» of housing within a system of one-way streets.

This was how Gio Ponti envisioned, at the end of the sixties, the growth of the city: new nuclei set amidst parks and gardens, detached from the old center but brought closer by rapid communications.

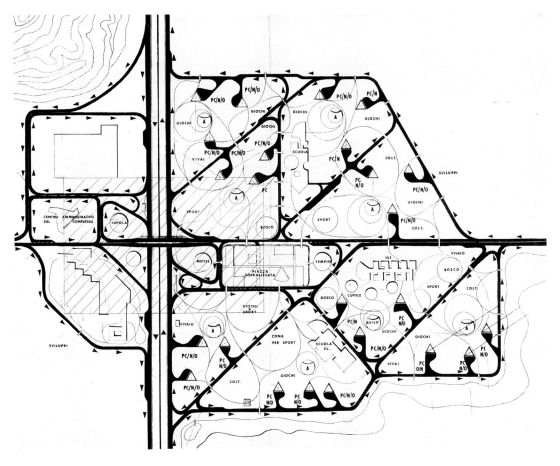

Left: «At the intersection between an *open* arterial expressway — that branches off from the metropolis and heads for open spaces in the countryside — and a minor arterial road» the new town is born, in which there is a differentiation between main routes for vehicular traffic, secondary routes, and pedestrian routes. *In the scheme top*, a variant.

239

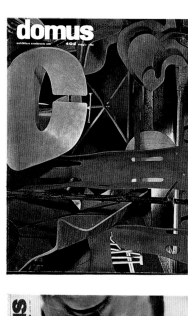
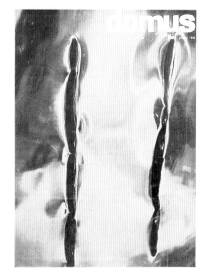

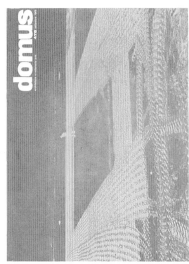

Covers of *Domus* in the sixties.

Domus in the sixties

The sixties began late, and ended even later.
There is an issue of Domus (477, August 1969) that has the «Instant City» by Archigram of London on the cover and, inside, a building designed by Gropius that had just been completed in Germany (it was his last): it could serve as a symbol of the sixties, a period in which three generations of architects were simultaneously in the limelight, and in which the «changes» took place right in front of everybody, experienced and communicated «at one and the same time.» Domus recorded them.
At the beginning of the decade Domus had adopted a change of scale, of layout (full-page images became the rule) and an almost monographic approach (a few «events,» given the maximum of visual exposure, with photographs by Casali and Mulas) that was an extension of Ponti's habit of paying «homage» to individual authors. Ponti, master/non-master, passed on the approach to the young Casati (who later became the managing editor of Domus): the world of Domus was still, in the Pontian manner, a world that operated on the basis of «authors,» placed in the same «front rank» of quality. In architecture, recognized talents and newly discovered talents (from Scarpa to Kahn and Hollein, from Coderch to Stirling and Isozaki, from Zvi Hecker to Piano, from Moretti to Van Eyck, Magistretti, Mangiarotti, and Enrico Castiglioni), or rediscovered talents (from Schindler to Chareau and Eileen Gray). The same for design, from Enzo Mari to Joe Colombo and from Alviani to the Archizoom. Even the critic Pierre Restany, who joined Domus in 1963, was an «author,» an individual artist like Yves Klein, Christo, and César, whom he brought with him. (And so, later on, was Celant an author, and then Bonito Oliva.) And Domus was a fine home for its authors. Indeed, they were the people who truly shaped the magazine: Eames, who photographed Saarinen's TWA for Domus as «crowded architecture,» and Wirkkala who photographed for Domus the Indian colors of Le Corbusier's architecture in Chandigarh; Melotti (a great adviser), who wrote in Domus as a poet; Sottsass (a great prompter), who made Domus into his own extraordinary diary; Fontana, who provided the covers (Fontana was a friend to Domus from its earliest years, the thirties, to the end of his life, in 1965).
Against this background, Domus itself was a case of «environmental creation,» by installments. (That «environmental creation» that Ponti advocated for architecture — in these years of debate over the «existing context» — and of which he wrote in Domus, in the first half of the decade.)
Gio Ponti and Domus: «... Although Domus did not participate in a number of tendencies, it still wanted to give an account of their expression whenever this represented truly 'original' values. This attitude of 'inner nonconformity' to my own tendencies (here it is myself that is in question) is perhaps being rewarded, for while I have been very worried about certain exuberances or digressions or deviations or revivals, I now have to recognize that digressions and revivals have — quite apart from their incidental expressions — represented a break and an opening toward a more natural, creative vivacity, and architectural imagination.»[1]
Thus Ponti gave Domus freedom to move, even in opposition. Ponti, even when he was «promoting» (his «colored
skyscrapers,» for example), was not a «visionary»: his future was a possibility of the present day. During this period Domus, on the other hand, in love with UFOs, was tempted by the Utopia as a symptom, and extended the antennae of fantasy. With the criterion of «multiplication», more objects than authors gradually found their way into the pages of Domus. The «Planet Vienna» appeared, and so did the «Rainbow over London,» the new Japanese scale, the simulated space, and the imaginary client (a population that would roam the planet in «mobile housing systems»).
And yet Domus carried on with everything. In this Domus «2001» the shrewd historical analyses of Pica (to whose critical talent Domus owes a great deal) and Rykwert were the «underground,» but they were there. In the same issue were Borromini and inflatable architecture.
But in the meantime the critic Tommaso Trini, who had joined Domus in 1966 under the camouflage of Op Art, had gradually established a new contact between Domus and art, a more direct one, and one that was diverging from design. Young artists like Merz, Paolini, and Pascali appeared in Domus in 1968 — preceded by a cover by Pistoletto in 1967, and unexpected images of Beuys's home in 1966.

Pages from *Domus* in the sixties.

The «armchair of little seat,» 1971.

The seventies: happiness

In 1970, the first centenary of the birth of Hoffmann and Loos, Gio Ponti was approaching eighty. In these closing years of his life he would complete two master works, Taranto Cathedral, 1970, and the Denver Museum, 1971. He also came up with a new object (an «armchair of little seat,» 1971) and a new way of designing fabrics (1970), tile floors (1976), and tile facades (1978). He wrote, drew, listened.

His thoughts, at this time, turned more and more around the «home,» around the act of living in a house. But his proposal of a «versatile» house with movable walls, never taken up, was something that went beyond the realm of design; it was the expression of a mode of thinking and living that was his final message, the one that he had always been trying to convey. «The house should be a simple affair. This can be judged from the *degree of delight* that one experiences when looking at it from the outside, and from the *degree of delight* that one experiences from living in it»[1] (Gio Ponti was alone in thinking in this way, in the hubbub of that time, 1971).

Right, detail of the Denver Art Museum facade, 1971. *Below*, drawing of the «sail» of Taranto Cathedral, 1970. *Bottom right*, bed on castors for Walter Ponti, 1970.

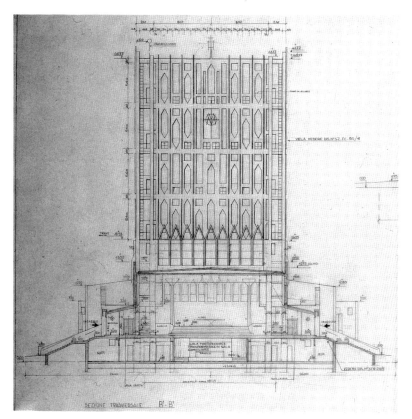

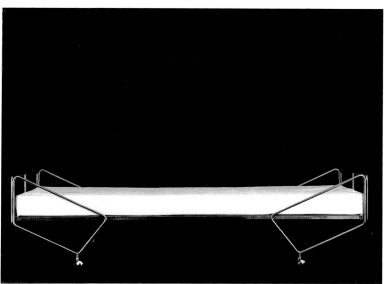

Velvet fabric for Jsa of Busto Arsizio, Varese, 1970.

The «Novedra» armchair for C&B, Novedrate, 1968—71

Designed in 1968[1] (Ponti was 77 years old), this small fiberglass armchair was presented at the exhibition «Torino Esposizioni» in 1971. On the unclad outside the deep diagonal stiffening ribs are in evidence. The fabric too is designed by Ponti (the armchair was presented on a floor carpeted with the same design, and «disappeared»). There exists another version of the armchair, with a plain outer surface and two fore castors.

«An armchair of little seat,» 1971

«In order to sit comfortably, with your legs crossed, you need little seat and a lot of back: slanted like this.» This «less is more» chair is not a variant, it is an invention. (Originally called «Gabriela» and made by Walter Ponti of San Biagio Po', it is now produced by Pallucco of Rome, under the name of «Pontiponti,» as a reminder of its history.[1])

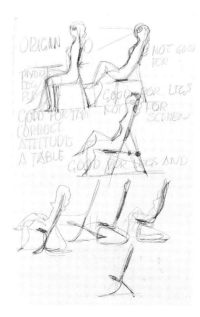

Montedoria building, Milan, 1970

*In this building, made up of two blocks of different shape
and size but linked together, Ponti has resorted to his typical solution for the facades of buildings in a city — where
the dimensions of fronts are strongly conditioned by the
building regulations: giving a «rhythm» to the front with
a sequence of vertical, modular sectors (and with a different pattern of windows within each sector). In addition to
this, slight changes of level in the plane of the facade, a
ceramic cladding that reflects the sunlight, and panes of
glass flush with the facade, reflecting the sky.*
*The project was the work of Gio Ponti and Antonio For-
naroli, on behalf of the Studio Ponti Fornaroli Rosselli.*

Top, the main front on Via Andrea Doria. *Right*, the back facade, with the low
block: lining of green tiles, smooth or
diamond-shaped.

246

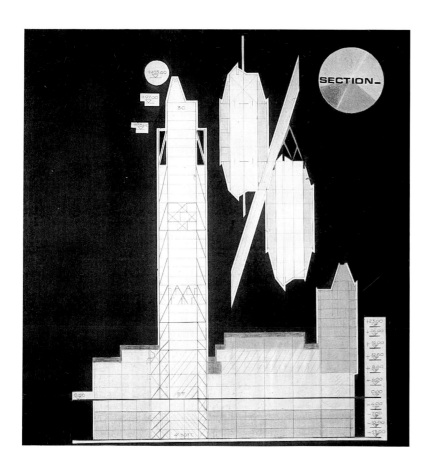

Competition project for an administrative center in Munich, 1970

The idea was to assemble the different constituent elements of the Center, each distinct and recognizable as such, on a single large platform laid out as a garden. These elements consisted of two slender, high-rise office blocks, two low blocks containing department stores, and a circular auditorium.

Left, the model. *Top*, section of the towers and plan.

247

From «La Casa Adatta,» 1970, to the «2 Elle» system, 1972

«La Casa Adatta» was a proposal presented by Gio Ponti at Eurodomus 3 («pilot exhibition of the modern house») in Milan, in 1970, and then at subsequent exhibitions. It is an example of a non-Utopian way of creating a «large» dwelling in a «small» area. For the «large» is necessary to man, as far as visible space (always a Pontian concept) is concerned, and the «small,» in terms of actual area, is inevitable today. Here, «in a small apartment of 80 m², 60 m² can be made visible at one time by opening the completely sliding partitions.»[1] Ponti, by putting this forward as a method, is proposing a custom: a mode of living in a «versatile» space, in which furnishings should be light, mobile and foldable. His small colored pieces of furniture weigh little, cost little, take up little space, and are great fun.

(The furniture was made to his design in 1970 by Walter Ponti of San Biagio Po':[2] the coincidence in their names was a source of merriment.[3]) The tables are small (with their leaves — painted leaves — raised, they become very large) and above all the cabinets are small (painted in two colors, and just over one meter high), an encouragement to «possess little.» There is one invention, the mini-desk for two people, incorporating two revolving seats. Everything is on castors, to allow a quick change of scene (later on he even thought of hanging partitions like curtains). This was Ponti's idea of living at the age of eighty (although he was looking forward to a «light, transparent style, linked to simplified social customs, and a possible free nomadism of ideas, in a land belonging to all»[4] back in the forties — he wrote about it in Stile).

And he did not stop there. In these years of solitude, he was constantly thinking up ideas for the building industry based on this type of apartment (proposals of multistory buildings for Feal, 1971)[5] and devised a system (that he proposed to Sacie, in 1972, and that would be given the name «2 Elle»)[6] for using these «versatile» apartments to construct tower-blocks, versatile themselves in their aggregation of housing units around the central core of vertical communications. (Towers set in parks: here there is a connection with Ponti's idea of creating new residential areas outside the city, based on the criterion of the «residential intersection,» see «Autilia,» 1968.[7]) His thoughts were taken up with the problem of housing: about the never-realized «2 Elle System» he might have said: «a design that comes from my earliest years, and that has emerged in my last ones» (1975).[8]

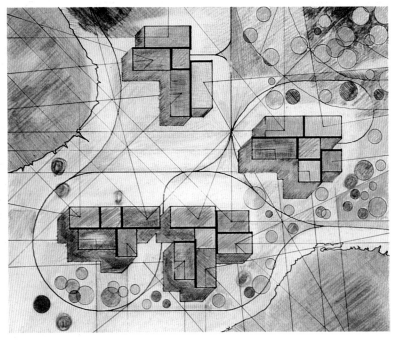

Top, model of a multistory building for FEAL, 1971; *right*, scheme of the «2 Elle» system, 1972.

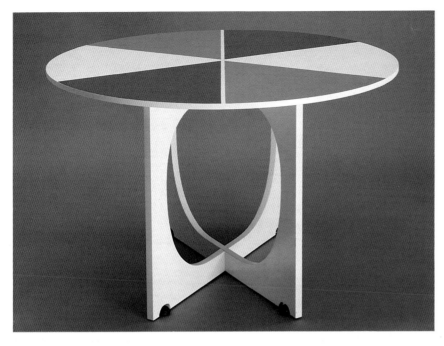

Furniture for «La casa adatta,» manufactured by Walter Ponti.

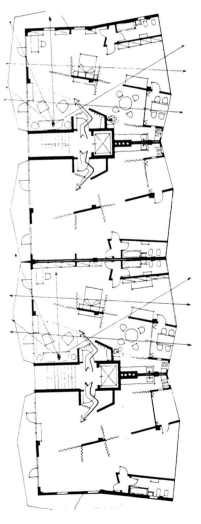

Above, plan for apartments with moving walls, in an idea of 1956 (*Domus*, 230).

Taranto Cathedral, 1970

Taranto Cathedral — which is beginning to supplant the Pirelli skyscraper in people's minds — is founded on an unprecedented idea: a «sail» (as people christened it straightaway) in place of a dome, or towers, as a landmark visible from afar.

The «sail» is a facade for the sky. In Ponti's words, «I thought: two facades. One, the smaller, at the top of a flight of steps, with doors giving access to the church. The other, larger, accessible only to the eye and the wind: a facade 'for the air,' with eighty windows opening onto immensity, the dimension of mystery.»[1]

«This almost immaterial structure (the 'sail') is itself, and by itself, the church,» was Luigi Moretti's comment.[2] He had grasped the non-liturgical, religious quality of this architecture, in which the «sail» that rises (to a height of 35 meters) above the church, and which has no internal connection with it, is an external «hymn», an external spectacle reflected and multiplied in the sheets of water located in front of the building: composed of two slender, parallel, perforated walls, set a meter apart, over which the light plays, it is an acrobatic exercise in architecture (a «blend of concreteness and air»[2]) dedicated to the sky. The congregation gathers inside the church (below deck): but here too the spirit is clear and light: a white and green space, perforated walls, an unbroken Pontian design to which the two frescoed images belong as well. There are no other decorations, nor contributions from anyone else. Archbishop Guglielmo Motolese, an enlightened client, protected «his» architect during the design process. The city, so far, has not been so careful with the building: the exterior of the cathedral, including the sheets of water, is now under siege from negligence and speculation — not «besieged by greenery,» as the architect had hoped.[3]

On the day of the cathedral's dedication, after the speeches made by the authorities, applauded as speeches, the architect's speech was «preceded» by applause — a long roll of thunder — from the crowd, and was listened to not as a speech but as the expression of a desire. And the next day the people of Taranto came to the cathedral with flowerpots and plants, in response to the architect's dream that the white walls of the cathedral would be covered with creepers.

(We kept the recording, not of the speech but of the applause, a full ten minutes of thunder.)

The side of the cathedral. *Opposite*, the «sail» is reflected in the sheets of water.

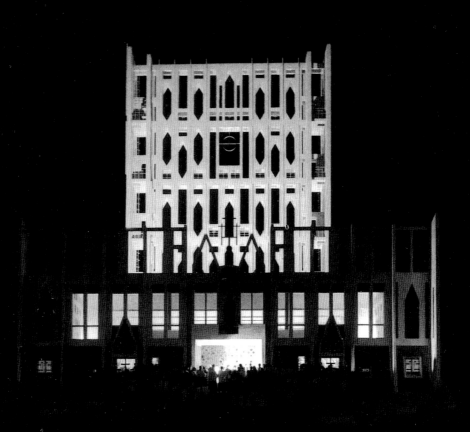

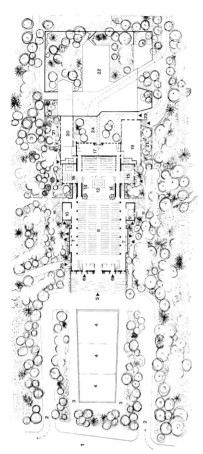

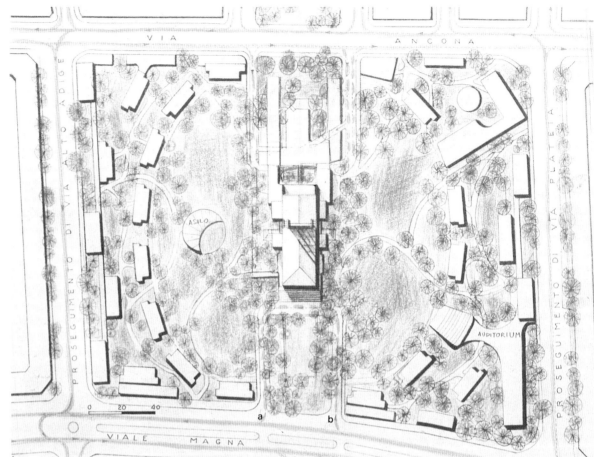

Taranto Cathedral, 1970. *Top*, plans of the cathedral, with the sheets of water in front, and scheme for a proposed «architectural setting around the cathedral.» *Right*, studies for the «sail.»

Top, external view and detail of the nave. *Left*, the altar.

253

Competition project for the Plateau Beaubourg, Paris, 1971

Ponti had noticed[1] that the great «landmarks» in the urban structure of Paris all lay in one prevailing direction, a roughly east-west direction, parallel to the central stretch of the Seine (which also corresponds to the axis of Nôtre Dame), and that the Plateau Beaubourg was located on the same axis as the complex of Les Halles. If Les Halles were to be connected with the Plateau Beaubourg (instead of being demolished), then another «landmark» would be created, a longitudinal feature following the axis of the Seine and on the same scale as the other great landmarks of the city.

This was the origin of the project: a project that was predominantly «architecture of the city,» and therefore completely at odds with the requirements of the competition, which were very clearly stated as the construction of a container for exhibitions and artistic activities. Thereby, Ponti put himself out of the running. But it was an interesting opportunity to react to the plan, already decided on, to knock down Baltard's (beautiful and empty) Les Halles — a plan that was already out of step with emerging cultural attitudes.

Ponti proposed that Les Halles should be used as an enormous exhibition space, linking them to the Plateau by a «garden» for open-air art (demolishing the two blocks that separated them) and locating the «brain» of the complex, that is the most delicate nerve centers of organization and management, on the Plateau. And on the Plateau was to stand the great «vertical» landmark that would conclude and arrest the «horizontal» movement coming from Les Halles: a high wall, its exterior covered with luminous and colored elevators (an echo of the project for the «Palace of Water and Light» at the «E42»?), a wall over which the beautiful light of Paris's changeable sky would play. In those years, after the «sail» of the Taranto cathedral, Ponti's thoughts were increasingly taken up with light.

The project was the work of Ponti and Alberto Ferrari.[2]

In the drawing, longitudinal and transversal section. In the models, the relationship between the Plateau and the surroundings.

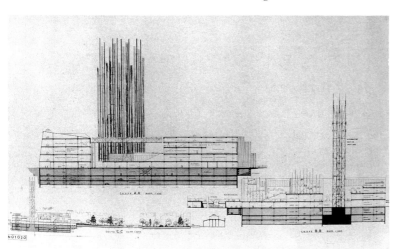

254

Denver Art Museum, Denver, Colorado, USA, 1971

«Why these curved profiles, at the top of the walls? Look at the plans and you will see that these profiles are the ideal vertical projection of a horizontal design, with its beautiful curves. They are the heavenly projection of the terrestrial profile of the plans.»[1]

This is possible (again according to Ponti) when the walls are, as here, purely an enclosure surrounding the volume within, an enclosure that rises above the level of the roof-garden. They are walls whose only function is to bring about a visual transformation of the static mass of the museum (two six-story cubes, juxtaposed) into a sequence of detached «vertical images,» changing with the play of shadows and filled with «traps to capture the light» (with their surfaces of diamond-cut tiles, «almost a million specially designed, faceted glass tiles, each hand set»).[2]

This vertical museum is artificially illuminated. The walls have no windows but, in typical Pontian fashion, slits. Slits through which one glimpses, from the inside, unexpected «narrow» views of the city and the distant Rocky Mountains. Slits that are lit up at night, a spectacle for the city. In Denver the museum was immediately christened «the castle, the fortress.» This pleased Gio Ponti («art is a treasure, and these thin but jealous walls defend it»), but it also led him to say: «Art should be inside museums only when the works are liable to suffer from light, heat, cold, water, snow, wind, and thieves. But living art should be outside, as in Venice, as in the villes d'art (why shouldn't Denver be one), with the architecture.»[1]

The design is by Gio Ponti with James Sudler and Joal Cronenwett, and in consultation with Otto Bach, curator of the museum.

Below, the external walls of the museum.

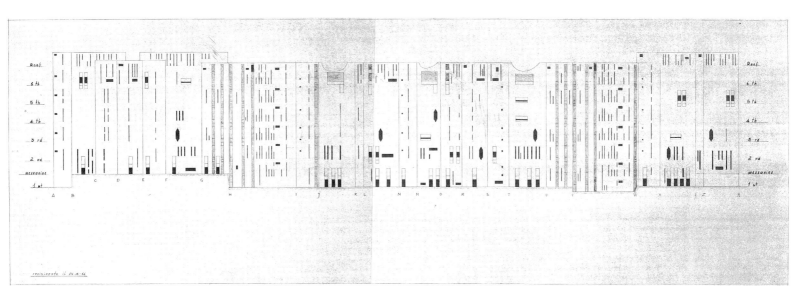

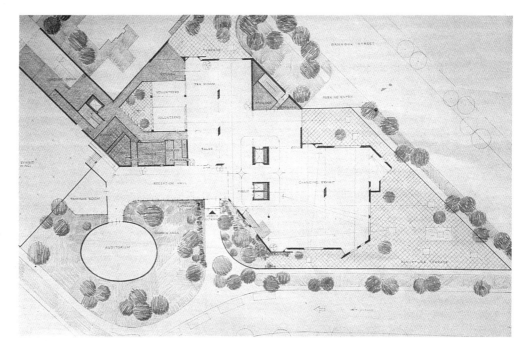

Denver Art Museum. *Below and right,* plan of the second floor and general plan.

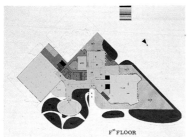

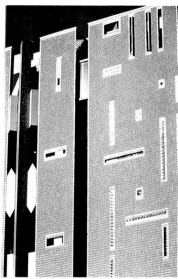

The slits in the facade, by day and by night, and the curved profile of the roof-garden wall.

257

Savoia Assicurazioni building, Milan, 1971

This was the last of Ponti's buildings to be constructed in Milan. In this work (which stands on the edge of the city, and is accompanied by a large garden, «an example to the city») Ponti liked to point to the effect of «verticality» produced by the variations in angle of the facades: this made the building look taller than it was. («In this power of illusion lies artistic reality.») «The effect of the architec- *ture depends more on surfaces than on masses: it is to be found in the reflections from the ceramic tiles, magical and not static, in their appearance and disappearance according to the direction of one's gaze.»*

«Architecture serves, when looked at, for what it reveals beyond its substance. Just like, as the sun turns, happens with all natural things, at each different moment....»[1]

Facade «with leaves,» Hong Kong, 1974

The giant leaves in colored ceramic pebbles running from floor to floor, playing with the windows, give an autonomous rhythm and scale to the small facade.

Floors in Salzburg, 1976, facade in Singapore, 1978: Ponti's colors in the seventies

In Gio Ponti's work, colors are born with the design. From his ceramics to his skyscraper projects of the last few years. But in architecture, his colors are never a «theoretical» signal (like the «gaieté artificielle» for which he sometimes criticized Le Corbusier: «it ought to be pointed out that gaiety of color should be expressed in the felicity of the architecture as a whole... to me these colors look suspiciously contrived....»)[1] Nor are they «applied supergraphics» (in the Japanese manner of the seventies): in his ceramic facade for a building in Singapore, 1978, the basis for the architectural design was a pattern of colors.

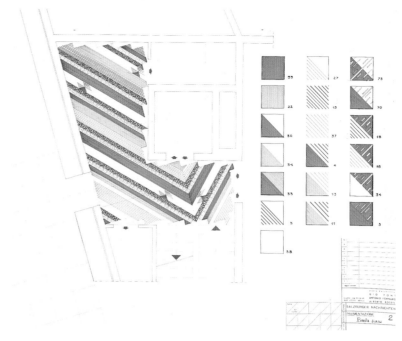

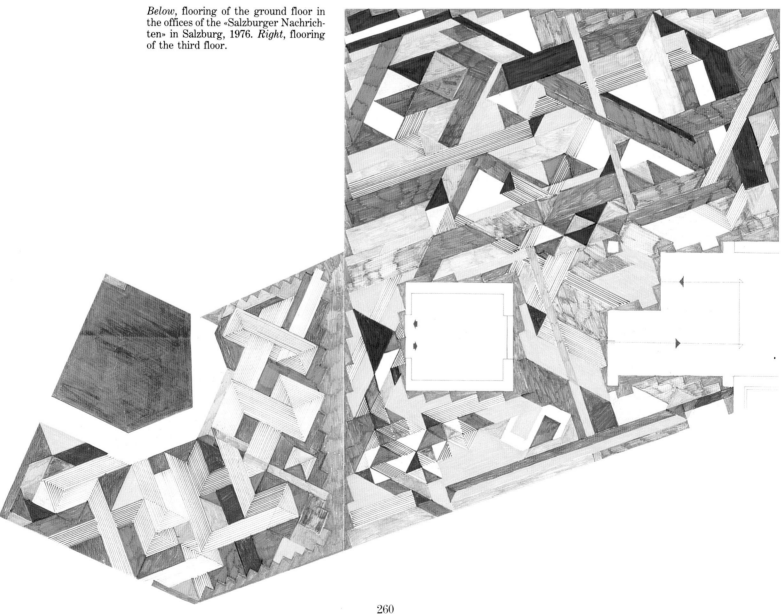

Below, flooring of the ground floor in the offices of the «Salzburger Nachrichten» in Salzburg, 1976. *Right*, flooring of the third floor.

Facade in D'Agostino tiles for the Shui-
Hing Department Store in Singapore,
1978. *Below*, the sketch for the facade.

261

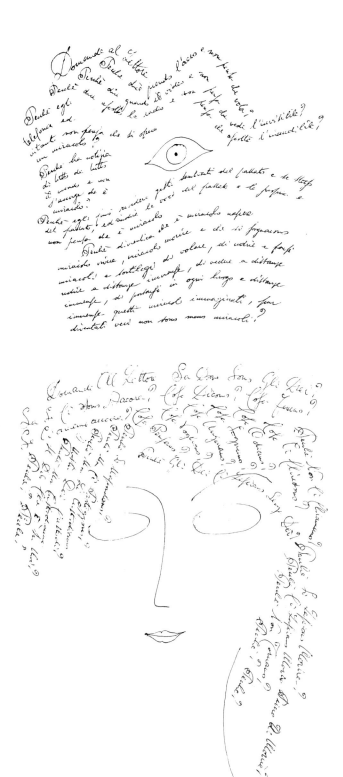

«Drawn Thoughts,» 1976 and «Cut Thought» (brass plate, *h* 70 cm), 1976 (A.G.P.).

Domus in the seventies

Having produced a first «self-portrait» in 1973, (when the magazine was invited to «put itself on display» at the Louvre[1]), in an attempt to view its own past as past, Domus[2] now turned to collective «problems» in architecture and design. Architecture and design that resembled one another, here and throughout the world. The impulse for this came from Casati. A layout tending to indifference and rapidity almost dismissed the «authors» (even though they included Fuller, Stirling, Hollein, and then Solsona, Isozaki, Lumsden, Gehry, Jahn, Kleihues, and Botta), and laid emphasis on the «objects.» There was now a direct encounter between industry and the public, a kind of ping-pong match. The «home» almost disappeared. Children invaded the museums.

The best example of this vision of the world, reflected all over the world, is Piano and Rogers's Beaubourg. Domus devoted more than one issue to it.[3] And yet the same Domus was giving space to an art that was indifferent to the Beaubourg: texts by critic-artists like Agnetti, and by artist-critics like Battcock, the poetical experiments of Corà; Mario Merz writing, Nicola de Maria appearing and a cover by Gino De Dominicis:[4] live art was making its way, with caution and enthusiasm, into the magazine. («The magazine is a particular place that art observes, while being observed by it,» Domus, 583, 1978.)

Gio Ponti looked on from the outside. He liked the poems of Marisa Merz.[5]

After the early seventies (when Taranto Cathedral, the Denver Art Museum, the «armchair of little seat,» the fairy-tale square in Eindhoven,[6] and the dream of «casa adatta» were published in the magazine), Ponti's work no longer appeared in Domus, *even though he continued to design. Perhaps at his age and from his celestial viewpoint* Domus *was no longer enough.*

Pages from *Domus* in the seventies.

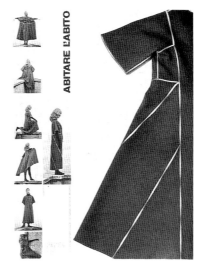

263

Covers of *Domus* in the seventies.

Selected writings

THE ITALIAN HOUSE
(from: Gio Ponti, *La casa all'italiana*, Editoriale Domus, Milan, 1933)

«Comfort» in the home lies in something higher, it lies in obtaining, through architecture, a measure for our own thoughts (p. 1).

Modernity is selection, is just active, impassioned, considered selection (p. 28).

There is a moral aspect to the evolution of architecture today... an idealistic resolve to create a purer *form* for our lives, and to comply with it (p. 40).

Italians should demand the *genuine*, antique and modern: the genuine antique is what it is, and it needs to be preserved, to be truly cherished and respected. But the genuine of today has to be modern; all that is made today, that is not modern, is false, just as what is made today «in the antique style» is fake. We have to purge ourselves forever from these harmful and humiliating falsehoods of taste (p. 65).

Woe betide the machine that reveals the exertion of its own labor; in machines, as in man, we appreciate the inscrutability of the organism, the skill of the work, the elegance of the effort (p. 107).

To have decorative value, painting should not be at all «decorative;» above all it should be painting, fine painting and only painting (p. 120).

It is a common view that modernity signifies the killing off of tradition. Instead it is the lazy exploiters of tradition who kill it off.... It is only on living — that is, modern — energies that tradition itself unfailingly relies.
The forces at work in tradition are hidden. From time to time we make them out even where they did not appear to be present, but they operate through the most *alive*: tradition is made up *solely* of authenticity. Those closest to it and serving it most ardently are not the ones who take advantage of it, but those who, having high and stern ambitions for themselves and for their own work and an incorruptible spirit, unconditionally devote the whole of their energy, the whole of their passion, to the expression of themselves and their own time (p. 150).

A MEETING WITH LE CORBUSIER
(from *Uomo*, a literary journal published by E. Gualdoni, Milan, October 1944)

I was with him at a «Volta Convention» on Architecture. An impassive, unemotional, youthful face, and thick-lensed glasses. I never met Stravinsky, but if Picasso had done a pen-and-ink portrait of Le Corbusier like the one he did of Stravinsky, it would have turned out to be a spitting image.
This man, architectural prophet and architect, talked about a museum for small towns, calmly displaying drawings of it in front of us — and cheating our expectations. He loved to *parler technique, parler métier*. A museum with a spiral plan in which additional elements could be included as time passed.
His exposition of this idea was imperturbable; as usual the idea and the exposition — in which any «liveliness» was deliberately avoided — were less interesting in themselves than as symptoms: as symptoms they had the value of carrying the discussion on architecture outside its customary terms, which for us at that time were academic terms (Ojetti) and anti-academic ones (Pagano), in a never-ending argument.

Then one day we went together to see, from the high scaffolding, the restoration, or rather the preservation, of the paintings on the ceiling of the Sistine chapel. He remained silent, with that face impervious to emotion, or at least to certain emotions. He kept quiet and almost seemed to be waiting for me while I talked about the fact that Michelangelo had not painted, there, «to be looked at from a distance, from below,» but *also* to be looked at with your nose right up against the wall. He painted for himself, in a wholly analytical way, hair by hair, wrinkle by wrinkle, in the faces, around the eyes and even in certain very small figures. There was no «syntheticism» in this giant, even though he was carrying out a great synthesis: which is only right for, while synthesis exists, «syntheticism» does not. Nothing in nature is synthetic: the mass of a wood is made up of the existence of a hundred thousand leaves of highly analytical (if it can be put in that way) and complicated, individual structure. Michelangelo, who was capable of a synthesis that has perhaps never been surpassed, did not even consider synthetic *effects* in his paintings. He worked in the same way as nature, where what is perfect close-up is perfect from a distance, and is always rich, full, and substantial.

Suddenly Le Corbusier said to me, in an impassive, ordinary voice, finishing off a thought that had been running through his mind: *«Donnez quatre ans de travail à un peintre d'aujourd'hui et il vous fera une chose pareille.»* [«Give a modern painter four years' work and he will do something similar.»] I experienced a violent inner rebellion against those words, which struck me as scandalous, as if I was hearing heresy or sacrilege. Inwardly I said, making myself the spokesman of a universal protest: *«C'est question d'un Michelange, pas de quatre ans!»* [«It's a matter of a Michelangelo, not four years!»], but the sound did not come out, as if quashed by the shocking nature of his assertion: a shock that worked within me, filled me

266

up, alive, unforgotten, insuppressible, victorious in the end. It represented a great lesson, for everyone, of faith in ourselves. *Quatre ans!* Why not, in fact? And I accused myself of cowardice for never having thought of this simple, true, natural thing: this strong and sure thing. I thought of Picasso and Sironi, but only of those two. And I thought that art is also opportunity: what a great poverty of our own time it is that it does not put artists to the test, does not let them try their hand at great works, at decisive undertakings, away from the isolation of a desperate personal life. We just put them on sale, at exhibitions. The ancients put great trust in artists, offering them great works, that is, immense and glorious ceilings, altars and palaces: we offer them art studios or those rows of rooms lined with jute — our exhibition «halls» — that we refer to, carelessly, as «artistic events,» while art *happens* outside, has happened with the *lives* of Modigliani, Van Gogh, and Gauguin.

THE TEACHING OF OTHERS AND THE FANTASY OF THE ITALIANS
(from *Domus*, 259, June 1951, on the subject of the 9th Milan Triennale)

The contribution that this country of ours — which has always had the happiness of youth and the strength of old age, and which embraces, to an extent that is always surprising and disquieting, both grace and barbarity — can make is to demonstrate to others the importance, indeed the indispensability, of the reckless gifts of freedom, independence, and improvisation, when one has to give concrete form to the imaginary....

Others teach the rules of life: with us however, who have been following rules in vain for centuries, life is expressed, is released in this way. There is no «time» in Italian things, but a charge of the unconscious (one could also say «foolhardiness»). Ours are improvised things, things which Italians have been unable to resist, in their courageous willingness to abandon themselves to unexpected temptations. In the things made by the hands of an Italian, there is not the thought and measure of a man, but the temptation, the sin, the abandonment of a man. This, we know, is the contribution filled with warmth that is principally brought by Italians and that is acknowledged as theirs: the fantasy of the Italians, their capacity for imagination, and the guts to give free rein to their fantasy and imagination in the most concrete and immediate ways.... Interpreters, in the most concrete ways, of the stuff of dreams, the Italians have always made, with their arts, the most powerful invitation to the peoples of the whole world to translate fantasy, without fear, into poetic reality, waking from sleep and capturing dreams, all dreams, beautiful and ugly. Our exhibitions are lively because they are dramatic; the more they are like this, the livelier and truer they are. They are admired even where they are dreadful, because of the revealing force of a lack of restraint....

At the Triennale, we have put in everything, the beautiful and the ugly (that is life). And for this too foreigners will thank us, for at times too strict a selection dries up the awareness and a lesson is also to be learned from unsuccessful, incorrect things: how many germs of life are sometimes to be found in them!

LE CORBUSIER'S YOUTHFULNESS OF TODAY OR SPLENDID AGE
(from *Domus*, 320, July 1956)

Someone, a young man himself, has sung the praises of the perennial and surprising youthfulness, or the «new youthfulness» of Le Corbusier, struck by the freedom, the playfulness, the imaginativeness, the «newness,» and the «state of grace» that his Ronchamp chapel and new constructions in India represent.

The truth is, I would say, that this «state of grace,» these expressions of genius, are typical of age, of the great age of maturity. The youthfulness of the masters, in our day, is «consummated» in its very zeal through their engagement in struggle and controversy, in movements, in *camaraderie*, in comradeship — in our era — in which there are no schools and masters as there were in the past to help us in our search for a technique. If all this is true for painters and sculptors of genius, it is even more dramatically so for architects of genius, for while painting and sculpture and literature and — up to a point — music and drama are produced independently of patronage, architecture is conditioned by the client. And while in the other arts revolutionary or trail-blazing works can appear and be rejected *afterwards* through lack of comprehension, innovative works of architecture are rejected through lack of comprehension *before*, and never appear. They remain desires *refoulés* [suppressed].

It is in old age, in the splendid age of maturity, in the individual isolation of this happy age that these geniuses, now wonderful old men, Le Corbusier, Wright, and Mies, masters of a technique that no longer holds secrets for them, in other words freed from it, freed from controversy, freed from struggle, freed even from the human ambitions and passions that are bound up with the arts, freed from comrades and pupils, freed from material necessities, now recognized by ordinary people, loved, asked to produce great works, it is in old age, in the splendid age, that they work at last in complete freedom, I would say with divine liberty and certainty and success: *felicitas et facilitas.*

And they have been granted the blessing of realizing *at last* things that they dreamed of in their youth or throughout their lives, things that were not wanted at the time, or that their contemporaries were not mature enough to accept. For the artist was absorbed in effort and argument, need and struggle, and the «dreamed-of things» stayed inside him like desires, like mysterious pregnancies, preserved in odd corners of the mind, in the «thesaurus» of each creator's life, where thoughts are accumulated and remain, in the certainty that their day will come; the day of their liberation, of their fulfillment. So it should not come as a surprise, but as something only to be expected, that Le Corbusier has finally taken out of his «thesaurus» what he had stored there, and the unfulfilled motifs and expressions of his own youth «of old.» He has taken them out for Ronchamp and for Ahmedabad.

What looks to others like a new youthfulness of today, or an up-to-date youthfulness in Le Corbusier's forms and expressions, is really the final surfacing of *his youthfulness of old*, of his own time. It is an ideal reuniting, and magnificent to behold, of now with *then*, when certain things were disclosed for the first time.

Le Corbusier the polemicist, the writer, the promoter, leader of a movement and involved with technique and prefabrication, with architecture and city planning in relation to a social ideal («*la ville radieuse,*» «*l'usine verte,*» and «*de logis pas des canons*» [«the radiant town,» «the green factory,» and «houses not arms»]), had pushed into the background, in our habitual way of thinking, Le Corbusier the artist, the pure, lyrical artist. Only his painting reminded us of the latter, in a direct way but one that was mistaken by many, and perhaps even by us, for a «hobby.»

Yet nothing could have been more serious than this painting and we should be grateful that in it are conserved his qualities as an artist, the old qualities of his youth, faithful to his youth. He used to say to me, «*je peins une heure chaque matin: c'est bon,*» as if he was talking about an exercise for keeping himself fit. This *boutade* [quip] was his way of keeping himself in art, maintaining a fidelity to art, to lyricism, to song («*il faut qu'une architecture chante,*» he wrote). Those who, like me, are almost the same age as Le Corbusier and whose familiarity with his work comes not from studying it now, but through a lifelong contact with it, will immediately recognize the degree to which the *époque* of «Esprit Nouveau,» of the Le Corbusier of that time, of his companions at that time, is present in the Le Corbusier of today, of Ronchamp or Ahmedabad.

These two works are not innovations of the present day, they are the marvelous ideas *refoulées* that have returned, fulfilled and liberated. Ahmedabad is, in some ways, «1919,» or the consequence of that 1919; it is — as art — *contemporary with that time*, it is the early Le Corbusier, not the late Le Corbusier. The same with Ronchamp. Ronchamp is that part of the age of Mendelsohn, of a post-art nouveau, of that 1919 that is — as art — unconsciously contemporaneous with Gaudí, which has at last, and gloriously, come to the surface in the Le Corbusier of today.

(And evidence for affinities, similarities with others, can be found. But I shrink, once again, from a criticism based on historical and technical documents and references, on coincidences of form, and am thinking instead of the intimate, vital, and personal processes — the only history that counts for an artist — in which everything surfaces, resurfaces, is given a new image, in coexistence — of course — with its own time, but, with the Great Masters, in the absolutely independent realm of their own personal history, a realm that is closed to others.)

But there is another comforting thing that we have to point out: controversy, technique, technicalities of economics and production, city planning, and proselytism, all had made us think, because of the «moralistic» or puritanical cast of some of Gropius and Le Corbusier's attitudes, of an architecture determined solely, and almost drained of feeling, by these factors — and only Mendelsohn and Mies van der Rohe represented a lyricism (whence the embracing of irrationalism by architects, whence the interest in Aalto and Niemeyer). But Le Corbusier does us the favor, not just in Ronchamp but also in these Indian buildings, and in the new city of Chandigarh that he has planned (although it is a city for ancient peoples, as Ronchamp is a church for an ancient religion, and in both cases a perennial humanity is revealed), the favor of revealing to us, powerfully and stout-heartedly, without equivocations and weaknesses, architecture as a lyrical entity. That is what it is.

AGAINST JOURNEYS BY WORKS OF ART
(from *Epoca*, 11 November 1956, in connection with the proposed sending of Renaissance masterpieces to New York)

There is no point in repeating other people's opinions — even ones as weighty as those of Berenson — in opposition to the travels of famous works of art, which ought to stay where history gave birth to them.

They are monuments of culture and monuments do not move, nor are they objects to be sent on *tournée*.

I am not moved by arguments about the cultural benefits for all those people who are given the chance to see works of art at home that they would be unable to see in their original location. Those who are interested in these great works love to go and see them wherever they are, out of respect or cultural devotion and to understand them better.

How many of us have been deeply disappointed to find the home of these masterpieces empty — *their* home — on going there to find them! And what comfort to know that they are back where they ought to be when we go and look for them again! And the act of traveling to their home increases the enjoyment and deepens the understanding. The rest is tourism: either of people on *tournée* running around our galleries, or of works on *tournée* running around the capitals of the world. It is all part of the restlessness of our age. I am a sufficiently active man not to be suspected of laziness and nostalgia when I speak of restlessness in this field of «cultural ex-

changes,» of «profits» in terms of prestige and propaganda, with the toing and froing of works — so that whoever loves them is obliged to turn to the published itineraries in order to track them down. This restlessness is part of a superficial activism which is wholly static and propagandistic, domineering, overwhelming, and optimistic, and which covers up painful truths. To judge by the ever-increasing numbers — in tens with regard to the countries taking part, in hundreds with regard to the visitors, in millions with regard to the sales — the Biennale in Venice ought to be more and more of a success. In reality it is in sad decline.

Instead of getting so agitated and shuffling around works of art in the superficial terms of a questionable propagandistic, promotional, or political approach to culture, let us pause to consider the serious and fundamental problems of art and culture with which we are faced.

EXISTING ENVIRONMENT AND CREATION OF THE ENVIRONMENT
(from *Domus*, 378, May 1961, on the subject of the Torre Velasca in Milan, designed by Belgiojoso, Peressutti, and Rogers — BBPR)

I admire, indeed love (the inevitable outcome of my judgement, when it is positive) the Velasca Tower....

While I am aware of, and have great respect for, the thoughts (as Nervi says, architecture is made out of thoughts) that inspired it as well as of its stylistic and environmental motivations, I love the Velasca Tower for the act and value of *architectural creativity* that it represents, and for the suggestion of form that is expressed and proposed in it, quite apart from references to the environment and tradition.

... Every possible (and facile) reference to remote forms has been of much less interest to me than recognizing in the Velasca Tower (keeping strictly to the realm of modern forms and those that may have a «future») an autonomous, structural and formal *invention* — or, if you prefer, a discovery — that opens up fascinating possibilities.

I find these autonomous values so predominant as to be able to say that the Velasca Tower has created instead, through its peremptory mass and peculiar form, an environment for itself, indeed an environment of its *own*, autonomous, and non-communicating, rather than submitting to or interpreting its surroundings. And so my imagination leaped to the *environmental creations* that the Velasca Tower could stimulate....

THIS IS THE GREAT AGE OF ARCHITECTURE
(from *Domus*, 389, April 1962)

... There is a historical culture, but there is also a culture that is more «involved» and just as fascinating as the historical one, and certainly more exciting, interlaced with revelations, advents, and intuitions. It is the one pertaining to awareness of the present and of that future which is in gestation in the present. «Trying out the future» with its studies and Utopias, it is a thrilling culture, the cultural conquest of the unknown. If the other culture represents the romance, sensational and inexhaustible (and therefore itself filled with prospects for the future), of the history of the whole of humanity over its millennia, centuries, years, seasons, and days, this one is *our* history, which brings the story of the past back to life, an immortal story of the dead, wonderfully revived in the present, that is in the very hours of the life of each one of us, for «today is history too,» and the marvelous adventure continues, and we are, in the realm of our activity and social life (and in the sweeping course of time) participants in and observers of it. But history cannot exist without love for history: thus its process decays into the mere fact of existence and is stripped of destiny and honor if the present and the future that lies in it are not loved. If it can be said of the marvelous past that what has been has been, then we will have to say that it is up to us whether the future will be marvelous; history is in our hands, in our consciousness, and in our yearning for civilization. If we consider what extraordinary means, what immense possibilities, what civilizing tasks, and what a share of human aspirations are today entrusted to architecture, which has not only to interpret and promote them, but also to give them «beautiful form,» then it could be said that the commitment of architecture has never been higher; and no age has ever been greater, or demanded more of architecture.

A PANORAMA OF DAWN, AWAKENING, AND THE NEW
(from *Domus*, 247, June 1965, on the subject of the «Habitat no. 3» by André Bloc)

... This «Habitat no. 3» [by André Bloc] was preceded by the ones published by *Architecture d'Aujourd'Hui* (issues no. 102 and no. 115); this gives me an opportunity to answer a question that is on everybody's lips but that gains authority from being framed by the prestige of this magazine: where is architecture going?

It is going in many directions at once, like all the arts today.

The «shortening» in the lifetime of styles has already been noted — lasting for millennia in ancient times, centuries since Christ, and years recently.

The fact of belonging to the present day is no longer indicated by *one* style but by the simultaneous development of diverse modes of expression; by the coexistence of all kinds of techniques, ways of thinking, opinions, and inspirations.

I have already said with regard to the ancient and modern, that everything in our culture is contemporaneous — Giotto and Picasso, because they are both present in it. This is even more true for what is being produced in the modern day, in an era in which every academicism, every formality and every form of conformity is dead.

If mechanized industrial civilization has led to a worldwide unity of means, it has its antidote in the unleashing (in the literal sense of releasing from their ties) of both the thoughts and the intellectual expressions of every human being; this is our freedom, and it has made us realize that there is architecture in monuments but not in monuments alone; that poetry is in poems but not in poems alone; that music is in its noble expressions but not only there, for it is in the songs of every land; that painting is in the works of the masters but it is not the property of the masters alone, and the same for sculpture, and for every genre, and for every literature, where each language is expressed through innumerable languages.

The panorama of today is a panorama from the creation of the world (a world is, in fact, being created), a panorama of dawn, of awakening, of the new. (Call it chaos even, for chaos is creative anticipation in all its natural vigor).

And in architecture the panorama is a very rich one, with works being produced contemporaneously — different from one another, and different for each architect — by men like Le Corbusier, Saarinen, Mies, Wright, Aalto, Nervi, Tange; and since each expression is an expression, and does not tolerate hierarchies, and since we are faced with the reality of the «forces of nature,» in this natural vigor there are also, simultaneously and equally — alongside those of the masters — the expressions of men like Morandi, Niemeyer, Candela, Castiglioni, Soleri, and Mangiarotti. And it is among these that Bloc's Habitats belong.

DOMUS IS HERE, HONORED IN PARIS
(from *1928/1973, Domus: 45 ans d'architecture, design, art*, catalogue of the Domus exhibition at the Musée des Arts Decoratifs, Palais du Louvre, Paris, May—September 1973)

Domus is here, you see it: honored in Paris.

And it is the first time, I believe, that a magazine has been invited to put itself on exhibition, and for its 45th anniversary.

Why 45th and not, for example, 50th? Fifty years smacks of a jubilee, of arrival. Forty-five indicates a process still under way.

Here one will be able to see — in the simultaneous presence of the past (of Domus's past), of the present (which is nothing but an anticipation of the future), and of the future (which lies somewhere between the unknown and the dream) — the extroverted editorial structure of Domus. But what matters is to grasp Domus's secret, its dream: in the hearts of the people who produce it, Domus is an art magazine that dreams of being a work of art. Its freshness? It lies in the fact that Domus's true age is the three months that it takes each time to put it together and bring it out. And its success indicates that it is what its readers were looking for — along with the artists, architects, designers, and writers, who by entrusting their work to the magazine have made their prestige its prestige. And we love them.

The world changes, in the dimensions of which it is composed; life changes, and customs with it. The mystery of man remains, in unchanged relation to the «original mystery» of existence. And culture? It tends to become simultaneous and universal, to be the unification of all differences of expression.

Convinced of this, and out of a natural optimism, I have gone along with the impulse to transform Domus: to change it from the magazine of Milanese improvisation that it has been since birth into a polyglot one; not by including translations but through the presence of texts in their original language, a direct expression of the simultaneous diversity of a living culture.

And Domus's tomorrow? It is bound up with its name: Domus—house.

The house is the origin of architecture, and the origin of art. It is the origin of culture, of the city, the origin of the individual, of his capacity to dream, of his ability to create. The home is at the source of the image of happiness that man, man alone among living creatures, knows how to create. It lies at the origin of life, which, within its human limits, is wonderfully unlimited.

For we are, we human beings, in the marvelous situation of being able to decide, once again, our own destiny. A sense of the possibility of happiness is essential to life. Today, when one talks about something too much, one puts it in danger: man, man, man... as if he had never existed!...

Since life is a dream (Calderon) and dreams are nothing but dreams, we start out from the dream (with art) to build our happiness, on what we can dream to be enduring, in the mystery of genesis, of reality.

If reality is the dream, and the mystery, let us accept the dream in order to live. A man in a state of grace, a poet [Ungaretti], on a night of war, was illuminated by the «boundless.»

He said, the same man: «I am looking for an innocent country.»

Everything depends on us. Innocence exists in childhood and in art, and art is the dream of he who creates. Are signs dreams? Or dreams signs? The signs left on us are terrible. Do you believe in signs? Or in dreams? I believe in dreams.

Happiness, man's last hope, is a dream. But nothing ever came to pass without being dreamed of first.

ABBREVIATIONS

P.L. Ponti Lancia — **P.F.S.** Ponti Fornaroli Soncini — **P.F.** Ponti Fornaroli — **P.S.** Ponti Soncini — **P.F.R.** Ponti Fornaroli Rosselli — **A.G.P.** Gio Ponti Archives — *Ad'I* Daria Guarnati (edited by), 'Espressione di Gio Ponti,' *Aria d'Italia*, VIII, 1954 — **CSAC** Centro Studi e Archivio della Comunicazione, University of Parma, Design Department

NOTES

THE TWENTIES

1. D. Guarnati (edited by), 'Espressione di Gio Ponti,' *Aria d'Italia*, VIII, 1954, p. 7.
2. «Aim of the new system is to provide, at modest prices, furniture of simple shape, but excellent taste and studied in detail so that the end product is endowed with all the most modern practical qualities and perfectly made,» *Domus*, 4, 1928, pp. 29—30.
'Concorso per l'ammobiliamento economico-Opera Nazionale Dopolavoro,' *Domus*, 8, 1929, p. 33.
'Le arti a Monza' (The lobby of the rooms of La Rinascente-Domus Nova), *Emporium*, August 1927.
Lidia Morelli, *La casa che vorrei avere*, Hoepli, Milan 1931.
A.D. Pica, *Storia della Triennale 1918-1957*, publ. by Il Milione, Milan, 1957.
3. Name suggested by Ugo Ojetti's daughter Paola (letter 6/3/1927 from P.O. to G.P. and answer 11/3/1927: «We have chosen, as a name: 'Labirinto,' as our ideas are always labyrinthine.» (A.G.P.).
Among the works produced by «Il Labirinto,» see: 'La Penna d'Oca' (restaurant in Milan), *Domus*, 2, 1928; *Domus*, 10, 1928; *International Studio*, 96, 1930; *Emporium*, August 1927.
4. «Milan, 4 November 1927=VI° / Dear Ponti, read this letter from Father Semeria and tell me how I can answer. Why do not you, or all the people in *Il Labirinto* together, take care of this magazine? Either send me an answer here in Milan by tomorrow, or send it to Florence. / Yours affectionately, Ojetti» (A.G.P.). For Father Semeria's relationship with Ponti and Ojetti, in connection with *Domus*, see also F. Irace, *Gio Ponti. La casa all'italiana*, Electa, Milan 1988, pp. 9 and 48—49.
5. G. Ponti, 'A Ugo Ritter'(dedication), *La casa all'italiana*, Ed. Domus, Milan 1933.
6. Unlike the Monument to the Fallen (in Milan's Piazza Sant'Ambrogio, 1927—28), a «collective» work from which Ponti dissociated himself in reality: «... I have not been 'fiercely' opposed to the project, yet opposed all the same.... Opposed in the first place because of the quality of the Monument... for the Basilica of Sant'Ambrogio, which, with its character of highly austere, early Christian simplicity, with its proportions so well composed, with its dark brown pile... can only be injured by its cumbersome neighbor — cumbersome in bulk and in color, stuck in that triangular area on which it only fits by force...,» letter from G. Ponti to U. Ojetti, n.d. (March—April 1927) (A.G.P.).
7. G. Ponti, *Autobiografia lampo-Quick self-biography or Gio Ponti story / beginning November 18, 1981 / probabile fine entro il 1981*, letter to James Plaut, 21/2/1977 (A.G.P.).

Bibliographic references:
R. Bossaglia, *L'Art Déco*, Laterza, Rome-Bari 1984.
R. Barilli, F. Solmi (edited by), *La Metafisica: gli Anni Venti* (Bologna 1980), Bologna 1980.
R. Bossaglia, *Omaggio a Gio Ponti* (Milan 1980), Decomania, Milan 1980.
R. Bossaglia, 'L'archivio Quarti: un secolo di storia e di cronaca dell'arredamento italiano,' *Rassegna di studi e di notizie*, year II, vol. III, Castello Sforzesco, Milan 1975.
A. Avon, 'Uno stile per l'abitare: attività e architetture di Gio Ponti fra gli anni 20 e gli anni 30,' *Casabella*, 253, 1986, pp. 44—53.
C. De Seta, *La cultura architettonica in Italia tra le due guerre*, Laterza, Rome-Bari 1972.
M.C. Tonelli Michail, *Il design in Italia 1925/43*, Laterza, Rome-Bari 1987

RICHARD-GINORI, 1923—30

1. G. Ponti, 'Le ceramiche,' *L'Italia all'Esposizione Internazionale di Arti Decorative e Industriali Moderne di Parigi 1925* (Paris 1925), Milan, 1926, pp. 69—89.
2. Cf. U. Nebbia, 'L'Italia all'Esposizione Internazionale di Parigi,' *Emporium*, 367, 1925, pp. 27—28.
3. *Ceramiche Moderne d'Arte / Modern Art Pottery, Richard Ginori*, Alfieri e Lacroix, Milan n.d. (160 pp., 500 ills., over 2000 pieces).
4. Cf. G. Nelson, 'Architects of Europe Today: Gio Ponti, Italy,' *Pencil Points*, May 1935, pp. 215—22.
5. From Gio Ponti's correspondence with Carlo Zerbi and Luigi Tazzini at the Doccia factory, Colonnata, Florence, in 1924—25 (Archives of the Museo delle Porcellane di Doccia, Sesto Fiorentino, and A.G.P.).

Bibliographic references:
Domino (R. Giolli), 'Sottovoce — Conversazione Classica,' *1927. Problemi d'arte attuale*, October 1927.
N. Zanni, 'Dal Palladianesimo al modernismo: Robert Adam, John Soane, Giovanni Muzio,' *Arte in Friuli — Arte a Trieste*, supp. to no. 7, 1984.
G. Liverani, *Il museo delle porcellane di Doccia*, Società Ceramica Italiana Richard-Ginori, Florence 1967.
P. Portoghesi, A. Pansera, *Gio Ponti alla Manifattura di Doccia* (Milan 1982), Sugarco, Milan 1982.
G.C. Bojani, *L'opera di Gio Ponti alla Manifattura di Doccia della Richard-Ginori* (Faenza 1977), Commune of Faenza 1977.
F. Pagliari, 'Gio Ponti, l'architettura e la ceramica: poesia e materia,' in G.C. Bojani, C. Piersanti, R. Rava (edited by), *Gio Ponti ceramica e architettura* (Bologna 1987), Centro Di, Florence 1987.
A. Mottola Molfino, *L'arte della porcellana in Italia*, Busto Arsizio 1976, nos. 499—501.
G. Pampaloni, 'Le occasioni del gusto,' *Gio Ponti. Ceramiche 1923-1930. Le opere del museo di Doccia* (Florence 1983), Electa, Milan 1983.
P.C. Santini, 'Gio Ponti: un innovatore,' *ibid.*
Catalogo della Prima Mostra Internazionale delle Arti Decorative (Monza 1923), Milan-Rome 1923.
G. Marangoni, *Catalogo della seconda Mostra Internazionale delle Arti Decorative* (Monza 1925), Milan 1925.
Terza Mostra Internazionale delle Arti Decorative, maggio-ottobre 1927 (Monza 1927), Milan-Rome 1927.
L.R., 'I grandi pezzi di Doccia,' *Stile*, 17, 1942, pp. 52—59.
G.L., 'Il XXXV Concorso Internazionale della ceramica d'arte contemporanea a Faenza,' *Faenza: bollettino del Museo*, 5, 1977, pp. 108 *et seq.*

HOUSE AT NO. 9, VIA RANDACCIO, MILAN, 1925

Bibliographic references:
F. Reggiori, 'Villa a Milano in via Randaccio degli architetti Emilio Lancia e Giovanni Ponti,' *Architettura e Arti Decorative*, VI, no. XII, 1926—27, pp. 568—74.
G. Muzio, 'Alcuni architetti d'oggi in Lombardia,' *Dedalo*, XI, August 1931, pp. 1082—119.

VILLA BOUILHET, GARCHES (PARIS), 1926

1. «... on page 5 take out 'with Lancia and Buzzi,' who in reality were not involved, and put 'for Mr Tony Bouilhet, of the Bouilhet family in Paris,'» G. Ponti, letter to Nathan Shapira, 28/10/1966 (A.G.P.) (correction to proof of article by N. Shapira, 'The Expression of Gio Ponti,' *Design Quarterly*, 69—70, 1967).

Bibliographic references:
M.M., 'L'Ange Volant, casa di campagna di Tony H. Bouilhet a Garches (Parigi),' *Domus*, 45, 1931, pp. 24—31.

THE THIRTIES

1. G. Ponti, letter to Nathan Shapira, 28/10/1966 (A.G.P.).
2. 'La Casa delle Vacanze alla Triennale di Monza,' *Domus*, 33, 1930.
E. Persico, 'Tendenze e realizzazioni,' *La Casa Bella*, 29, 1930.
3. G. Ponti, E.A. Griffini, L.M. Caneva, *Progetti di ville di architetti italiani all'Esposizione triennale internazionale delle arti decorative e industriali moderne alla Villa Reale di Monza*, Bestetti-Tumminelli, Milan 1930—31.

Bibliographic references:
A. Pansera, *Storia e cronaca della Triennale*, Longanesi, Milan 1978.
P. Farina, 'Gio Ponti: anni Trenta e dintorni,' *Ottagono*, 82, 1986, pp. 60—65.
G. Ciucci, 'Il dibattito sulla architettura e la città fasciste,' *Storia dell'arte italiana*, VII, *Il Novecento*, Einaudi, Turin 1982.
E. Persico, 'Il gusto italiano,' *L'Italia Letteraria*, 4 June 1933.
E. Persico, 'L'architetto Gio Ponti,' *L'Italia Letteraria*, 29 April 1934.
A. Pica, *Architettura moderna in Italia*, Hoepli, Milan 1936.
A. Pica *Nuova Architettura Italiana*, Hoepli, Milan 1941.
Var. authors, *Anni Trenta. Arte e cultura in Italia*, Mazzotta, Milan 1982.
Var. authors, *Milano 70/70, 2° dal 1915 al 1945* (Milan 1971), Museo Poldi Pezzoli, Milan 1971.
G. Pagano, 'Potremo salvarci dalle false tradizioni e dalle ossessioni monumentali?,' *Costruzioni Casabella*, 157, 1941, pp. 2—7.
G. Nelson, 'Architects of Europe Today. 1 — Gio Ponti, Italy,' *Pencil Points*, May 1935, pp. 215—22.
G. Ponti, 'Un appartamento risistemato a Milano' (Casa Vanzetti), *Domus*, 131, 1938, pp. 10—28.
G. and R. Fanelli, *Il tessuto moderno*, Vallecchi, Florence 1976.
The International Studio, 96, May 1930, p. 65.
London Studio, 9, June 1935, p. 343.

FURNITURE AND OBJECTS FOR THE FONTANA FIRM, MILAN, FROM 1930

1. 'Alla Triennale di Monza,' *Domus*, July 1930, p. 36.
2. 'Mobili di eccezione,' *Domus*, 44, 1931, p. 40.
3. 'La modernità più audace nella tecnica vetraria,' advertisement by Luigi Fontana & Co., *Domus*, 42, 1932, p. 5.
4. *Ad.I*, p. 120.

Bibliographic references:
'Mobili d'arte in specchio,' *Domus*, 41, 1931, pp. 80—81.
Special issue devoted to glass, *Stile*, 5—6, 1941.

BORLETTI CHAPEL IN THE CIMITERO MONUMENTALE, MILAN, 1931

1. 'Ingegneria e architettura,' *Domus*, 313, 1955, pp. 1—3.

Bibliographic references:
'L'arte nostra nei cimiteri,' *Domus*, 59, 1932, p. 652.
'Tomba Borletti dell'architetto Gio Ponti,' *Architettura*, 1932, pp. 590—93.
R. Aloi, *Architettura funeraria moderna*, Hoepli, Milan, 1941, pp. 177—79.

HOUSE AT NO. 1, VIA DOMENICHINO, MILAN, 1930

Bibliographic references:
'Aspetti di architetture contemporanee,'*Domus*, 35, 1930, p. 21.

F. Reggiori, 'Casa a Milano in via Domenichino angolo Monterosa,' *Architettura e Arti Decorative*, X (1930—31), v. II, pp. 547—56.
F. Irace, 'La casa all'italiana 1928—1933. Gio Ponti e la progettazione delle Case Tipiche,' in O. Selvafolta (edited by), *Costruire in Lombardia. Edilizia residenziale*, Electa, Milan 1985, pp. 183—202.
A. Avon, 'Uno stile per l'abitare,' *Casabella*, 253, 1986, pp. 44—53.
P. Farina, 'Gio Ponti, anni Trenta e dintorni,' *Ottagono*, 82, 1986, pp. 60—65.
V. Gregotti, 'Architettura italiana, 1900—45' in *Arte Italiana. Presenze, 1900—1945*, Bompiani, Milan 1989, p. 272.

PROJECT FOR «AN APARTMENT HOUSE IN TOWN,» 1931

Bibliographic references:
'Progetto di una casa d'abitazione in città con appartamenti su due piani,' *Domus*, 41, 1931, pp. 59—62.

«DOMUSES,» OR «TYPICAL HOUSES,» MILAN, 1931—36

1. G. Ponti, 'Interpretazioni dell'abitazione moderna. Case economiche ad appartamenti grandi,' *Domus*, 77, 1934, pp. 8—9.
2. G. Ponti, 'Una abitazione dimostrativa alla VI Triennale,' *Domus*, 103, 1936, p. 10.

Bibliographic references:
G. Ponti, 'Concezione dell'edificio d'abitazione,' *Domus*, 52, 1932, p. 187.
'L'Italia che si rinnova,' *Domus*, 72, 1933, p. 626.
G. Ponti, 'Le idee che ho seguito in alcune costruzioni,' *Domus*, 84, 1934, pp. 3—14.
F. Irace, 'La «casa all'italiana» 1928—1933. Gio Ponti e la progettazione delle «case tipiche,»' in O. Selvafolta (edited by), *Costruire in Lombardia. Edilizia residenziale*, Electa, Milan 1985, pp. 183—202.
'Una casa in condominio costruita da Gio Ponti,' *Domus*, 126, 1938.
G. Ponti, 'Fortuna dei Floricoltori,' *Corriere della Sera*, 7/1/1937.
F. Irace, 'Gio Ponti e la casa attrezzata,' *Ottagono*, 82, 1986, pp. 50—59.
B. Moretti, *Case d'abitazione in Italia*, Hoepli, Milan 1939, pp. 111—13 (Via Cicognara); pp. 114—15 (Via De Togni); pp. 118—19 (Via Letizia); p. 120 (Viale Coni Zugna).

CERAMIC PANELS FOR THE FERRARIO TAVERN, MILAN, 1932

1. G. Ponti, 'Rivestimenti ceramici,' *Stile*, 10, 1941, pp. 49—56.

Bibliographic references:
'L'arte moderna riporta il rivestimento ceramico agli antichi onori quale tecnica ricca di risorse di colore e di smalti per le grandi figurazioni murali,' *Domus*, 50, 1932, p. 100—101.

BREDA ELECTRIC TRAIN ETR 200, 1933

1. Cf. G.K. Koenig, in 'Il disegno del veicolo ferroviario, automotrici ed elettrotreni,' *Ferrovie dello Stato 1900-1940, Rassegna*, 2, 1980, p. 70.
A. Nulli, 'Il disegno della velocità: elettrotreno ETR 200,' in V. Gregotti (edited by), *Il disegno del prodotto industriale in Italia: 1860-1980*, Electa, Milan 1981, p. 213.
2. 'Verso un nuovo arredamento dei nostri vagoni?,' *Domus*, 94, 1935, pp. 22—23.
3. *Domus* had always reflected Ponti's interest in trains — from American innovations in the thirties to the Italian OM self-propelling observation car produced by Zavanella in 1948. Cf. among others: 'Nuovi vagoni delle Ferrovie Austriache arredati de Josef Hoffmann,' *Domus*, 51, 1932, pp. 164—65; 'M.10.001 New York — Los Angeles,' *Domus*, 87, 1935, pp. 18—21; 'Come si trasforma un'architettura,' *Domus*, 136, 1939, p. 92; 'Viaggiare per guardare,' *Domus*, 229, 1948, pp. 6—9.

Bibliographic references:
C. De Seta, *L'Architettura del Novecento*, Utet, Turin 1981.

TORRE LITTORIA IN THE PARK, MILAN, 1933

1. E. Persico, 'La torre al Parco,' *Casabella*, August—September 1933.

Bibliographic references:
C. Chiodi, 'La Torre Littoria di Milano,' *Politecnico*, 8, 1933, pp. 3—22.
A. Pica, *V Triennale di Milano, Catalogo ufficiale*, Ceschina, Milan 1933.
Emporium, December 1933.
'Notizie,' *Ponteggi Dalmine*, 2, 1985.
T. Molinari, 'Da Torre Littoria a Torre del Parco a Torrebranca,' *Abitare*, 279, 1989, pp. 172-75.

CASA RASINI, MILAN, 1933

1. A. Isozaki, 'Gio Ponti's journey through the decades,' *Gio Ponti 1891-1979 from the Human-Scale to Post-Modernism* (Tokyo 1986), Seibu/Kajima, Tokyo 1986, p. 12.
2. 'Gio Ponti' (monographic issue), *Space Design*, 200, 1981, p. 31.
3. A. Savinio, *Ascolto il tuo cuore, città*, Bompiani, Milan 1944, p. 76.

Bibliographic references:
'Una casa torre sui giardini,' *Domus*, 88, 1935, pp. 26—27.
'Grattacielo a Milano,' *Casabella*, August 1936.
G. Ponti, 'Divagazioni sulle terrazze,' *Corriere della Sera*, 23/1/34.
'Per l'industria del marmo' (Lasa advertisement), *Domus*, 85, 1935, p. XXI.
G. Ponti, 'Le idee che ho seguito in alcune costruzioni,' *Domus*, 84, 1934, pp. 3—14.
G. Ponti, 'Terrazze e piscine sul tetto,' *Domus*, 92, August 1935, pp. 10—12.
P. Masera, 'Cento case a Milano,' *Edilizia Moderna*, 21—22, 1936.
F. Irace, 'La casa sospesa,' in var. authors, *Gli Anni Trenta, Arte e cultura in Italia*, Mazzotta, Milan 1982, pp. 217 et seq.

B. Moretti, *Case d'abitazione in Italia*, Hoepli, Milan 1939, pp. 104—10.
F. Irace, 'Through the Thirties,' *Domus*, 624, 1982.

«LIGHTER-THAN-AIR» ROOM AT THE AERONAUTICS EXHIBITION, MILAN, 1934

Bibliographic references:
A.M. Mazzucchelli, 'Stile di una mostra,' *Casabella*, 80, 1934, pp. 6 et seq.
V. Costantini, (on the Aeronautics Exhibition), *Emporium*, August 1934, pp. 119—21.
F. Reggiori, 'L'Esposizione dell'Aeronautica Italiana nel Palazzo dell'Arte di Milano,' *Architettura*, 9, 1934, pp. 532—40.

«ITALCIMA» FACTORY, MILAN, 1935

1. G. Pagano, 'Uno stabilimento industriale moderno a Milano,' *Casabella*, March 1933, pp. 43—44.

Bibliographic references:
F. Irace, *Gio Ponti. La Casa all'italiana*, Electa, Milan 1988, p. 188.
F. Irace, 'Un'esempio di architettura industriale degli anni Trenta: lo stabilimento ItalCima a Milano,' in O. Selvafolta (edited by), *Costruire in Lombardia*, Electa, Milan 1985.
G. Nelson, 'Architects of Europe Today. 1 — Gio Ponti, Italy,' *Pencil Points*, May 1935, pp. 215—22.
P. Rampa, 'Luciano Baldessari, complesso industriale ItalCima, Milano, 1932-36,' *Domus*, 705, 1989, pp. 52—59.

CASA MARMONT, MILAN, 1934

1. G. Ponti, 'Una casa,' *Domus*, 94, 1935, pp. 1—16.

Bibliographic references:
G. Ponti, 'Le idee che ho seguito in alcune costruzioni,' *Domus*, 84, 1934, pp. 3—14.
'Elementi per l'architettura della casa,' *Domus*, 92, 1935, p. 13.
B. Moretti, *Case d'abitazione in Italia*, Hoepli, Milan 1939, pp. 116—17.

SCHOOL OF MATHEMATICS AT THE NEW UNIVERSITY CAMPUS, ROME, 1934

1. 'La città universitaria di Roma,' *Architettura*, (special issue), 1935.
2. Cf. G. Ponti, *Amate l'Architettura*, Vitali e Ghianda, Genoa, 1957, p. 56.

Bibliographic references:
R. Pacini, 'Il grandioso progetto della Città Universitaria di Roma,' *Emporium*, March 1933, pp. 177—82.
A. Melis, 'La Scuola di Matematica alla R. Università di Roma,' *L'Architettura Italiana*, August 1936, pp. 171—82.
(The university campus in Rome), *Emporium*, January 1936, pp. 18—24.
G. Nelson, 'Architects of Europe Today. 1 — Gio Ponti, Italy,' *Pencil Points*, May 1935, pp. 215—22.
'School of Mathematics. University of Rome,' *Architectural Review*, 80, 1936, pp. 204—206.

A. Pica, *Nuova Architettura Italiana*, Hoepli, Milan 1936.

COMPETITION PROJECT FOR THE «PALAZZO DEL LITTORIO,» ROME, 1934

1. G. Ponti (Competition for the «Palazzo del Littorio») project report, *Casabella*, 82, 1934, pp. 36—39.
2. G.P., 'Risultato felice di un concorso perduto,' *Domus*, 438, 1966, pp. 6—11.
3. G. Pagano, 'Palazzo del Littorio: atto primo,' *Casabella*, 79, 1934, pp. 2—3.
4. G. Ciucci, 'Il dibattito sull'architettura e la città fasciste,' in *Storia dell'arte Italiana*, VII, *Il Novecento*, Einaudi, Turin 1982, pp. 358—60.

Bibliographic references:
(Domus Littoria), *Emporium*, October 1934, pp. 233—37.
(Domus Littoria), *L'Architettura Italiana*, November 1934.

STANDARD FOR THE OSPEDALE MAGGIORE IN MILAN, 1935

1. Ad'I, pp. 20—21.

Bibliographic references:
(Ospedale Maggiore: Standard), *Domus*, 83, 1934, p. 13.
'Il Gonfalone dell'Ospedale Maggiore di Milano,' *Domus*, 91, 1935, pp. 6—7.
'Un ricamo monumentale,' *Domus*, 145, 1940, pp. 28—31.

INTERIORS OF THE FÜRSTENBERG PALACE, VIENNA, 1936

1. «I learned it from Loos: Adolf Loos, whom I knew personally. The foot and leg of a chair and of a piece of furniture, he used to tell me, should always be a bit 'too slender,' a spire a bit 'too high,' a bridge always a bit 'too stretched': an eternal challenge: you make (this is the lesson of the obelisk)...,» G. Ponti, *Amate l'Architettura*, Vitali e Ghianda, Genoa 1957, p. 127.
2. On Oswald Haerdtl's exhibition in Vienna, unpublished text, 18/1/77 (A.G.P.).
3. 'Austria,' *Domus*, 260, 1951, pp. 18—21.

Bibliographic references:
L. Langseth Christensen, *A Design for Living. Vienna in the Twenties*, dedicated to Carmela Haerdtl, Viking Penguin Inc., New York, 1987.

UNIVERSAL EXHIBITION OF THE CATHOLIC PRESS, VATICAN CITY, 1936

1. 'Un avvenimento significativo,' *Domus*, 104, 1936, pp. 13—19.
G. Ponti, 'La Mostra della Stampa Cattolica,' *Emporium*, XIV, October 1936, pp. 198—205.
2. G. Ponti, *Amate l'Architettura*, Vitali e Ghianda, Genoa 1957, p. 134.
3. M. Labò, 'Mostra Universale della Stampa Cattolica al Vaticano,' *Casabella*, 105, 1936, pp. 18—25.
4. M. Piacentini, 'Esposizione Mondiale della Stampa Cattolica nella Città del Vaicano,' *Architettura*, July 1936, cover, pp. 297—309.

Bibliographic references:
(Ausstellung der katholischen Presse in Vatikan), *Innen-Dekoration*, January 1937.
R. Aloi, *Esposizioni*, Hoepli, Milan 1960, p. XXIII.

CASA LAPORTE, MILAN, 1936

1. G. Ponti, 'Una abitazione dimostrativa alla VI Triennale,' *Domus*, 103, 1936, pp. 14—22, and also in *Casabella*, April 1934, pp. 2—5; *Emporium*, 500, 1936, pp. 64—115; *L'architettura*, February 1937, pp. 65—87; *Architettura Italiana*, May 1937, pp. 146—49.
2. G. Ponti, 'Una villa a tre appartamenti in Milano,' *Domus*, 111, 1937, pp. 2—9.
3. *Ibid.*

Bibliographic references:
B. Moretti, 'Die eigene Wohnung eines Architekten,' *Innen-Dekoration*, 6, 1937, pp. 196—207.
T. Lundgren, 'Funktionalism i sin prydno,' *Svenska Hem*, vol. 27, 1939, pp. 199—204.
F. Irace, 'Gio Ponti e la casa attrezzata,' *Ottagono*, 82, 1986, pp. 50—59.

PROJECT FOR A DAY NURSERY AT BRUZZANO, MILAN, 1934

Bibliographic references:
E. Persico, 'Un progetto di Ponti,' *Casabella*, 88, 1935.
'Edificio per l'Opera Maternità e Infanzia,' *Case d'oggi*, 2, 1936.

PROJECT FOR THE VILLA MARZOTTO, VALDAGNO, 1936

1. *Ad'I*, p. 7.

Bibliographic references:
Ad'I, p. 13.
A. Erseghe, G. Ferrari, M. Ricci, *Francesco Bonfanti Architetto*, Electa, Milan 1986, p. 78.

VANZETTI FURNISHINGS, MILAN, 1938

Bibliographic references:
'Un appartamento risistemato a Milano,' *Domus*, 131, 1938, pp. 10—28.

FIRST MONTECATINI BUILDING, MILAN, 1936

1. G. Pagano, 'Alcune note sul Palazzo della Montecatini,' *Casabella*, 138-139-140, 1939 (monographs), pp. 3—6.
2. Cf. Ponti-Donegani correspondence, 1936—43 (A.G.P.).
3. Cf. 'Villa a Milano' (architect, I. Gardella), *Domus*, 263, 1951, pp. 28—33.
4. C. Malaparte, 'Un palazzo d'acqua e foglie,' *Aria d'Italia*, May 1940.
5. «It is the building of silence. It is a building constructed out of coagulated water. It is a building of sugar polished and turned slightly green by the frost,» in A. Savinio, *Ascolto il tuo cuore, città*, Bompiani, Milan 1944, p. 153.
6. Cf. G. Ponti, *Amate l'Architettura*, Vitali e Ghianda, Genoa 1957, p. 149.
7. *Casabella*, 138-139-140, 1939 (monographs).

8. Cf. G. Ponti, 'Come è nato l'edificio,' *Casabella*, 138-139-140, 1939 (monographs), p. 11.
9. Cf. G. Ponti, *Amate l'Architettura*, Vitali e Ghianda, Genoa 1957, pp. 56—57.
10. G. Ponti, 'Alcune considerazioni sugli edifici per uffici,' *Edilizia Moderna*, 49, 1952, pp. 11—19.
11. Cf. D. Buzzati, in *Antologia Rivista Pirelli*, publ. by Scheiwiller, Pizzi e Pizio, Milan 1987, p. 83.

Bibliographic references:
'Un palazzo del lavoro,' *Domus*, 135, 1939, pp. 36—43.
M. De Giorgi, 'Il Palazzo Montecatini a Milano,' in O. Selvafolta (edited by), *Costruire in Lombardia*, Electa, Milan 1983.
Il Palazzo per uffici Montecatini, Pizzi e Pizio, Milan 1938.
G. Zucconi, 'L'imperativo del Capitolato,' *Rassegna*, 24, 1985, pp. 55—66.
G. Ponti, 'Ingegneria e architettura,' *Domus*, 313, 1955, pp. 1—3.
Casabella, 138-139-140, 1939 (monographs).

THE LIVIANO, PADUA, 1937

1. G. Ponti, quoted in *Ad'I*, p. 69.
2. S. Bettini, 'Campigli al Liviano,' *Calendario*, Cassa di Risparmio di Padova e Rovigo, 1979.

Bibliographic references:
'Concorso per il Palazzo della Facoltà di Lettere in Piazza Capitaniato in Padova,' *L'Architettura Italiana*, 1934, September, pp. 302—307.
'Concorso edilizio per la sistemazione della Università di Padova,' *Architettura*, 9, 1934, pp. 548 *et seq.*
R. Pallucchini, 'Affreschi padovani di Massimo Campigli,' *Le Arti*, V—VI, 1940, pp. 346—50, plates CXLIV—CXLV.
I. Favaretto, *Il Museo del Liviano a Padova*, Cedam, Padova, 1976.
G. Ponti, 'Opere durature agli artisti, non solo premi ed esposizioni,' *Stile*, 13, 1942, pp. 7—28.
'Il marmo in fotografia,' *Domus*, 292, 1954, p. 'i concorsi.'

VILLA MARCHESANO, BORDIGHERA, 1938

Bibliographic references:
G. Ponti, 'Villa M. a Bordighera,' *Domus*, 138, 1939, pp. 36—39.
B. Moretti, *Ville*, 2, Hoepli, Milan 1942, pp. 24—29.
Ad'I, p. 29.

PROJECT FOR A «HOTEL IN THE WOOD,» ON CAPRI, 1938

1. G. Ponti in *Ad'I*, p. 25.
2. See G. Ponti, 'Casa a Posillipo,' *Domus*, 120, 1937, pp. 6—15.
3. G. Ponti, 'Albergo di San Michele o nel bosco all'Isola di Capri,' *Architettura*, June 1940, pp. 1—14.
4. See B. Rudofsky, 'Introduzione al Giappone,' *Domus*, 319, 1956, pp. 45—49.

Bibliographic references:
See 'Un nuovo tipo d'albergo progettato da Ponti e Rudofsky per le coste e le isole del Tirreno e che può essere ideale per la Dalmazia,' *Stile*, 8, 1941, pp. 16—19.
Plans of bungalows for Eden Roc, Hotel du Cap, Antibes, 1939 (with Carlo Pagani), publ. in *Ad'I*, p. 28.

HOTEL PROJECT FOR THE ADRIATIC COAST, 1938

Bibliographic references:
R.G., 'Albergo per il Lido Adriatico,' *Casabella*, 125-26, 1938, pp. 8—11.
See also, R.G., 'Progetto di albergo per il Lido Tirreno,' *Casabella*, 125—26, 1938, pp. 4—7.

PROJECT FOR THE MASTER PLAN OF ADDIS ABABA, 1936

1. On the margin of a drawing, today kept at the CSAC, Parma.

Bibliographic references:
G. Pagano, 'Il piano regolatore di Addis Abeba degli ingegneri Valle e Guidi,' *Casabella*, 107, 1936, pp. 16—23.

URBAN DEVELOPMENT SCHEME FOR THE AREA OF THE FORMER SEMPIONE STATION, MILAN, 1937—48

1. Program for an urban development scheme, unpublished text, (1937) (A.G.P.).
Cf. G. Ponti, 'Possibilità di grandi realizzazioni edilizie,' *Corriere della Sera*, 30 April 1937.
G. Ponti, 'Consenso dei milanesi a una realizzazione urbanistica degna del tempo di Mussolini,' *Corriere della Sera*, 29 November 1937.
G. Ponti, 'Via libera,' *Corriere della Sera*, 24 December 1937.
2. Cf. G. De Finetti, 'Piano per la ricostruzione 1944.46,' publ. in G. Cislaghi, M. De Benedetti, P. Marabelli (edited by), *Giuseppe De Finetti*, Clup, Milan 1981, pp. 118—19.
3. See 'Giuseppe Vaccaro: la casa a collina e la città nuova,' *Domus*, 113, 1937, p. 33 (republished in *Domus*, 501, 1971).
4. Letter from G.P. to Mazzocchi-Minoletti-De Smaele-Guagliumi-Gandolfi, Milan, 4 September 1948 (CSAC, Parma).
'Fiume verde all'ex-Scalo Sempione,' *Corriere della Sera*, 14 October 1948.
(Garden district at the former Sempione Station), *Corriere d'Informazione*, 14—15 October 1948.
'L'isola verde al Sempione,' *L'Umanità*, 14 October 1948.
5. «In Milan there is only one axis of penetration that leads directly to the Cathedral through an extraordinary sequence of monuments. The new modern district, three times as deep as the diameter of Foro Bonaparte, is grafted onto this major urban system and will be a grandiose element in it...,» caption to ill. No. 2, presentation layout of the scheme, 1948 (CSAC, Parma).

6. G. Ponti, 'Sull'edilizia popolare — l'edilizia popolare è un fatto transitorio,' *Domus*, 314, 1956, p. 6.

COMPETITION PROJECT FOR THE FOREIGN MINISTRY, ROME, 1939

1. All Ponti's comments are taken from the presentation album of the competition project (A.G.P.).

Bibliographic references:
Ad'I, pp.14—15.

TATARU VILLA, CLUJ, ROMANIA, 1939

Bibliographic references:
'Due progetti per la villa del Prof. Tataru,' *Domus*, 111, 1937, pp. 12—15.
'Una villa in Romania,' *Domus*, 136, 1939.

«AN IDEAL SMALL HOUSE,» 1939

1. G. Ponti, 'Una piccola casa ideale,' *Domus*, 138, 1939, pp. 40—46.

Bibliographic references:
Ponti systematically published projects for houses by the sea in *Domus* and *Stile*. See, among others:
'Una casetta al mare,' *Domus*, 140, 1939, pp. 34—35.
'Proposta di una casa al mare,' *Domus*, 138, 1939, pp. 48—49.
'Quattro progetti di case al mare,' *Stile*, 8, 1941, pp. 24—26.
'Immaginate la vostra casa al mare,' *Stile*, 10, 1941, pp. 8—12.
'Invenzione per una villa sul Pacifico,' *Stile*, 14, 1942, pp. 7—9.
'Studio per una casa sul Pacifico,' *Stile*, 15, 1942, pp. 8—9.
'Un progetto «anteguerra» che dedichiamo ad Arturo Benedetti-Michelangeli,' *Stile*, 37, 1944, pp. 36—39.
'Risoluzione di una casa in riviera,' *Stile*, 1, 1946, pp. 8—11 (with V. Viganò).

PROJECT FOR THE PALAZZO MARZOTTO, MILAN, 1939

1. Cf. 'Genesi di un perfezionamento,' *Stile*, 25, 1943, p. 16.
2. G. Ponti, 'Dieci anni fa come oggi e la questione delle opere d'arte nell'architettura,' *Domus*, 270, 1952, pp. 18—19.

Bibliographic references:
A. Erseghe, G. Ferrari, M. Ricci, *Francesco Bonfanti architetto*, Electa, Milan 1986, pp. 78—138.
G. Pagano, 'Potremo salvarci dalle false tradizioni e dalle ossessioni monumentali?,' *Costruzioni Casabella*, 157, 1941, pp. 2—7.

EIAR BUILDING, NOW RAI BUILDING, MILAN, 1939

Bibliographic references:
G. Ponti, N. Bertolaia, *Relazione del progetto* entered for the competition for the new seat of the Ente Italiano Audizioni Radiofoniche in Milan, 1939 (A.G.P.).
'Genesi di un perfezionamento,' *Stile*, , 25, 1943, p. 16.

COMPETITION PROJECT FOR THE PALACE OF WATER AND LIGHT AT THE «E42» EXHIBITION, ROME, 1939

1. The project drawings are now kept at the CSAC, Parma.
2. Cf. the report of the Jury publ. in R. Mariani, *E42, un progetto per l'Ordine Nuovo*, publ. by Comunità, Milan 1987, pp. 137—39 and 160.

DOMUS, 1928—40

1. G. Michelucci, 'Contatti fra architetture antiche e moderne,' *Domus*, 51, 1932, pp. 134—37.
2. *Domus*, August 1930, pp. 61—63.
3. 'Applicazioni del cristallo nell'arredamento moderno,' *Domus*, 58, 1932, p. 603.
4. Multicolored sculpture for the swimming pool of 'La villa-studio per un artista' (architects, Pollini and Figini), *Domus*, 67, 1933, p. 357.
5. E. Persico, 'Punto e da capo per l'architettura,' in G. Ponti, 'Lo stile nell'architettura e nell'arredamento moderno,' *Domus*, 83, 1934, pp. 1—9.

THE FORTIES

1. V. Bini, G. Ponti, *Cifre Parlanti: ciò che dobbiamo conoscere per ricostruire il Paese*, Vesta, Milan 1944.
2. Bosisio, Libera, Ponti, Pozzi, Soncini, Vaccaro, Villa, Beretta, *Verso la casa esatta*, Editrice Italiana, Milan 1945.

Bibliographic references:
R. Aloi, *L'arredamento moderno*, Hoepli, Milan 1952.
M.C. Tonelli Michail, *Il design in Italia, 1925—43*, Laterza, Rome-Bari 1987.

SCENES AND COSTUMES FOR STRAVINSKY'S «PULCINEL-LA» AND FOR GLUCK'S «ORPHEUS, 1940—47

1. They comprised:
1939 Scenes and costumes for the ballet *La vispa Teresa* by Ettore Zapparoli, choreographed by Walter Toscanini, in San Remo.
1940 Scenes and costumes for the ballet *Pulcinella* by Igor Stravinsky at the Teatro della Triennale, Milan (directed by Carletto Tieben).
1944 Scenes and costumes for the ballet *Festa romantica* by Giuseppe Piccioli, for La Scala, Milan (prima ballerina, Vanda Sciaccaluga).
1945 Scenes and costumes for the ballet *Mondo Tondo* by Ennio Porrino at La Scala, Milan (not performed).
1947 Scenes and costumes for Gluck's *Orpheus* at La Scala, Milan (directed by Fritz Schuh, choreography by Erika Hanka, orchestra conducted by Ionel Perlea; Orpheus, Ebe Stignani; Eurydice, Suzanne Danco).
1951 Scenes and costumes for Scarlatti's *Mitridate* at La Scala, Milan (not performed).
2. *Ad'I*, pp. 60—63.
3. *Ad'I*, p. 6.

4. G. Ponti, 'Il teatro di Appia, o l'opera d'arte vivente,' *Il Teatro*, Il Convegno, Milan 1923, pp. 62—81.
5. See *Ad'I*, p. 44, and in general Ponti's work for the magazine *Bellezza*, from 1941 to 1943.
6. Gio Ponti drew or painted many Harlequins in the twenties (for Richard-Ginori) and in the fifties.
7. G. Ponti, *Il Coro — cronache immaginarie*, Uomo, Milan 1944.

VILLA DONEGANI IN BORDIGHERA, 1940

Bibliographic references:
'Architettura mediterranea,' *Stile*, 7, 1941, pp. 2—13.

GRAND FRESCOED STAIRCASE IN PALAZZO DEL BO, PADUA, 1940

Bibliographic references:
G. Ponti, 'Opere durature agli artisti, non solo premi ed esposizioni — anticipazioni di Padova,' *Stile*, 13, 1942, pp. 7—29.
L. Ponti, 'L'ultima statua di Martini,' *Domus*, 226, 1948, pp. 40—41.
Ad'I, pp. 46—49.
M. Universo, *Gio Ponti designer; Padova 1936-1941*, preface by Lionello Puppi, Laterza, Rome-Bari 1989.
U. La Pietra (edited by), *Gio Ponti: l'arte si innamora dell'industria*, Coliseum, Milan 1988, pp. 117—25.

COLUMBUS CLINIC, MILAN, 1940—48

1. *Ad'I*, p. 6.
2. G. Fonti, 'Clinica Columbus,' *Domus*, 240, 1949, pp. 12—25.
3. Archias (G. Ponti), *Ringrazio Iddio che le cose non vanno a modo mio*, Antoniazzi, Milan 1946.

Bibliographic references:
G. Ponti, 'Clinica Columbus,' *Edilizia Moderna*, 43, 1949.
G. Ponti, 'Superfici,' *Stile*, 2, 1941, pp. 16—17.
Stile, 8, 1942, cover.

FRESCOES IN THE «POPOLO D'ITALIA» BUILDING, MILAN, 1940

Bibliographic references:
Ad'I, p. 47.

«HENRY IV,» IDEA FOR A FILM, 1940

Bibliographic references:
Ad'I, p. 65.
U. La Pietra (edited by), *Gio Ponti: l'arte si innamora dell'industria*, Coliseum, Milan 1988, pp. 130—31.

«BELLEZZA,» 1941—43, FASHION, WOMEN

1. See in particular the issues: January—July/August—October 1941; April 1942; December 1943.

In the field of fashion, Elena Celani (Parigi), Federico Berzewiczy-Pallavicini (Vienna), Brunetta (Milan) were the designers contributing to *Bellezza* for whom Ponti had a predilection, as he did for Elena Kuster Rosselli, editor of the magazine *Fili*.
2. G. Ponti, 'Voi o donne,' *Stile*, 3, 1941, p. 63.
3. G. Ponti, 'Alle lettrici [per] Antologia di Frank Lloyd Wright,' *Stile*, 1, 1946, pp. 1—5.

FURNITURE WITH ENAMEL DECORATIONS BY PAOLO DE POLI, PADUA, 1941

1. G. Ponti, *De Poli: smalti*, Guarnati, Milan 1958 (introduction).
2. *Ad'I*, pp. 64-65; 'Alcune opere d'arte sul Conte Grande,' *Domus*, 244, 1950, pp. 16—17.
3. A. Pica, 'Paolo De Poli e Milano,' in *L'Arte dello Smalto — Paolo De Poli*, Padua 1984, pp. 21—22.

CASA PONTI AT CIVATE, BRIANZA, 1944

1. 'Casa in Brianza,' *Domus*, 245, 1950, pp. 30—32.

DESIGNS FOR VENINI, MURANO, 1946—49

1. See here 'The Twenties' (introduction).
2. G. Ponti, 'Venini,' *Domus*, 361, 1959, pp. 31—48.

Bibliographic references:
Var. authors, *Venini. Murano 1921*, Franco Maria Ricci, Milan 1989.

«ASSEMBLING» AND «LIGHTENING,» 1948—50

1. *Ad'I*, p. 72.
(Collection of objects, books, and prints), 'Casa B., Milano,' *Domus*, 226, 1948, p. 61.
2. 'La testiera-cruscotto,' *Domus*, 227, 1948, pp. 36—37.
G. Ponti, 'Una proposizione per la modernità dei mobili,' *Stile*, 10, 1946, pp. 16—17.
3. 'Il pannello-cruscotto per la scrivania di un dirigente d'azienda,' *Domus*, 228, 1948, pp. 22—23.
'Lo studio di un dirigente d'azienda,' *Domus*, 257, 1951, pp. 30—31.
4. 'La finestra arredata,' *Domus*, 298, 1954, pp. 17—20.
5. Cf. G. Ponti, 'Il modello della villa Planchart in costruzione a Caracas,' *Domus*, 303, 1955, pp. 8—14.

LA PAVONI, COFFEE MACHINE, MILAN, 1948

1. 'Forme,' *Domus*, 228, 1948, p. 50.

Bibliographic references:
'Industrial design italiano,' *Domus*, 252—53, 1950, p. 74.

A. Nulli, 'Le macchine per fare il caffè,' in V. Gregotti (edited by), *Il disegno del prodotto industriale in Italia, 1860-1980*, Electa, Milan 1981, p. 164.
G. Bosoni, 'Le macchine per fare il caffè,' in V. Gregotti (edited by), *Il disegno del prodotto industriale in Italia, 1860-1980*, Electa, Milan 1981, pp. 294—95.

SWIMMING POOL AT THE HOTEL ROYAL, SAN REMO, 1948

1. G. Ponti, 'Che cosa può significare la parola «funzionale» (discorso su une piscina),' *Domus*, 229, 1948, pp. 10—13.
G. Ponti, *Quick self-biography...*, letter to J. Plaut, 21/2/1977 (A.G.P.).

Bibliographic references:
Ad'I, pp. 34 and 36.
Swimming-pool project for the roof garden of the Hotel Royal in Naples, *Domus*, 291, 1954, cover (see here p. 165).

«AMUSEMENT» AND «DISQUIET FANTASY,» 1948—50

1. G. Ponti 'Considerazioni su alcuni mobili' (Casa Cremaschi), *Domus*, 243, 1950, pp. 26—29.
G. Ponti, 'Una casa non finisce mai,' *Domus*, 238, 1949, pp. 13—17.
'Una sala da pranzo da guardare,' *Domus*, 252-53, 1950, pp. 28—29.
2. G. Ponti, 'Casa di fantasia' (Casa Lucano), *Domus*, 270, 1952, pp. 28—38.
3. 'Un negozio grafico,' *Domus*, 246, 1950, pp. 6—9.
4. G. Ponti, 'Omaggio ad una mostra eccezionale,' *Domus*, 252—53, 1950, pp. 25—74.

Bibliographic references:
'Particolari di una casa' (Casa Ceccato), *Domus*, 256, 1951, pp. 28—32 (see here p. 145).
'Eleganza dell'alluminio, della vipla, della gomma' (interiors of the San Remo Casino), *Domus*, 258, 1951, pp. 22—25 (see here p. 144).
M.R. Rogers, W.D. Teagne, *Italy at Work: Her Renaissance in Design Today*, exhibition at the Brooklyn Museum and in various other museums, 1950—51, Compagnia Nazionale Artigiana, Rome 1950.

STILE, 1941—47

1. *Verve* (artistic and literary review appearing four times a year). Dírécteur: E. Tériade, *Éditions de la Revue Verve*, no. 1, Paris, December 1937.
2. G. Ponti, 'Storia di oggi e artisti di oggi,' *Stile*, 17, 1942, p. 3.
3. See *Stile*, 35, 1943, p. 1; see also Archias (G. Ponti), 'Politica dell'architettura,' *Idearii*, Garzanti, Milan 1944. With other words, the subject (architects and post-war reconstruction) was also treated by Alberto Sartoris in his essay in *Stile*, 37, 1944, 'Momento dell'architettura.'

4. Motto on the cover of V. Bini, G. Ponti, *Cifre Parlanti: ciò che dobbiamo conoscere per ricostruire il Paese*, Vesta, Milan 1944.
5. Cf. in the scheduling for the *Idearii* (publ. by Garzanti), no. 2: 'Dobbiamo ricostruire la Scala?'
6. 'Documenti sulle idee del nostro tempo' (letter by Van Gogh), *Stile*, 36, 1943, p. 27.
7. The young Ligurian poet, writer and critic, fallen in 1945.
8. Alighiero Boetti.
9. Four of these were put on show in the exhibition 'Arte Italiana. Presenze 1900-1945,' organized by Pontus Hulten and Germano Celant, Palazzo Grassi, Venice, April—November 1989.

SHIP INTERIORS, 1948—52

Bibliographic references:
'Alcune opere d'arte sul Conte Grande,' *Domus*, 244, 1950, pp. 14—20.
'Informazione su alcuni ambienti del Conte Biancamano,' *Domus*, 245, 1950, pp. 3—19.
G. Ponti, 'Confronto' (Conte Grande/Ile de France), *Domus*, 246, 1950, pp. 2—3.
G. Ponti, 'Alcuni interni dell'Andrea Doria,' *Domus*, 281, 1953, pp. 17—24.
G. Ponti, 'Occorre che nei nostri bastimenti gli stranieri imparino l'Italia,' *Corriere della Sera*, 21 March 1950.
G. Pristerà, 'Studio storico della progettazione degli arredi navali di Gio Ponti,' now in U. La Pietra (edited by), *Gio Ponti: l'arte si innamora dell'industria*, Coliseum, Milan 1988, pp. 206—25.

THE FIFTIES

1. D. Guarnati (edited by), 'Espressione di Gio Ponti,' *Aria d'Italia*, VIII, 1954.
2. W. Gropius, 'Agli allievi di Harvard,' *Domus*, 346, 1958, pp. 5—6.

Bibliographic references:
O. Gueft, 'Ascetic and sybarite: the masks of Ponti,' *Interiors*, vol. 112, December 1952, pp. 74—77.
L.L. Ponti, E. Ritter (edited by), *Mobili e interni di architetti italiani*, Editoriale Domus, Milan 1952.
Centro Kappa (edited by), *Il design italiano degli anni '50* (Binasco/Milan 1981), Igis Edizioni, Milan 1981.
C. Borngräber, *Stilnovo, design in den 50er Jahren*, Fricke, Frankfurt 1979.
A. Pica, *Forme nuove in Italia*, Bestetti, Milan 1957.
W. Hofmann, U. Kultermann, *Italy after 1950*, Viking Press, New York 1970, pp. 374—77.
P. Maenz, *Die fünfziger Jahre*, Du Mont Verlag, Cologne 1978.
V. Gregotti, 'Le désir de réalité,' in var. authors, *Les Années 50*, Centre Georges Pompidou, Paris 1988.
Architectural Record, 120, December 1956, pp. 155—64.
The Architectural Review, 121, April 1957, pp. 272—73.

DRAWN LETTERS, 1950—79

1. S. Sermisoni (edited by), *Gio Ponti:*

Cento lettere (Milan, Galleria Jannone, 1987), Rosellina Archinto, Milan 1987.

«AMUSEMENTS» WITH FORNASETTI IN SAN REMO, TURIN, GENOA, 1950

1. 'Eleganza dell'alluminio, della vipla, della gomma,' *Domus*, 258, 1951, pp. 22—25.

Bibliographic references:
'Chiarezza, unità, visibilità totale negli uffici modernissimi,' *Domus*, 270, 1952, pp. 20—27.
Ad'I, pp. 78—79, 84—85.

CECCATO FURNISHINGS, MILAN, 1950

Bibliographic references:
'Particolari di una casa,' *Domus*, 256, 1951, pp. 28—32.
Ad'I, p. 58.

HARRAR-DESSIÉ HOUSING DEVELOPMENT, MILAN, 1950

1. G. Ponti, 'Sull'edilizia popolare, l'edilizia popolare è un fatto transitorio,' *Domus*, 314, 1956, pp. 2—6.
2. «In my view, for schemes of city planning to be realized straightaway, and [that are] complete, a degree of geometric order is justified, while certain undulating, vermiform layouts are the non-spontaneous — romantic — imitation of a 'spontaneous generation' for subsequent naturalistic developments; these imitations are an affectation,» G. Ponti, *ibid.*

Bibliographic references:
Ad'I, pp. 114—15.
'Il Quartiere Ina-Casa in via Dessié a Milano,' *Domus*, 270, 1952, pp. 9—15.
G. Ponti, 'Paesaggio moderno di Milano,' *Domus*, 313, 1955, pp. 7—10.

SECOND MONTECATINI BUILDING, MILAN, 1951

1. G. Ponti, 'Considerazioni sugli edifici per uffici,' *Edilizia Moderna*, 49, 1952, pp. 11—18.
2. G. Ponti, *Amate l'Architettura*, Vitali e Ghianda, Genoa 1957, p. 173.
3. *Ad'I*, pp. 106—109.

Bibliographic references:
G. Ponti, 'Cristalli e palazzi per uffici,' *Vitrum*, 51, 1954.

HOTEL BEDROOM AT THE 9TH MILAN TRIENNALE, 1951

1. G. Ponti, 'Camera d'albergo,' *Domus*, 264—65, 1951, pp. 12—13.

Bibliographic references:
Ad'I, pp. 82—83.

LUCANO FURNISHINGS, MILAN, 1951

1. «If it were worthwhile to chronicle my life as an architect, a chapter (beginning in 1950) could be: 'Passion for

---

Fornasetti.' What does Fornasetti give me? With his prodigious printing process... an effect of lightness and evocative magic. Everything becomes weightless...» G. Ponti, in 'Una casa di fantasia,' *Domus*, 270, 1952, pp. 28—38.

Bibliographic references:
Ad'I, pp. 57—58.

EDISON POWER PLANT, SANTA GIUSTINA, 1952

1. In the same chapter of *Ad'I*, only seven further works are mentioned: another power plant, the School of Mathematics at the University Campus, Rome, Casa Laporte, Columbus Clinic, Harrar-Dessié housing development, Milan, and two projects, Palazzo Marzotto, 1940, and Mondadori factory, Milan 1943.

Bibliographic references:
Ad'I, pp. 120—21.

VILLA ARATA, NAPLES, 1952

1. In the same chapter of *Ad'I*, only the hotel in the wood, Capri (with Rudowsky), the bungalows of Eden Roc at Cap d'Antibes (with Pagani), the Marchesano and Donegani villas, the swimming-pools of the Hotel Royal in San Remo and Naples.

GIO PONTI'S STUDIO AT NO. 49, VIA DEZZA, MILAN, 1952

1. 'Da autorimessa a studio d'architettura, redazione, scuola,' *Domus*, 276—77, 1952, pp. 59—66.
2. «Lisa, if the issue is done for me, the titles can run like this:
«Form for skyscrapers
«Form for an automobile
«Form for an inhabited crossroad
«Form for a museum
«Form for a cathedral» (from G. Ponti, handwritten note for L.L.P., n.d.) (A.G.P.).
3. G. Ponti, 'Le produzioni moderne per l'architettura sono chiamate ad intervenire nella efficienza dell'insegnamento di una nuova scuola moderna di architettura,' *Domus*, 296, 1954, pp. 1—8.

PROJECT FOR THE LANCIA BUILDING, TURIN, 1953

Bibliographic references:
Ad'I, pp. 126—29.

PROJECT FOR THE TAGLIANETTI HOUSE, SÃO PAULO, 1953

Bibliographic references:
G. Ponti, 'Idea per la casa del dottor T. a San Paolo,' *Domus*, 283, 1953, pp. 8—11.
Ad'I, pp. 130—31.

PROJECT FOR THE SWIMMING-POOL OF THE HOTEL ROYAL, NAPLES, 1953

Bibliographic references:
Cover of *Domus*, 291, 1954.

PROJECT FOR THE «PREDIO ITALIA» (ITALO—BRAZILIAN CENTER) IN SÃO PAULO, 1953

Bibliographic references:
G. Ponti, 'Si fa coi pensieri,' *Domus*, 379, 1961, pp. 1—30 (see p. 2).
G. Ponti, 'Prima e dopo la Pirelli,' *Domus*, 379, 1961, pp. 31—34 (see p. 31).
Ad'I, pp. 140—45.
G. Ponti, *Amate l'Architettura*, Vitali e Ghianda, Genoa 1957, pp. 176—77.

PROJECT FOR THE FACULTY OF NUCLEAR PHYSICS AT THE UNIVERSITY OF SÃO PAULO, 1953

1. 'Istituto di Fisica Nucleare a San Paolo,' *Domus*, 284, 1953, pp. 16—21.

Bibliographic references:
Ad'I, pp. 134—39.
G. Ponti, *Amate l'Architettura*, Vitali e Ghianda, Genoa 1957, pp. 174—75.

IDEAL STANDARD SANITARY FIXTURES, MILAN, 1953

1. 'Nuovi apparecchi sanitari,' *Domus*, 304, 1955, pp. 34—35 and 70.
2. V. Gregotti, (introduction), in V. Gregotti (edited by), *Il disegno del prodotto industriale, cit.*, Electa, Milan 1981, p. 138.
A. Nulli, 'Apparecchi sanitari,' in V. Gregotti (edited by), *Il disegno del prodotto industriale, cit.*, Electa, Milan 1981, pp. 200—201.
3. 'Disegno per l'industria,' *Domus*, 283, 1953, p. 59.
4. 'Ideal Standard' ('Le immagini più significative della prima Eurodomus'), *Domus*, 440, 1966.

Bibliographic references:
Ad'I, pp. 92—93.
'Una nuova serie di apparecchi sanitari,' *Domus*, 308, 1955, pp. 55—56.
G.C. Bojani, C. Piersanti, R. Rava (edited by), *Gio Ponti: ceramica e architettura* (Bologna 1987), Centro Di, Florence 1987, p. 68.
M. Goldschmiedt, 'Gio Ponti,' *Il bagno oggi e domani*, Nov/Dec 1985, pp. 462—65.
G. Bosoni, 'Gli apparecchi sanitari,' in V. Gregotti (edited by), *Il disegno del prodotto industriale, cit.*, Electa, Milan 1981, pp. 280—81.

«FURNISHED WINDOW,» 1954

1. 'La finestra «arredata,»' *Domus*, 298, 1954, pp. 17—20.

Bibliographic references:
'Alloggio uniambientale alla Triennale,' *Domus*, 301, 1954, pp. 31—35.
F. Irace, 'Gio Ponti e la casa attrezzata,' *Ottagono*, 82, 1986, pp. 50—59.

AUTOMOBILE BODY PROPOSAL FOR CARROZZERIA TOURING, MILAN, 1952—53

1. «The Touring automobile body developed by Ponti in 1953 has become a for-

mula for what was known as the European reaction to the exuberance of Detroit.... The Touring body was never introduced as Ponti designed it, but one can see it adapted — it is a question of degree — in the cars by Fiat, Peugeot and Austin, where a continental coherence has had its influence on the development of the compact car in the United States.» (Nathan Shapira, 'The expression of Gio Ponti,' *Design Quarterly*, 69—70, 1967, pp. 9 and 13).
2. 'Borax,' *Domus*, 230, 1948, p. 52.
3. G. Ponti, typewritten texts, 17/10/73 and 16/11/73 (A.G.P.).
4. *Ad'I*, pp. 96—97.

Bibliographic references:
Quattroruote, February 1977, p. 135.

PROJECT FOR THE TOGNI SYSTEM OF LIGHTWEIGHT PREFABRICATION AT THE 10TH MILAN TRIENNALE, 1954

Bibliographic references:
'Prototipo di casa per la serie,' *Domus*, 297, 1954, pp. 20—21.
'Casa unifamiliare di serie, alla Triennale,' *Domus*, 301, 1954, pp. 23—27.

HOUSE IN THE PINE WOOD, ARENZANO, 1955

1. Cf. bibliographic references for 'An ideal small house, 1939,' p. 113.

Bibliographic references:
'Una casa nella pineta: la pianta e alcuni aspetti,' *Domus*, 395, 1962, pp. 13—19.

VILLA PLANCHART, CARACAS, 1955

1. G. Ponti, 'Il modello della villa Planchart in costruzione a Caracas,' *Domus*, 303, 1955, pp. 8—14.
2. G. Ponti, 'Una villa fiorentina,' *Domus*, 375, 1961, pp. 1—40.
3. Ponti and Melotti were to go on working together, in Italy and elsewhere. Among the fruits of their collaboration were the Alitalia offices on Fifth Avenue in New York (cf. *Domus*, 354, 1959, pp. 7—11; see here p. 186) and the Villa Nemazee in Teheran (cf. *Domus*, 422, 1965, pp. 14—19).
4. G.P., 'A Teheran, una villa,' *Domus*, 422, 1965, pp. 14—19 (see here p. 208).

Bibliographic references:
F. Irace 'Caracas, Villa Planchart,' *Abitare*, 253, 1987.
'Casa Planchart di Gio Ponti: come una enorme scultura astratta,' *Casa Vogue*, March 1987, pp. 98 *et seq.*
Axel Stein (edited by), *Gio Ponti, 1891—1979, Obra en Caracas* (Caracas November '86 — January '87), Sala Mendoza / Fundacion Anala y Armando Planchart, Caracas, cat. no. 5, 1986.
Johann Ossott, 'Gio Ponti y la villa Planchart,' *Revista M*, 88, monographic issue, 1988.
Roberto Guevara, 'Legado de Ponti en Caracas,' *El Nacional*, 25 November 1986.
Beatrice Hernandez, 'Leticia Ponti: Gio

Ponti Quedò Enamorado de Caracas para Siempre,' *El Universal*, 22 November 1986.
F. Irace, 'Corrispondenze: la villa Planchart di Gio Ponti a Caracas,' *Lotus International*, 60, 1989, pp. 84—105.
G. Chiaramonte, 'Villa Planchart: tre canoni e l'immancabile Duchamp,' *Lotus International*, 60, 1989, pp. 106—11.

ITALIAN CULTURAL INSTITUTE, LERICI FOUNDATION, STOCKHOLM, 1954

1. 'Un edificio italiano a Stoccolma,' *Domus*, 288, 1953, pp. 8—11.
2. G. Ponti, 'Architettura italiana a Stoccolma,' *Domus*, 355, 1959, pp. 1—8.

Bibliographic references:
Ad'I, pp. 132—33.
'Italia in Svezia,' *Domus*, 324, 1956, p. 1.

PROJECT FOR THE TOWN HALL IN CESENATICO, 1959

Bibliographic references:
B. Zevi, 'Cesenatico si ribella alle vele in ferro battuto,' *Cronache di architettura*, III, Laterza, Rome—Bari 1959.

FACULTY OF ARCHITECTURE AT THE MILAN POLYTECHNIC, 1956

1. (G. Ponti), 'Le produzioni moderne per l'architettura sono chiamate ad intervenire nella efficienza dell'insegnamento di una nuova scuola moderna di architettura,' *Domus*, 296, 1954, pp. 1—8.

Bibliographic references:
'La ricostruzione edilizia dell'Università degli Studi,' *Corriere della Sera*, 7 April 1951.
G. Ponti, 'Un nuovo primato. La scuola d'architettura,' *Corriere della Sera*, 24 April 1953.
G. Ponti, 'Le scuole di architettura,' *Corriere della Sera*, 20 May 1953.
G. Ponti, 'Contributo alla modernizzazione delle scuole di architettura,' *Atti del Collegio Regionale Lombardo degli Architetti*, Milan 1959.
'Non è ancora terminata dopo otto anni la sede della Facoltà di Architettura,' *Corriere della Sera*, 22 February 1961.

THE «SUPERLEGGERA» CHAIR FOR CASSINA, MEDA, 1957

1. 'Una sedia, una poltrona,' *Domus*, 240, 1949, p. 29.
2. G. Ponti, 'Senza aggettivi,' *Domus*, 268, 1952, p. 1.
3. 'La sedia «Superleggera» di Gio Ponti,' *Domus*, 352, 1959, pp. 44—45.

Bibliographic references:
Centro Kappa (edited by), *Il design italiano degli anni '50* (Binasco/Milan 1981), Igis Edizioni, Milan 1981, pp. 109—10.
G. Bosoni, 'Lo stile italiano nella casa,'

in V. Gregotti (edited by), *Il disegno del prodotto industriale, cit.*, Electa, Milan 1981, pp. 348—49.
E. Bellini, E. Morteo, M. Romanelli, 'Storie di sedie. Il progetto italiano dopo il 1947,' *Domus*, 708, 1989, pp. 94—119.

DOOR-PAINTING, 1955, AND PRINTED DOOR-PAINTING, 1957

1. G. Ponti, 'Porta-pittura,' *Domus*, 313, 1955, p. 57.
2. 'Sulle porte, pannelli in stoffa stampata,' *Domus*, 330, 1957, pp. 44—45.

Bibliographic references:
P. Magnesi, *Tessuti d'Autore degli anni Cinquanta* (Turin 1987), Avigdor, Turin 1987.

OBJECTS IN ENAMELED COPPER FOR DE POLI, PADUA, 1956

Bibliographic references:
G. Ponti, *De Poli, smalti*, Guarnati, Milan 1958.
P. Fantelli, G. Segato (edited by), *L'arte dello smalto. Paolo De Poli* (Padua 1984), 1984.
U. La Pietra (edited by), *Gio Ponti: l'arte si innamora dell'industria*, Coliseum, Milan 1988, pp. 310—16, 318—19.
'Nella mostra «Formes Idées d'Italia» a Parigi,' *Domus*, 329, 1957, p. 25.

VILLA ARREAZA, CARACAS, 1956

Bibliographic references:
G. Ponti, 'Modello per la villa Arreaza nel Country Club a Caracas,' *Domus*, 304, 1955, pp. 3—5.
G. Ponti, 'Villa «La Diamantina» nel Country Club a Caracas,' *Domus*, 349, 1958, pp. 5—19.

STEEL FLATWARE FOR KRUPP ITALIANA, MILAN, 1951

1. G. Ponti, 'Smalti e metalli alla Triennale,' *Domus*, 263, 1951, pp. 18—19.

Bibliographic references:
'Vetrina di Krupp,' *Stile*, 10, 1941, pp. 46—47.
'Al Centro Domus: in acciaio inox e alpacca argentata,' *Domus*, 511, 1972, p. d/545.
P. Scarzella, *Il bel metallo*, Arcadia edizioni, Milan 1985.
A. Nulli, M. Mainó, 'La posata: senza apprezzabili variazioni,' *Domus*, 695, 1988, pp. 60—84.

FLATWARE FOR CHRISTOFLE, PARIS, 1955

1. 'Nella mostra «Formes Idées d'Italia» a Parigi,' *Domus*, 329, 1957, pp. 25—30.

Bibliographic references:
'Proposte per la casa alla XI Triennale,' *Domus*, 337, 1957, pp. 31—35 (see p. 33).

U. La Pietra (edited by), *Gio Ponti: l'arte si innamora dell'industria*, Coliseum, Milan 1988, pp. 300—309.
Patrizia Scarzella, *Il bel metallo*, Arcadia edizioni, Milan 1985, p. 136.
F. Alison, 'Lino Sabattini,' *Domus*, 711, 1989, pp. 64—65.

PIRELLI SKYSCRAPER, MILAN, 1956

1. G. Ponti, 'Espressione dell'edificio Pirelli in costruzione a Milano,' *Domus*, 316, 1956, pp. 1—16 (see p. 8).
2. R. Banham, 'The newest invasion of Europe,' *Horizon*, November 1960.
3. Which uses three plans (ground floor, 16th floor, and 31st floor); cf. *Domus*, 316, 1956, cover and p. 1.
4. «A giant billboard,» «a piece of advertising architecture» (Reyner Banham, 'Pirelli Criticism,' *The Architectural Review*, 129, 1961, pp. 194—200; 'powerful tower, delicate shell' (Walter McQuade, *idem, Architectural Forum*, February 1961, p. 90); 'it consolidates the gains of three generations' (Edgar Kaufmann, 'Scraping the Skies of Italy,' *Art News*, 54, 1956, p. 39); 'un mobile bar ingrandito a scala di grattacielo' (Bruno Zevi, letter to Ponti, 20 November 1959 [A.G.P.] and *L'Architettura*, 50, V, 8, December 1959, p. 512).
5. P.L. Nervi, 'L'ossatura,' *Edilizia Moderna* (special issue devoted to the Pirelli Center), 71, 1960, pp. 35—39.
6. 'Modello grattacielo Nuova Sede Pirelli,' *bollettino ISMES*, Begamo, October 1955.
7. G. Ponti, 'Si fa coi pensieri,' *Domus*, 379, 1961, pp. 1—30.
8. *Ibid.*, p. 2.
9. G. Ponti, 'Favola americana,' *Domus*, 272, 1952, pp. 6—10.
10. 'Brasile: da Le Corbusier architetto allo «stile Le Corbusier,»' *Domus*, 229, 1948, p. 1.
11. G. Ponti, 'Stile di Niemeyer,' *Domus*, 278, 1953, pp. 8—9.
12. Ponti recognized the difference between talent and genius. He used to say: Gaudí a genius, Wright a (barbarian) genius, Niemeyer a genius (all his errors are permitted him), Le Corbusier a genius, Aalto a very great architect artist, Mies a very great architect, Neutra a very great architect, Perret a master, Gropius a very great master (cf. *Amate l'Architettura*, p. 230). And his admiration for Saarinen's TWA was boundless («in Domus itself, which has the informative obligation of holding up a mirror to architecture, I repudiate inessential architecture for its cost, silly [works of architecture] for their forms, which are also costly — such as the building in the shape of a clown's hat which makes beautiful San Francisco ridiculous — I repudiate the twofold giantism of Yamasaki — an economic catastrophe on top of everything. Although Saarinen's TWA was expensive it remains an unsurpassed masterpiece and satisfies the supreme requirements of architecture and of art; it is a form the contains forms marvelously; it is a mise-en-scène on an open stage; it has no precedents and no consequents; it is a work of art, one of

a kind» (G. Ponti, notes, handwritten notebook, 1975, A.G.P.)

Bibliographic references:
Special issue devoted to the Pirelli Center, *Edilizia Moderna*, 71, 1960.
A. Belluzzi, C. Conforti, *Architettura italiana 1944-1984*, Laterza, Rome-Bari, 1985, pp. 123—29.
C. De Carli, 'La nuova sede Pirelli,' *Pirelli*, 3, 1955, pp. 18—25.
F. Irace, *Gio Ponti. La casa all'italiana*, Electa, Milan 1988, pp. 162—71.
'Free floor concrete tower,' *Architectural Forum*, November 1955, pp. 138—39.
'An industrial tower,' *Arts & Architecture*, 79, 1962, pp. 10 and 28.
'Pirelli completed,' *The Architectural Review*, 127, 1960, p. 4.
'Powerful construction details mark Milan skyscraper,' *Progressive Architecture*, 40, 1959, p. 95.
'The Pirelli skyscraper....,' *The Architectural Review*, 126, 1959, p. 4.
'Ponti and the Pirelli building,' *Architectural Record*, 120, 1956, pp. 155—64.
V. Viganò, 'Immeuble Pirelli, Milan,' *Architecture d'Aujourd'hui*, 127, March 1956, pp. 1—5.
'Gratte-ciel de bureaux à Milan: Immeuble Pirelli, Tour Galfa,' *Architecture d'Aujourd'hui*, 30, 1959, pp. 44—45.
'Pirelli Hochhaus in Mailand,' *Werk*, October 1956, pp. 312—13.
P.C. Santini, 'Deux gratte-ciels à Milan,' *Zodiac*, 1, 1957, pp. 200—205.
G. Veronesi, 'L'architettura dei grattacieli a Milano,' *Comunità*, 74, 1959, pp. 78—91.
Werner Hoffmann, Udo Kultermann, *Modern Architecture in Color*, Viking Press, New York 1970, pp. 374—75.
G. Ponti, 'Perpetuità di un edificio' (1970), *La rivista Pirelli* (anthology), Scheiwiller, Milan 1988, p. 82.
'Italian Skyscraper Nears Completion,' *The New York Times*, 24 August, 1958.
'Europe's tallest,' *The Sunday Times*, 26 October, 1958.
M.W. Rosenthal, 'Thoughts on Ponti's Pirelli Building,' *The Journal of the RIBA*, vol. 64, no. 7, 1957.
R.v.O., 'De hoogste Wolkenkrabber van Europa,' *De Linie*, 7 July, 1956.
'Edificio Pirelli,' *Informes de la Construccion*, 84, 1956.
Kenzo Tange (the Pirelli office building), *Shinkentiku*, March 1956.
A.C., 'Nowy Drapacz Nieba W Mediolania,' *Stolica*, Warsaw, 5 July 1956.

CASA MELANDRI, MILAN, 1957

1. G. Ponti, typewritten text, 26 October 1957 (A.G.P.).

Bibliographic references:
'Una casa, una scala,' *Domus*, 345, 1958, pp. 31—34.
G. Ponti, *Amate l'Architettura*, Vitali e Ghianda, Genoa 1957, p. 133.
C. Perogalli, *Case e appartamenti in Italia*, Görlich, Milan 1959, pp. 273—76.

PROJECT FOR THE VILLA GORRONDONA, CARACAS, 1957

Bibliographic references:
'Progetto di una villa per il Venezuela,' *Domus*, 333, 1957, pp. 15—16.

GIO PONTI'S APARTMENT IN VIA DEZZA, MILAN, 1957

1. 'Una casa a pareti apribili,' *Domus*, 334, 1957, pp. 31—35.
2. See here p. 151.
3. Painted, with Francesca Willers, in 1977—78, the twenty angels on perspex were then sent to Hong Kong, to Ponti's beloved client Daniel Koo, who used them as a temporary decoration for the facade of his Department Store, on 16 December 1978, and then handed them over to the city's Catholic church.
4. G. Ponti, 'Giorno e notte,' *Domus*, 320, 1956, p. 7.

Bibliographic references:
'La parete organizzata,' *Domus*, 266, 1952, p. 25.
'Alloggio uniambientale alla Triennale,' *Domus*, 301, 1954, pp. 31—35.
'La finestra arredata,' *Domus*, 298, 1954, pp. 17—20.
'Proposte per la casa alla XI Triennale,' *Domus*, 337, 1957, pp. 31—35.
'Una porta e nuovi mobili,' *Domus*, 321, 1956, pp. 21—24.
'Alloggio uniambientale per quattro persone,' *Domus*, 320, 1956, pp. 27—28.
G. Corsini (edited by), 'Incontro con Gio Ponti: l'architettura è fatta per essere guardata,' *Casa Vogue*, November 1978, pp. 138—47.

PROPOSALS FOR THE HOUSE AT THE 11TH MILAN TRIENNALE, 1957

Bibliographic references:
'Proposte per la casa alla XI Triennale,' *Domus*, 337, 1957, pp. 31—35.
C. Corsini, G. Wiskemann, 'Indagine alla Joo,' *Stile Industria*, 30, 1961.

FABRICS FOR THE JSA FACTORY, BUSTO ARSIZIO, 1950—58

1. G. Ponti, 'Profezie sulla pittura,' *Domus*, 319, 1956, pp. 37—38.

Bibliographic references:
Pinuccia Magnesi, *Tessuti d'Autore degli anni Cinquanta* (Turin 1987), Avigdor, Turin 1987, cover and plates 60, 61, and 62.
U. La Pietra (edited by), *Gio Ponti: l'arte si innamora dell'industria*, Coliseum, Milan 1988, pp. 292—98.
Domus, 252—53, 1950, p. 83 ('Balletto Scala' fabric).
Rassegna Domus, *Domus*, 313, 1955 ('Arlecchino' fabric).
Rassegna Domus, *Domus*, 322, 1956 ('Rilievo' fabric).
Cover, *Domus*, 328, 1957 ('Eclisse' fabric).
'Sulle porte , pannelli in stoffa stampata,' *Domus*, 330, 1957, pp. 44—45 ('Estate mediterranea' and 'Geometria' fabrics).

'Tovaglie stampate e nuove stoffe,' *Domus*, 330, 1957, pp. 46—47 ('Eclisse,' 'Estate,' 'Cristalli,' and 'Luci' fabrics).
Rassegna Domus, *Domus*, 331, 1957 ('Vita degli angeli' fabric).
'Mostra a Villa Olmo,' *Domus*, 335, 1957, pp. 33—48 (see p. 43).
'Una nuova stoffa,' *Domus*, 383, 1961, p. 52 ('Dafne' fabric).

CARMELITE CONVENT OF BONMOSCHETTO, SAN REMO, 1958

1. 'Bonmoschetto, Convent by Gio Ponti,' *The Architectural Review*, 127, March 1960, pp. 149—50.
2. Cf. G. Ponti, 'Il Carmelo di Bonmoschetto, monastero delle Carmelitane Scalze in San Remo,' *Domus*, 361, 1959, pp. 1—16.
3. Unpublished correspondence (A.G.P.).
4. Handwritten letter to Gio Ponti from the Reverend Mothers Marie de Jesus and Marie Bernard de Jesus, 3 September 1965 (A.G.P.).

Bibliographic references:
G. Ponti, 'Religione e architetti,' *Domus*, 372, 1960, insert between pp. 40 and 41.
G. Ponti, 'Invito ad andare a Ronchamp,' *Domus*, 323, 1956, pp. 1—2.
Une fille d'Èlie, mère Marie Bernard de Jesus au Carmel de Saint Èlie, San Remo, Editions du Cloître, Jouques 1983.

BUILDING FOR GOVERNMENT OFFICES, BAGHDAD, 1958

1. G. Ponti, 'Prima e dopo la Pirelli,' *Domus*, 379, 1961, pp. 31 *et seq.*

Bibliographic references:
G. Ponti, 'Progetto per l'edificio del Development Board in Baghdad,' *Domus*, 370, 1960, pp. 1—6.

AUDITORIUM ON THE EIGHTH FLOOR OF THE TIME AND LIFE BUILDING, NEW YORK, 1959

Bibliographic references:
'Al piano ottavo del Time-Life Building, New York,' *Domus*, 383, 1961, pp. 5—6.
'The Ponti pavilion in Time and Life Building,' *Architectural Forum*, vol. 113, August 1960, p. 81.
N.H. Shapira, 'The expression of Gio Ponti,' *Design Quarterly*, 69/70, 1967, p. 13.

DOMUS IN THE FIFTIES

1. G. Ponti, 'Picasso convertirà alla ceramica. Ma noi, dice Lucio Fontana, s'era già cominciato,' *Domus*, 226, 1948, pp. 24—38.
2. *Domus*, 236, 1949.
3. Lucio Fontana, unpublished typescript, 1951 (A.G.P.).
4. For the Pirelli flooring, see for example the Vembi offices in Genoa, *Domus*, 270, 1952, cover, and 'Chiarezza, unità, visibilità totale negli uffici modernissimi,' pp. 20—27; see here p. 152).

THE SIXTIES

1. G. Ponti, 'Giovinezza d'oggi o splendida età di Le Corbusier?,' *Domus*, 320, 1956, pp. 1—4.
2. G. Ponti, 'Henry Van de Velde: il nuovo, e il suo apporto alla architettura e alle arti industriali' (1929), *Domus*, 373, 1960, opening pages.
3. The architects included Libera, Saarinen, Rietveld, Le Corbusier, Lescaze, Gropius, and Mies; the artists, Yves Klein, Braque, Manzoni, Cocteau, Morandi, Fontana, Duchamp, Milani, and Leoncillo.
4. G. Ponti, 'L'Habitat n.3 di André Bloc,' *Domus*, 427, 1965, pp. 22 *et seq.*
5. G. Ponti, 'Per le città fumose con vie strette: facciate lucenti illuminate dal cielo,' *Domus*, 469, 1968, pp. 20—21.

Bibliographic references:
Progressive Architecture, 41, November 1960, p. 63
Architectural Record, 139, April 1966, pp. 204—6.
The Architectural Review, 123, February 1968, p. 149.
Architecture d'Aujourd'hui, March 1960, p. 1.
Architecture d'Aujourd'hui, April 1960, p. 102—5.
Architecture d'Aujourd'hui, September 1960, pp. 156—58.
Arts and Architecture, 84, March 1967, pp. 16—21.
Architecture d'Aujourd'hui, 128, October 1967, pp. 82—83.
Craft horizon, 21, March 1961.
Industrial Design, 14, May 1967, pp. 48—51.

VILLA NEMAZEE, TEHERAN, 1960

G. Ponti, 'A Teheran una villa,' *Domus*, 1965, pp. 14—19.

OFFICE BUILDING FOR THE RAS (RIUNIONE ADRIATICA DI SICURTA'), MILAN, 1962

1. G. Ponti, 'Nuova sede della Riunione Adriatica di Sicurtà in Milano,' *Domus*, 397, 1962, pp. 1—12.

Bibliographic references:
G. Ponti, 'La nuova sede della RAS a Milano,' *Edilizia Moderna*, 79, 1963.

HALL IN THE MONTECATINI PAVILION AT THE MILAN TRADE FAIR, 1961

Bibliographic references:
'Allestimenti,' *Domus*, 382, 1961, p. 42.
'Allestimenti per la Montecatini alla Fiera del 1961,' *Allestimenti Moderni*, Görlich, Milan, 1961, in particular pp. 58—59.

LAYOUT OF THE INTERNATIONAL EXHIBITION OF LABOR («ITALIA '61») IN TURIN, 1961

Bibliographic references:
'Dentro l'immane struttura,' *Domus*, 374, 1961, pp. 1–6.
'E.I.L.: momenti di uno spettacolo, prima dell'apertura,' *Domus*, 380, 1961, pp. 1–18.
'Italia '61 a Torino: immagini della Esposizione del Lavoro,' *Domus*, 381, 1961, pp. 3–12.
'Nervi, Ponti Design, Italian Centennial Pavilion,' *Progressive Architecture*, vol. 41, November 1960, p. 63.
'Turin 1961 exposition news: Nervi and Ponti design Exposition Palace,' *Interiors*, vol. 120, December 1960, p. 16.

HOTEL PARCO DEI PRINCIPI, ROME, 1964

1. G. Ponti, 'Cielo azzurro, mare azzurro, isole azzurre, maioliche azzurre, piante verdi, rose ai piedi della principessa, orma di danzatrice,' *Domus*, 415, 1964, pp. 29 *et seq.* («... Is all this true? It was in the mind of the architect; it is not — except for the white and the blue — in reality. So he works, works, works, and does not succeed in expressing himself,» p. 33).
2. G. Ponti, 'Il nuovo albergo Parco dei Principi in Roma,' *Domus*, 425, 1965, pp. 47–54.

Bibliographic references:
U. La Pietra (edited by), *Gio Ponti: l'arte si innamora dell'industria*, Coliseum, Milan 1988, pp. 274–75, 360–67, and 368–73.
G.C. Bojani, C. Piersanti, R. Rava (edited by), *Gio Ponti: ceramica e architettura* (Bologna 1987), Centro Di, Florence 1987, pp. 69, and 72–73.

HOUSES AT CAPO PERLA, ISLAND OF ELBA, 1962

Bibliographic references:
M. Ferrari, S. Castagni (edited by), *Gio Ponti. I progetti dell'Elba, 1960-62*, Editrice Azzurra, Cavalese (Trento) 1988.

PROJECT FOR THE MONTREAL TOWERS, 1961

1. G. Ponti, 'Prima e dopo la Pirelli,' *Domus*, 379, 1961, pp. 31–34.

Bibliographic references:
N.H. Shapira, 'The expression of Gio Ponti,' *Design Quarterly*, 69/70, 1967, pp. 11–12 and 55.

FOR ISLAMABAD, THE IDEA OF A COUNTER-FACADE TO SERVE AS A «BRISE-SOLEIL,» 1962

1. G. Ponti, article for *Domus*, draft, n.d. (A.G.P.).

Bibliographic references:
Space Design, 200 (monographic issue: Gio Ponti), 1981, p. 61.

FACADE OF THE SHUI-HING DEPARTMENT STORE, HONG KONG, 1963

1. C. Mollino, F. Vadacchino, *Architettura, Arte e Tecnica*, Chiantore, Turin, n.d., p. 27.

Bibliographic references:
'Per Hong Kong,' *Domus*, 385, 1961, insert at beginning.
'Hong-Kong: luci sulla facciata,' *Domus*, 459, 1968, p. 16.

VILLA FOR DANIEL KOO, HONG KONG, 1963

Bibliographic references:
Space Design, 200, 1981 (monographic issue: Gio Ponti), p. 70.

SECOND PONTI HOUSE IN CIVATE (BRIANZA), 1963

Bibliographic references:
G. Ponti, 'Immagini di una casa di campagna, in Brianza,' *Domus*, 411, 1964, pp. 36–42.

CHURCH OF SAN FRANCESCO, MILAN, 1964

1. G. Ponti, (the church of San Francesco), *Il Fopponino*, year III, no. 4, 1961 (monthly publ. by the Parish).
2. From a conversation between LLP and the parochial vicar, 11 July 1988.

Bibliographic references:
G.C. Bojani, C. Piersanti, R. Rava (edited by), *Gio Ponti: ceramica e architettura* (Bologna 1987), Centro Di, Florence 1987, pp. 70–71.

THE OBELISKS OF THE SIXTIES

1. *Domus*, 48, 1963, cover and 'Gli obelischi di Domus,' opening page. G.P., 'Il nostro premio, gli Obelischi di Domus,' *Domus*, 409, 1963, pp. 3–4.
2. 'Espressioni. Un negozio di idee a Milano.' *Domus*, 415, 1964, pp. 16–20. 'Espressioni, a Milano, nel «negozio di idee» della Ideal Standard,' *Domus*, 423, 1965, pp. 44–45.

COMPETITION PROJECT FOR THE ANTON BRUCKNER CULTURAL CENTER, LINZ, 1963

1. G. Ponti, 'Risultato felice di un concorso perduto,' *Domus*, 438, 1966, pp. 6–11.

TILES FOR SORRENTO, 1964

1. G. Ponti, 'Giochi con i rivestimenti di Salerno,' *Domus*, 414, 1964, pp. 47 *et seq.*

Bibliographic references:
G. Ponti, 'Cielo azzurro, mare azzurro, isole azzurre, maioliche azzurre, piante verdi, rose ai piedi della principessa, orma di danzatrice,' *Domus*, 415, 1964, pp. 29 *et seq.*

«A BEETLE UNDER A LEAF,» 1964

1. 'Uno scarabeo sotto una foglia,' *Domus*, 414, 1964, pp. 17–23.
2. 'Una collezione in una casa,' *Domus*, 482, 1970, pp. 32–36.

MINISTRIES IN ISLAMABAD, PAKISTAN, 1964

1. Project notes and reports (typescripts), n.d. (A.G.P.).

CHURCH FOR THE HOSPITAL OF SAN CARLO, MILAN, 1966

Bibliographic references:
G. Ponti, 'La cappella del nuovo ospedale di San Carlo a Milano,' *Domus*, 445, 1966, pp. 2–14.
G.C. Bojani, C. Piersanti, R. Rava (edited by), *Gio Ponti: ceramica e architettura* (Bologna 1987), Centro Di, Florence 1987, pp. 74–75.
E. Villa, 'Metodologia dell'Urbanistica Pastorale,' *Nuove Chiese*, 4, 1966, pp. 29–45 (photo p. 41).

CIBORIUM IN THE BASILICA OF OROPA, 1966

1. G. Ponti, 'Architettura di invenzione: serve per guardarla,' *Domus*, 445, 1966, pp. 16 *et seq.*

GIO PONTI AT THE NIEUBOURG GALLERY, MILAN, 1967

1. Tommaso Trini, 'Una galleria per l'uomo dalle idee,' *Domus*, 459, 1968, pp. 42–50.
2. «... in the course of the exhibition *Gio Ponti*, an international collective of new sculpture has been organized as a framework for the presentation of Udo Kultermann's book *Nuove dimensioni della scultura*, published by Feltrinelli ... there were works by Christo, Marzot, Gilardi, Pistoletto, Piacentino, Mario Merz, Del Pezzo, Nanda Vigo, Van Hoeydonck, and Pizzo Greco. The book was presented by Sottsass, Gilardi, and Trini,» *Domus, ibid.*, p. 47.

Bibliographic references:
'1977-1979,' (Galleria Toselli, Via de Castillia, 28), Milan 1980, p. 27.
'1979-1982,' (Franco Toselli, Via del Carmine), Milan 1983, p. 33.

«THICK STAINED-GLASS WINDOWS» FOR VENINI, MURANO, 1966

1. G. Ponti, 'Le vetrate grosse alla Ponti, da Venini,' *Domus*, 436, 1966, pp. 25–29.

DINNER SET FOR CERAMICA FRANCO POZZI, GALLARATE, 1967

Bibliographic references:
Domus, 454, 1967, cover and 'Nuove ceramiche italiane,' pp. 41–46.

FACADE OF THE BIJENKORF DEPARTMENT STORE, EINDHOVEN, THE NETHERLANDS, 1967

Bibliographic references:
G. Ponti, '3 promozioni in Eindhoven e 1 episodio,' *Domus*, 472, 1969, pp. 5-10.
G. Ponti, 'A Eindhoven, la piazza dei bimbi acrobati,' *Domus*, 511, 1972, p. 8.
G.C. Bojani, C. Piersanti, R. Rava (edited by), *Gio Ponti: ceramica e architettura* (Bologna 1987), Centro Di, Florence 1987, p. 79.

THE FACADES OF THE INA BUILDING AT NO. 7, VIA SAN PAOLO, MILAN, 1967

1. G. Ponti, 'Per le città fumose con vie strette: facciate lucenti illuminate dal cielo,' *Domus*, 469, 1968, pp. 20–21.

Bibliographic references:
G.C. Bojani, C. Piersanti, R. Rava (edited by), *Gio Ponti: ceramica e architettura* (Bologna 1987), Centro Di, Florence 1987, pp. 76–77.

COUCH FOR ARFLEX, MILAN, 1966

Bibliographic references:
'Un altra novità alla Eurodomus,' *Domus*, 440, 1966.

PROJECT FOR A VILLA FOR DANIEL KOO, MARIN COUNTY, CALIFORNIA, 1969

1. Ponti collection.

Bibliographic references:
Space Design, 200, 1981 (monographic issue: Gio Ponti), p. 72.
Gio Ponti 1891-1979 from the Human-Scale to the Post-Modernism (Tokyo 1986), Seibu/Kajima, Tokyo 1986, p. 167.
U. La Pietra (edited by), *Gio Ponti: l'arte si innamora dell'industria*, Coliseum, Milan 1988, pp. 354–56.

COLORED SKYSCRAPERS, ON A TRIANGULAR PLAN, 1967

1. G. Ponti, 'Perchè no? Apparizioni di grattacieli,' *Domus*, 470, 1969, pp. 7–11.
2. This was the title ('Grattacieli Immaginati') of the exhibition held at the Galleria Marcatrè, Milan, organized by Silvana Sermisoni, with contributions from Vittoriano Viganò and Giulio Ernesti, in March 1987.

Bibliographic references:
Tommaso Trini, 'Una galleria per l'uomo dalle idee,' *Domus*, 459, 1968, pp. 44–45.
Space Design, 200, 1981 (monographic issue: Gio Ponti), p. 72.

«AUTILIA,» 1968

Bibliographic references:
G. Ponti, 'Per un rapporto moderno fra strade, veicoli e abitazioni,' *Domus*,

461, 1968 (at beginning: Eurodomus 2 insert).
'Eurodomus 2: mostra pilota della casa moderna,' *Domus*, 463, 1968, pp. 5—6.

DOMUS IN THE SIXTIES

1. G. Ponti, introduction to 'Domus X 400,' *Domus*, 406, 1963, at beginning.

THE SEVENTIES

1. G.P., 'Vogliamo promuovere due esigenze,' *Domus*, 504, 1971 ('manifesto' for Eurodomus 4).

Bibliographic references:
D. Mosconi, *Design Italia '70*, Achille Mauri editore, Milan 1970.
A. Pica, 'Gio Ponti,' *I grandi designers* (catalogue of selective furniture exhibition), Cantù, 1973.
A. Branzi, 'Elogio della discontinuità,' *Modo*, 13, 1978, p. 68.
The Architect and Building News, 20, May 1970.
Connaissance des Arts, February 1976.
Industrial Design, 19, July 1972, p. 47.
Newsweek, 17, September 1973, pp. 88—89.
Progressive Architecture, 53, February 1972, p. 46.
Art Journal, 31—1, Fall 1971, p. 82.
Architectural Record, 151, March 1972, pp. 87—92.
Time, 1 October 1979, p. 97.

THE «NOVEDRA» ARMACHAIR FOR C&B, NOVEDRATE, 1968—71

1. P. Vidari, 'Progetto n. 114. Poltrona Novedra,' *Un'industria per il design*, Ed. Lybra, Milan 1983, pp. 52—53.

«AN ARMCHAIR OF LITTLE SEAT,» 1971

1. «An extraordinary case of the Mantuan East Po: I get a nice little letter from San Biagio di Mantova that runs like this: 'Why, Mister Architect, don't you design some modern furniture for us? Our father Walter is worried that our traditional furniture is not up to the mark': signed Maria Chinaglia Ponti. (Ponti? exactly, like me). But that is not all: I go there: lovely people, these Walter Pontis, very skillful in their work.... This furniture (what passion!) is a comfort in my season of four times twenty, to use Ungaretti's phrase. I wanted to call this furniture 'Pontiponti' like those famous old American companies 'Sullivan, Sullivan, Sullivan and Co.,' but then people would think that I had gone *into* industry while what I like is to work *for* industry (when they ask me to) and for craftsmen, all people who have helped me to get over difficult problems [of design...],» G. Ponti, 'East Po River Story,' *Domus*, 490, 1970, p. 30.

Bibliographic references:
'Una poltrona di poco sedile,' *Domus*, 510, 1972, p. 34.

MONTEDORIA BUILDING, MILAN, 1970

Bibliographic references:
A. Mendini, 'Tre pareri e una casa,' *Modo*, 43, 1981, pp. 39—45.
Space Design, 200, 1981 (monographic issue: Gio Ponti), p. 16.
G.C. Bojani, C. Piersanti, R. Rava (edited by), *Gio Ponti: ceramica e architettura* (Bologna 1987), Centro Di, Florence 1987, pp. 80—81.

COMPETITION PROJECT FOR AN ADMINISTRATIVE CENTER IN MUNICH, 1970

Bibliographic references:
Space Design, 200, 1981 (monographic issue: Gio Ponti), p. 14.

FROM «LA CASA ADATTA,» 1970, TO THE «2 ELLE» SYSTEM, 1972

1. G. Ponti, 'Maggior spazio godibile in minor superficie,' *Domus*, 490, 1970, pp. 22—24.
2. 'I mobili della serie Apta ideati da Gio Ponti, prodotti dalla Walter Ponti di San Biagio Mantova, in vendita alla Rinascente,' *Domus*, 490, 1970, pp. 25—30.
3. See note 1 to «An armchair of little seat.»
4. G. Ponti, 'Come sarà lo stile architettonico futuro?', *Stile*, 8, 1946, p. 11.
5. G. Ponti, 'Perchè si?,' *Domus*, 500, 1971, pp. 2—3.
6. G. Ponti, 'Ricerca di un nuovo spazio di abitazione' (Eurodomus 4), *Domus*, 512, 1972.
7. See bibliographic references to «Autilia.»
8. G. Ponti, notes, handwritten notebook, 1975 (A.G.P.).

Bibliographic references:
G. Ponti, 'La casa adatta,' *Domus*, 488, 1970, p. 15.
U. La Pietra (edited by), *Gio Ponti: l'arte si innamora dell'industria*, Coliseum, Milan 1988, pp. 378—80.

TARANTO CATHEDRAL, 1970

1. G. Ponti, 'La religione, il sacro,' *Domus*, 497, 1971, pp. 15—16.
2. Luigi Moretti, 'Il fastigio della cattedrale,' *Domus*, 497, 1971, pp. 11—23.
3. Draft of letter from Ponti to Archbishop Motolese, n.d. (A.G.P.) (and also «the risk is that the thing would end up in this shabby way, with lots of ugly houses in view and the sail no longer against the sky and the landscape of God, but against a background of houses, houses, houses...,» original in capital letters). In recent times, see also the correspondence between the Ponti family and Alessandro Mendini and the Comune di Taranto (summer 1984): it was a protest against the negligence that had turned the mirroring sheets of water in front of the building into empty basins. In autumn 1989 the people of Taranto unanimously rebelled against the blitz of the Commune, that

had suddenly demolished the abandoned basins (A.G.P.).

COMPETITION PROJECT FOR THE PLATEAU BEAUBOURG, PARIS, 1971

1. From a conversation between LLP and Alberto Ferrari, 10 June 1988.
2. The plans are now kept at the CSAC, Parma.

DENVER ART MUSEUM, DENVER, COLORADO, USA, 1971

1. G. Ponti, 'A Denver,' *Domus*, 511, 1972, pp. 1—7.
2. B. Chancellor, 'Denver Art Museum,' *Guestguide*, winter/spring 1971, p. 62.

Bibliographic references:
G. Ponti, 'America: the happy Denver Museum,' *Domus*, 485, 1970, p. 36.
D. Davis, 'The Museum Explosion,' *Newsweek*, 17 September 1973, pp. 88—89.
E. McCoy, 'Architecture West,' *Progressive Architecture*, 53, February 1972, p. 46.
'All that glitters,' *Architectural Forum*, 135, July 1971, p. 5.
'Western Culture,' *Architectural Forum*, 135, December 1971, p. 5.
'Denver Art Museum: spirited and unconventional,' *Architectural Record*, 1951, March 1972, pp. 87—92.
'Denver: the cage for stacking galleries,' *Architectural Record*, 139, April 1966.
H. Stubbs, 'Art in artificial light,' *The Architect & Building News*, May 20, 1970.
'Denver's new art museum,' *Design*, autumn 1971, p. 12.
'Denver Art Museum,' *Art Journal*, 31-1, fall 1971, p. 82.
'The Westernness of Western Art,' *Art in America*, 5, September—October 1972.

SAVOIA ASSICURAZIONI BUILDING, MILAN, 1971

1. G. Ponti, unpublished typescript, 15 May 1972 (A.G.P.).

FACADE «WITH LEAVES,» HONG KONG, 1974

Bibliographic references:
G.C. Bojani, C. Piersanti, R. Rava (edited by), *Gio Ponti, Ceramica e architettura* (Bologna 1987), Centro Di, Florence 1987, p. 84.
Space Design, 200, 1981 (monographic issue: Gio Ponti), p. 17.

FLOORS IN SALZBURG, 1976, FACADE IN SINGAPORE, 1978: PONTI'S COLORS IN THE SEVENTIES

1. G. Ponti, 'La «gaieté artificielle,»' *Domus*, 286, 1953, p. 1.

Bibliographic references:
Gio Ponti 1891-1979 from the Human-Scale to the Post-Modernism (Tokyo 1986), Seibu/Kajima, Tokyo 1986, pp. 170—71 and 190—91.
G.C. Bojani, C. Piersanti, R. Rava (edited by), *Gio Ponti: ceramica e architettura* (Bologna 1987), Centro Di, Florence 1987, pp. 85—87.

DOMUS IN THE SEVENTIES

1. C. Casati, A. Pica, C.E. Ponzio, G. Ratto, P. Restany (edited by), *1928/1973. Domus: 45 ans d'architecture, design, art* (Musée des Arts Décoratifs, Paris 1973), Ed. Domus, Milan 1973, 2 vols.
2. Ponti's *Domus* falls into two periods. The first, from its foundation in 1928 to 1940. The second (after the interval during which Ponti was the editor of *Stile* (Ponti took over from Rogers, editor from 1946—47) until 1979, the year of Ponti's death.
In the first period, the magazine — whose subtitle was «art in the house» (in English, French, and German in 1933) and «art in the house and garden» in 1937 — listed in 1931 as regular contributors Gherardo Bosio in Florence, Luigi Vietti in Genoa, Carmela Haerdtl in Vienna, Luigi Piccinato in Rome, Gustavo Pulitzer in Trieste, Ugo Nebbia in Venice, and Roberto Pane in Naples. The magazine was edited by Giancarlo Palanti until the end of 1933.
In the second period, the editorial staff of the magazine — whose subtitles varied from «art and style in the house» in 1952 to «art in the house, industrial design» in 1954, and «architecture, furnishing, art» from 1955 onward, until the English subtitle «monthly magazine of architecture, design, art» was introduced in 1977 — included Mario Tedeschi and Lisa L. Ponti in the fifties, and Enrichetta Ritter from 1951. The staff was to change in the sixties (Gillo Dorfles was editor for a year, in 1961) and from 1965 onward consisted of LLP (assistant editor), Cesare Casati, Marianne Lorenz, Anna Marchi, and Gianni Ratto for special initiatives. From 1965 to 1972, *Domus* listed Carmela Haerdtl, Pica, Restany, Rykwert, Sottsass, Ray and Charles Eames, Kho Liang Ie, Rudofsky, Nelson, Melotti, Trini, and Rut and Tapio Wirkkala as regular contributors. With Ponti still editor, Casati became managing editor in 1976, retaining the post until June 1979. He was then replaced by Alessandro Mendini, who edited the magazine, on Ponti's death (16 September 1979), until 1986.
3. 'Piano + Rogers = Beaubourg,' *Domus*, 503, 1971, pp. 1—7.
Renzo Piano, Richard Rogers, 'A Parigi, per i parigini,' *Domus*, 511, 1972, pp. 9—13.
P. Restany, 'Per il nuovo Centre Pompidou' (interview with Renzo Piano, Richard Rogers, and Peter Rice), *Domus*, 566, 1977, pp. 5—37.
4. *Domus*, 596, 1979.
5. *Domus*, 579, 1978, p. 50.
6. G. Ponti, 'Eindhoven, la piazza dei bimbi acrobati,' *Domus*, 511, 1972, p. 8.

BIBLIOGRAPHY

SELECTED ARTICLES WRITTEN BY GIO PONTI

1923
'Il teatro di Appia o l'opera d'arte vivente,' *Il Teatro*, Editoriale Il Convegno, Milan

1926
'Le ceramiche,' *L'Italia alla Esposizione Internazionale di Arti Decorative e Industriali Moderne di Parigi* (Paris 1925), Milan

1928
'La casa all'italiana,' *Domus*, 1

1930
'Sul Novocomum di Terragni a Como,' *Domus*, 4
'Il Palazzo Gualino,' *Domus*, 6
'La Casa delle Vacanze,' *Domus*, 9
'Il fattore italianità nelle nostre arti applicate moderne,' *Domus*, 11

1931
'Palazzina al Lungotevere Arnaldo da Brescia' (by Capponi), *Domus*, 37
'Gli italiani alla Triennale di Milano,' *Domus*, 37
'Per l'Italia e per la modernità' (on the Triennale), *Domus*, 44
'Stile e civiltà' (on the Triennale), *Domus*, 45
'L'arredamento navale oggi e domani' (on the motorship *Victoria*), *Domus*, 46
'Occorre dare un mercato nazionale alla produzione moderna italiana,' *Domus*, 48

1932
'Quale sarà la nostra casa domani?,' *Domus*, 49
'Casa Ferrarin a Milano' (by Albini), *Domus*, 50
'Morte e vita della tradizione,' *Domus*, 51
'Nuovi vagoni per le Ferrovie austriache arredati da Josef Hoffmann,' *Domus*, 51
'Concezione dell'edificio d'abitazione,' *Domus*, 52
'Giudicare lo stile moderno,' *Domus*, 53
'Una casa di campagna per uomo di studio' (by De Renzi, Moretti, Paniconi, Pediconi, and Tufaroli), *Domus*, 55
'A proposito delle dimensioni degli ambienti nelle case,' *Domus*, 56
'Una abitazione moderna senza architetto,' *Domus*, 57
'Caratteri di interni all'estero' (on Strnad and Frank), *Domus*, 57
'Ieri e oggi' (on Lingeri), *Domus*, 58
'Una bella casa' (on Luigi Moretti), *Domus*, 58
'Verso gli artisti,' *Domus*, 59
'30 all'ora o 130 all'ora,' *Domus*, 60

1933
'Una nave. Il Conte di Savoia di Pulitzer,' *Domus*, 63
'Antico e moderno,' *Domus*, 65
'Architettura, pittura, scultura' (on the frescoes at the 5th Triennale), *Domus*, 66
'La villa-studio per un artista' (by Figini and Pollini, at the 5th Triennale), *Domus*, 67
'L'arredamento alla Triennale' (on Ulrich), *Domus*, 67
'Casa moderna, città moderna,' *Domus*, 70
'Esempio del lusso' (on Ulrich), *Domus*, 71
'Formazione del gusto,' *Domus*, 71
'Architecture of the New Italy: a Presentation of the Architectural Features of the Exposition Held Every Three Years in Milan,' *The Architectural Forum*, August
'Architettura,' *L'Illustrazione Italiana*, October
'La Triennale di Milano,' *Nuova Antologia*, 1, October
'Distribuzioni e propozioni degli ambienti,' *Corriere della Sera*, 22 October
'Divagazioni su un ambiente,' *Corriere della Sera*, 5 November
'Ambienti in trasformazione,' *Corriere della Sera*, 21 November
'Primo ospite, la bellezza,' *Corriere della Sera*, 14 December
'I colori dell'arredamento,' *Corriere della Sera*, 31 December

1934
'Responsibilità dell'edilizia,' *Domus*, 77
'Interpretazione dell'abitazione moderna. Case economiche ad appartamenti grandi,' *Domus*, 77
'Interpretazioni della abitazione moderna. Villa del Sole,' *Domus*, 79
'Una villa alla pompeiana,' *Domus*, 79
'Verso funzioni nuove,' *Domus*, 82
'Due recenti opere di architetti milanesi' (Muzio, Albini), *Domus*, 82
'Lo stile nell'architettura e nell'arredamento moderno' (on Persico's essay 'Punto e da capo per l'architettura'), *Domus*, 83
'Possiamo costruire delle chiese?' *Domus*, 83
'Le idee che ho seguito in alcune costruzioni,' *Domus*, 84
'Relazione del progetto di concorso per il Palazzo del Littorio,' *Casabella*, 82
'Divagazioni sulle terrazze,' *Corriere della Sera*, 23 January
'Case per famiglie numerose,' *Corriere della Sera*, 19 April
'L'arredamento semplice,' *Corriere della Sera*, 7 June
'Comperando un appartamento,' *Corriere della Sera*, 18 October
'L'ubicazione della casa in rapporto al verde,' *Corriere della Sera*, 4 December

1935
'Espressioni tipiche costruttive' (on Libera's house in Ostia), *Domus*, 86
'M.10.001 New York-Los Angeles,' *Domus*, 87
'Due ville al Forte' (by Marelli), *Domus*, 90
'Il gusto di Hoffmann,' *Domus*, 93
'Una casa' (Casa Marmont), *Domus*, 94
'Architettura per noi,' *Corriere della Sera*, 10 February
'Le porte,' *Corriere della Sera*, 22 February
'Pavimenti e tappeti,' *Corriere della Sera*, 14 June

1936
'Casa in Milano di Lingeri e Terragni,' *Domus*, 102
'Capovolgimenti' (on Vaccaro), *Domus*, 102
'Una abitazione dimostrativa' (at the 6th Triennale), *Domus*, 103
'La sala della Vittoria' (at the 6th Triennale), *Domus*, 103
'Martini e Sironi' (at the 6th Triennale), *Domus*, 103
'La battaglia di Parigi' (on the exhibition in Paris, 1937), *Domus*, 106
'La mostra della Stampa Cattolica,' *Emporium*, October
'Per la casa che costruite,' *Corriere della Sera*, 11 October
'Case comode per gente ordinata,' *Corriere della Sera*, 3 November

1937
'Una villa a tre appartamenti in Milano,' *Domus*, 111
'Casa a Posilippo' (on Cosenza and Rudofsky), *Domus*, 120
'Fortuna dei floricoltori,' *Corriere della Sera*, 3 January
'Possibilità di grandi realizzazioni edilizie,' *Corriere della Sera*, 30 April
'Consenso dei milanesi a una realizzazione urbanistica degna del tempo di Mussolini,' *Corriere della Sera*, 29 November
'Via libera,' *Corriere della Sera*, 24 December

1938
'Un appartamento risistemato a Milano' (Casa Vanzetti), *Domus*, 131
'Cieli americani,' *Domus*, 135
'Come è nato l'edificio' (the Montecatini building), *Casabella*, 138-139-140
'Introduzione alla vita degli angeli,' *Aria d'Italia*, December
'Mobilitiamo le nostre produzioni d'arte,' *Corriere della Sera*, 17 February
'Mobilitare le produzioni d'arte con un piano per potenziarle,' *Corriere della Sera*, 23 February

1940
'Strade,' *Aria d'Italia*, summer
'Albergo San Michele, o nel bosco, all'isola di Capri,' *Architettura*, June
'Vocazione architettonica degli italiani,' *Il Libro Italiano nel Mondo*, December

1941
'Oroscopi sulla moda,' *Bellezza*, 1
'Noi donne e l'arte,' *Bellezza*, 1
'La signora arredatrice,' *Bellezza*, July-August
'La casa vivente,' *Bellezza*, October
'Architettura *nel* cinema. Idee,' *Aria d'Italia*, winter
'Chiudendo queste pagine...,' *Aria d'Italia*, spring
'Presentazione', *Stile*, 1
'Progetto per una villa in città,' *Stile*, 2
'Senza architetto,' *Stile*, 2
'Una mostra perfetta' (on Scipione at Brera), *Stile*, 3
'Stile di Caccia,' *Stile*, 3
(Serangelo) 'La eccezionale stagione scenografica alla Scala. Cronache immaginarie,' *Stile*, 3
'Invito a far collezione di incisioni di Bartolini,' *Stile*, 3
'Voi o donne,' *Stile*, 3

'L'Apocalisse illustrata da de Chirico,' *Stile*, 4
'Primizie' (on Arturo Martini), *Stile*, 4
'L'età del vetro,' *Stile*, 5-6
'Un arredamento di Carlo Mollino,' *Stile*, 5-6
'Architettura mediterranea,' *Stile*, 7
'Turismo mediterraneo italiano,' *Stile*, 8
'Una casa di Libera: una opinione sulla architettura,' *Stile*, 9
'Immaginate la vostra casa al mare,' *Stile*, 10

1942
'Scelta di Bellezza,' *Bellezza*, April
'Per un gusto nostrano nelle stoffe stampate,' *Bellezza*, April
'Opere durature agli artisti, non solo premi ed esposizioni,' *Stile*, 13
'Sulla polemica Bontempelli-de Chirico,' *Stile*, 15
'Storia di oggi, artisti di oggi,' *Stile*, 17
'Stile di Libera,' *Stile*, 17
'L'arte di Marino è stile,' *Stile*, 17
'Dove noi architetti abbiamo mancato,' *Stile*, 19-20
'Italiani collezionate incisioni di Viviani,' *Stile*, 21
'Italiani aggiornatevi sulle opinioni italiane' (on Malaparte's *Prospettive*), *Stile*, 21
'Buona architettura e cattiva edilizia,' *Stile*, 24
'Industrie d'arte in tempo di guerra,' *Corriere della Sera*, 15 February

1943
'Abbigliamento e arredamento,' *Bellezza*, December
'I concorsi urbanistici della Triennale,' *Stile*, 25
'Stile di Ridolfi,' *Stile*, 25
'Due ipotesi: stazioni e ospedali,' *Stile*, 26
'Stile di Daneri,' *Stile*, 26
'Stile di Vaccaro,' *Stile*, 27
'L'architettura, le altre arti e l'uomo della strada,' *Stile*, 27
'Cieli di Giotto, maledizione di noi,' *Stile*, 28
'Civiltà' (on Albini), *Stile*, 28
'Bisogna credere alle ragioni della architettura,' *Stile*, 30
'Distruzione e ricostruzione. Industria ed edilizia futura,' *Stile*, 32-33-34
'Stile di Pagano,' *Stile*, 32-33-34
'Equivoci sulla architettura moderna,' *Stile*, 32-33-34
'Politica dell'architettura,' *Stile*, 35
'Stile di domani' (on Asnago and Vender), *Stile*, 35
'La casa deve costare meno,' *Stile*, 36
'Il monumento mausoleo ad Ataturk, opera di un architetto italiano' (Foschini), *Il Popolo d'Italia*, 25 March
'Per tutti, anzi per ciascuno. Appello di tre architetti per la Carta della casa' (A. Libera, G. Ponti, G. Vaccaro), *Il Popolo d'Italia*, 15 June
'Più bello e splendente risorgerà ciò che fu distrutto,' *Il Popolo d'Italia*, 13 April
'Umanità della casa,' *Corriere della Sera*, 2 January
'Funzione degli architetti,' *Corriere della Sera*, 12 January
'Ritratto dell'artigiano,' *Corriere della Sera*, 22 January
'Architettura dell'avvenire,' *Corriere della Sera*, 22 February

'Elogio dell'uniformità,' *Corriere della Sera*, 22 March

'La casa moderna e il restauro dei monumenti lesi,' *Corriere della Sera*, 29 March

'Esatto cioè bello,' *Corriere della Sera*, 28 April

'Poco inchiostro su molta carta,' *Corriere della Sera*, 28 May

'Architetture italiane di domani,' *Corriere della Sera*, 15 June

'Ad ogni famiglia la sua casa,' *Corriere della Sera*, 1 July

'Dicono gli architetti...,' *Corriere della Sera*, 2 December

'Invito agli scrittori,' *L'Italia*, 24 October

'Invito all'urbanistica e all'architettura,' *L'Italia*, 2 December

'Carità cristiana e solidarietà umana,' *L'Italia*, 4 December

'La città di domani e l'esempio negativo di Milano,' *L'Italia*, 28 December

'Rapporto su Budapest,' *Il Gazzettino*, 14 May

1944

'Utilità della casa,' *Bellezza*, May

'Regaliamo all'impresa X due progetti di case a piccole abitazioni,' *Stile*, 37

'È necessario il formarsi di una opinione pubblica sui problemi dell'architettura per affrontare quelli della ricostruzione' (on Sartori's essay 'Momento della architettura'), *Stile*, 37

'Architettura per l'industria,' *Stile*, 37

'Invenzione di una architettura composita,' *Stile*, 39

'Evocazione di noi,' *Stile*, 40

'Proposta generale per la ricostruzione,' *Stile*, 41

'Affrontiamo il problema della scuola,' *Stile*, 42—43

'Quanto costa preparare la ricostruzione (e chi paga?),' *Stile*, 42

'Ristabilire la rete antica delle vie o interromperla con nuclei nuovi?' *Stile*, 42

'Affrontiamo il problema del paesaggio?' *Stile*, 42

'Proposizioni architettoniche di Mollino,' *Stile*, 43

'Cimiteri,' *Stile*, 43

'Ungaretti,' *Stile*, 44

'Milanesi, come vi si rifarà Milano?' *Stile*, 9

'Offriamo ai costruttori elementi di casa popolare per centri di campagna,' *Stile*, 12

'La casa deve costare meno,' *Corriere della Sera*, 7-8 January

'Ragioni dell'architettura,' *Corriere della Sera*, 2 February

'La città di domani. Riforme che maturano,' *L'Italia*, 11 January

'Problemi della ricostruzione,' *L'Italia*, 8 February

'Richieste ai Podestà (preliminari della ricostruzione),' *L'Italia*, 22 February, 7 March, 21 March, and 4 April

'Spirito della ricostruzione,' *L'Italia*, 18 April

'Quello che il pubblico deve chiedere alla ricostruzione,' *L'Italia*, 14 May

'Proposta generale per la ricostruzione,' *L'Italia*, 1 June

'La ricostruzione è pericolosa,' *L'Italia*, 11 July

'La riunione degli architetti,' *L'Italia*, 25 July

'Quel che chiedono gli architetti al Co-

mune di Milano,' *L'Italia*, 8 August

'Gli studi delle assicurazioni sul problema fiscale e finanziario della ricostruzione,' *L'Italia*, 5 September

'L'università per i migliori,' *L'Italia*, 7 September

'Milano vera o falsa,' *L'Italia*, 17 October

'I messaggi sociali e lo spirito della ricostruzione,' *L'Italia*, 13 December

'Un milione di lire destinato agli ingegneri e agli architetti per preparare i testi per la ricostruzione,' *L'Italia*, 24 December

1945

'Chi ci darà la casa prefabbricata?' *Stile*, 3

'E dopo la guerra, che faranno gli artigiani?' *L'Italia*, 21 January

'Pratiche iniziative per la futura città,' *L'Italia*, 1 April

'Vocazione cattolica d'una civiltà italiana,' *L'Italia*, 6 May

1946

'Alle lettrici' (on Frank Lloyd Wright's *Anthology*), *Stile*, 1

'Dobbiamo trasferire lo studio della casa su altri termini,' *Stile*, 8

'In che consiste l'avanguardia americana?' *Stile*, 8

'Come sarà lo *stile* architettonico futuro?' *Stile*, 8

'In che consiste l'avanguardia russa?' *Stile*, 10

'La ricostruzione, e Palmiro, Pietro ed Alcide,' *Stile*, 10

'Una proposizione per la modernità dei mobili,' *Stile*, 10

'L'arte è un gesto prima di morire,' *Stile*, 11

'Come ricostruirebbero i partiti?' *Cronache*, 14 and 21 September

1947

'Artigianato, aristocrazia del lavoro italiano,' *Cronache*, 15 March

1948

'Picasso convertirà alla ceramica. Ma noi, dice Lucio Fontana, s'era già cominciato,' *Domus*, 226

'Brasile. Da Le Corbusier architetto allo stile Le Corbusier,' *Domus*, 229

'Che cosa può significare la parola «funzionale»' (discussion of a swimming pool), *Domus*, 229

'Il rustico è architettura' (on Moretti), *Domus*, 231

'Finestre tutte uguali nelle case del Piano Fanfani,' *Corriere della Sera*, 25 August

'Gli architetti firmeranno le case, come i pittori fanno con i loro quadri,' *Corriere della Sera*, 12 September

'Fiume verde all'ex-Scalo Sempione,' *Corriere della Sera*, 14 October

'Padrone di pagarsi il lusso chi pretende il fuori serie,' *Corriere della Sera*, 20 October

'Mancano agli italiani venti milioni di stanze,' *Corriere della Sera*, 1 December

'Un'isola verde al Sempione,' *L'Umanità*, 14 October

'Dove va l'architettura,' *Il Popolo*, 12 September

1949

'Le città debbono tornare naturali,' *Domus*, 232

'Architettura vera ed architettura sognata,' *Domus*, 233

'L'opera di Pietro Chiesa,' *Domus*, 234

'Architettura e costume,' *Domus*, 234

'Andiamo a Marsiglia?' *Domus*, 235

'Clinica Columbus,' *Domus*, 240

'L'era dell'alluminio,' *Corriere della Sera*, 12 April

1950

'Oro sul Conte Grande,' *Domus*, 244

'Un negozio «grafico»' (on the Dulciora store), *Domus*, 246

'Forma,' *Domus*, 250

'Omaggio ad una mostra eccezionale' (on the MUSA exhibition), *Domus*, 252—53

'Il Carlo Felice di Genova, progetto di Paolo A. Chessa,' *Domus*, 252—53

'Occorre che nei nostri bastimenti gli stranieri imparino l'Italia,' *Corriere della Sera*, 21 March

'Tutti sono urbanisti,' *Corriere della Sera*, 2—3 May

1951

'Eleganza dell'alluminio, della vipla, della gomma,' *Domus*, 258

'Insegnamento altrui e fantasia degli italiani' (on the 9th Triennale), *Domus*, 259

'Austria,' *Domus*, 260

'Spagna,'*Domus*, 260

'La Triennale nel suo quartiere sperimentale QT8,' *Domus*, 263

'Villa a Milano' (on Gardella), *Domus*, 263

'I mobili, l'insegnamento e la vocazione di Albini,' *Domus*, 263

'Ci vuole a Milano un museo della tecnica,' *Corriere della Sera*, 25—26 June

'Svalutando l'artificiale l'uomo svaluta se stesso,' *Corriere della Sera*, 2 September

'De divina et humana proportione. Dalle simmetrie classiche alla architettura contemporanea,' *Corriere della Sera*, 24—25 September

'Esperienze d'architetto,' *Pirelli*, 6

1952

'Giappone modernissimo: Kenzo Tange,' *Domus*, 262

'Senza aggettivi' (on the 'leggera' chair), *Domus*, 268

'Casa di fantasia' (Casa Lucano), *Domus*, 70

'Chiarezza, unità, visibilità totale negli uffici modernissimi,' *Domus*, 270

'Dieci anni fa come oggi, e la questione delle opere d'arte nella architettura,' *Domus*, 270

'Favola americana' (on the UN and Lever House), *Domus*, 272

'San Paolo cresce e divora se stessa,' *Corriere della Sera*, 21 September

'La vitrea muraglia dell'ONU ha chiuso l'era dei grattacieli,' *Corriere della Sera*, 31 August

1953

'Stile di Niemeyer,' *Domus*, 278

'Il «termine» del grattacielo,' *Domus*, 278

'Burle Marx o dei giardini brasiliani,' *Domus*, 279

'Il Pedregal di Luis Barragan a Città

del Messico,' *Domus*, 280

'Una grande esposizione semplice ideata da Niemeyer,' *Domus*, 281

'La professione dell'architetto,' *Domus*, 282

'Mobili italiani a Stoccolma,' *Domus*, 282

'Istituto di Fisica Nucleare a San Paolo,' *Domus*, 284

'La gaieté artificielle,' *Domus*, 286

'Segnano il passo le idee di molti nostri architetti,' *Corriere della Sera*, 20 January

'Più sottili i muri, più bella la casa,' *Corriere della Sera*, 1 April

'Un nuovo primato, la Scuola di architettura,' *Corriere della Sera*, 24 April

'Non monumenti ma vecchie case i grattacieli di New York,' *Corriere della Sera*, 12 July

'La vera casa moderna deve essere un organismo,' *Corriere della Sera*, 17 July

'Si faranno case fluorescenti,' *Corriere della Sera*, 25 November

1954

'Coraggio del Venezuela,' *Domus*, 295

'Idea per Caracas,' *Domus*, 295

'Espressione di Gardella, espressione di Rouault,' *Domus*, 295

'Le produzioni moderne per l'architettura sono chiamate ad intervenire nella efficienza dell'insegnamento di una nuova scuola moderna di architettura,' *Domus*, 296

'Reveron, o la vita allo stato di sogno,' *Domus*, 296

'Prototipo di casa per la serie,' *Domus*, 297

'La finestra arredata,' *Domus*, 298

'Casa unifamigliare di serie alla Triennale,' *Domus*, 301

'Alloggio uniambientale alla Triennale,' *Domus*, 301

'Alloggio uniambientale per 4 persone,' *Domus*, 302

'Considerazioni sui rapporti fra forma e funzionalità,' *Stile Industria*, 2

'Finestre e porte unificate per realizzare il Piano Romita,' *Corriere della Sera*, 27 April

'Le case d'oggi sono fatte come se si fosse tutti uguali,' *Corriere della Sera*, 3 August

1955

'Il modello della villa Planchart in costruzione a Caracas,' *Domus*, 303

'Invito a considerare tutta l'architettura come «spontanea»,' *Domus*, 304

'Una nuova serie di apparecchi sanitari,' *Domus*, 308

'Milano definita da un giornale inglese la «città più moderna del mondo»,' *Corriere della Sera*, 30 October

1956

'Sull'edilizia popolare. L'edilizia popolare è un fatto transitorio,' *Domus*, 314

'Espressione dell'edificio Pirelli in costruzione a Milano,' *Domus*, 316

'Vocazione iberica per la forma' (on Torroja), *Domus*, 317

'Profezie sulla pittura,' *Domus*, 319

'Giovinezza d'oggi o splendida età di Le Corbusier?' *Domus*, 320

'Invito ad andare a Ronchamp,' *Domus*, 323

'Esemplare strumento di civiltà il nuo-

vo regolamento edilizio,' *Corriere della Sera*, 2–3 October
'Contro i viaggi delle opere d'arte famose,' *Epoca*, 11 November
'Out of a Philosophy of Architecture,' *Architectural Record*, December
'Una mostra permanente di disegno industriale al Museo della Scienza e della Tecnica,' *Stile-Industria*, 9

1957
'Il colore nella vita moderna,' in var. authors, Proceedings 1st Congress *Il Colore dell'ambiente umano*, Padua
'Il Piano Territoriale, strumento di coordinamento e collaborazione,' *Corriere della Sera*, 27 July

1958
'Una casa, una scala' (Casa Melandri), *Domus*, 345
'Villa La Diamantina nel Country Club a Caracas,' *Domus*, 349
'Il problema dell'air terminal,' *Corriere della Sera*, 22 October
'L'architettura moderna nelle case e nelle chiese,' *Corriere della Sera*, 31 December

1959
'Espressioni di Nervi a Milano,' *Domus*, 352
'La nuova sede dell'Italia a New York,' *Domus*, 354
'Il Carmelo di Bonmoschetto, monastero delle Carmelitane scalze in San Remo,' *Domus*, 361
'Venini,' *Domus*, 361
'Inchiesta sull'artigianato,' *Zodiac*, 4
'Incompleto senza l'air terminal il nuovo sistema aeroportuale,' *Corriere della Sera*, 8 January
'Mito e realtà di Le Corbusier,' *Corriere della Sera*, 27–28 April
'Come preparare gli architetti che servano veramente il Paese,' *Corriere della Sera*, 5 November
'Contributo alla modernizzazione delle scuole di architettura,' in var. authors, *Atti del Collegio Regionale Lombardo degli Architetti*, Milan, July
'Estetica e tecnica,' inaugural lecture at the third annual congress of the *European Foundation for Culture*, Vienna, November
'Gli sviluppi di Milano,' in var. authors, Proceedings of the congress of the same name (*Collegio Regionale Lombardo degli Architetti*), ed. Politecnica Tamburini

1960
'Grattacielo sul Reno' (on Schneider Esleben), *Domus*, 362
'Grattacielo a Düsseldorf' (on Hentrich and Pettschnigg), *Domus*, 372
'Religione e architetti,' *Domus*, 372
'Per Van de Velde,' *Domus*, 373
'Divagando per la Triennale,' *Domus*, 373
'La scuola inglese alla Triennale, esemplare monito per gli italiani,' *Corriere della Sera*, 13 October
'Sugli sviluppi di Milano, secondo Convegno nel '60,' *Corriere della Sera*, 23 November

1961
'Una villa fiorentina' (Villa Planchart), *Domus*, 375

'Estetica e tecnica nei pensieri di un architetto,' *Domus*, 376
'Esistenza ambientale, Conservazione ambientale, Creazione ambientale' (on the Velasca Tower), *Domus*, 378
'Si fa coi pensieri' (on the Pirelli Tower), *Domus*, 379
'Prima e dopo la Pirelli,' *Domus*, 379
'La ceramica è un tegumento leggero...' (for Joo), *Stile Industria*, 30
'Milan: in search of the new,' *Craft Horizon*, March

1962
'Questa è la grande epoca della architettura,' *Domus*, 389
'Picasso a Barcellona,' *Domus*, 392
'Una chiesa lombarda' (on Enrico Castiglioni), *Domus*, 397
'Le «planimetrias» di Vilacasas,' *Domus*, 394
'Nuova sede della Riunione Adriatica di Sicurtà in Milano,' *Domus*, 397
'La Triennale in pericolo per i ritardi burocratici,' *Corriere della Sera*, 24 October
'Milano, ultima tappa della mostra d'arte iraniana,' *Domus*, 404
'Domus X 400,' *Domus*, 406
'Le scale di Gentili,' *Domus*, 407
'Il nostro premio, gli Obelischi di Domus,' *Domus*, 409

1964
'Su Felix Candela,' *Domus*, 410
'A Michelucci, sulla chiesa di San Giovanni,' *Domus*, 413
'Giochi con i rivestimenti di Salerno,' *Domus*, 414
'Il Pylonen, grattacielo a Stoccolma,' *Domus*, 414
'The world in Vogue,' *Domus*, 414
'Uno scarabeo sotto una foglia,' *Domus*, 414
'Cielo azzurro, mare azzurro, isole azzurre, maioliche azzurre, piante verdi, rose ai piedi della principessa, orma di danzatrice,' *Domus*, 415
'Against uniformity,' *Domus*, 416
'Tre architetture di Luigi Moretti,' *Domus*, 419
'Una moderna scuola statale d'arte in Svezia,' *Domus*, 421

1965
'A Teheran, una villa,' *Domus*, 422
'Questo è il mondo di forme meravigliose, anche enormi, nel quale viviamo' (on Arne Jacobsen), *Domus*, 423
'Sulla prima raccolta degli scritti di Persico,' *Domus*, 424
'Su Gino Ghiringhelli,' *Domus*, 426
'Il gioco del pallone,' *Domus*, 427
'Un panorama di alba, di risveglio, di inediti,' *Domus*, 427
'Su Mollino, per il Palazzo degli Affari,' *Domus*, 427
'Morte di Le Corbusier,' *Domus*, 430
(On Rauschenberg and Dante's *Inferno*), *Domus*, 431
'Architettura senza architetto,' *Domus*, 431
(On the 'proposal of a linear development for Milan'), *Domus*, 432

1966
'Il Kolleg St. Joseph, seminario a Salisburgo,' *Domus*, 433
'Le vetrate grosse alla Ponti, da Venini,' *Domus*, 436

'Risultato felice di un concorso perduto,' *Domus*, 438
'La cappella del nuovo ospedale di San Carlo a Milano,' *Domus*, 445
'Architettura di invenzione: serve per guardarla,' *Domus*, 445

1967
'Musei americani,' *Domus*, 446
'Invenzioni di Manzù,' *Domus*, 455

1968
'Tokyo: Imperial Hotel, 1922-1967,' *Domus*, 459
'Per un rapporto moderno fra strade, veicoli, abitazioni,' *Domus*, 461
'Le torri di Dreyfuss,' *Domus*, 465
'Lucio Fontana,' *Domus*, 466
'I muri di Barragan,' *Domus*, 468
'Per le città fumose con vie strette: facciate lucenti illuminate dal cielo,' *Domus*, 469

1969
'Perchè no? Apparizioni di grattacieli,' *Domus*, 470
'3 promozioni a Eindhoven, e 1 episodio,' *Domus*, 472
'Leoncillo,' *Domus*, 479

1970
'Alexandra,' *Domus*, 485
'America. The happy Denver Museum,' *Domus*, 485
'Rudofskying,' *Domus*, 486
'La casa adatta,' *Domus*, 488
'Discorso introduttivo ad Eurodomus 3,' *Domus*, 488
'Maggior spazio godibile in minor superficie,' *Domus*, 490
'East Po River Story,' *Domus*, 490
'Perpetuità di un edificio,' *Pirelli*, now in *Antologia*, Scheiwiller, Milan 1988

1971
'Nuove immagini della casa,' *Domus*, 496
'La cattedrale di Taranto,' *Domus*, 497
'Perchè si?' (on Feal houses), *Domus*, 500
'Vogliamo promuovere due esigenze,' *Domus*, 504

1972
'A Denver' (on the Denver Museum), *Domus*, 511
'A Eindhoven, la piazza dei bimbi acrobati,' *Domus*, 511
'Ricerca di un nuovo spazio di abitazione' (on Sacie), *Domus*, 512

1973
'Fuori Parigi, costruita in tre mesi' (on Henri Bouilhet), *Domus*, 522
'Per quale casa,' *Prefabbricare. Edilizia in evoluzione*
'Architettura finlandese,' catalogue of the exhibition at 'Torino Esposizioni,' Turin 10–13 December

BOOKS WRITTEN BY GIO PONTI

La casa all'italiana, Domus, Milan 1933
Il Coro, Uomo, Milan, 1944
(With V. Bini), *Cifre Parlanti*, Vesta, Milan 1944
Archias (alias G. Ponti), *Politica dell'Architettura*, Garzanti, Milan 1944

L'Architettura è un cristallo, Editrice Italiana, Milan 1945
(With A. Libera, G. Vaccaro, *et al.*), *Verso la Casa Esatta*, Editrice Italiana, Milan 1945
Ringrazio Iddio che le cose non vanno a modo mio, Antoniazzi, Milan 1946
Paradiso Perduto, Daria Guarnati, Milan 1946
Amate l'Architettura, Vitali e Ghianda, Genoa 1957 (American edition: *In Praise of Architecture*, F.W. Dodge Corporation, New York 1960; Japanese edition: *Bijutsu Shuppau-sha*, Tokyo 1963)
Nuvole sono immagini, Scheiwiller, Milan 1968

PUBLICATIONS EDITED BY GIO PONTI

(With F. Albini), *Quaderni artigiani*, ENAPI, Milan 1932
99 e più disegni inediti di mobili d'oggi, Domus, Milan 1932
Lamberto Vitali (edited by), *Scritti e disegni dedicati a Scheiwiller*, Officina d'Arte Grafica A. Lucini & C., Milan 1937
(With L. Sinisgalli), *Italiani*, Domus, Milan 1937–39
Poesie di Lisa Ponti, and drawings by Luigi Bartolini, Massimo Campigli, Domenico Cantatore, Carlo Carrà, Fabrizio Clerici, Giorgio de Chirico, Filippo De Pisis, Leoncillo Leonardi, Leo Longanesi, Giacomo Manzù, Marino Marini, Arturo Martini, Quinto Martini, Giorgio Morandi, Mino Rosi, Aligi Sassu, Gino Severini, Mario Sironi, Orfeo Tamburi, Arturo Tosi, Giuseppe Viviani, Toni Zancanare, and Gio Ponti, Alfieri & Lacroix, Milan 1941
(With A. Libera, G. Vaccaro), *Scale pronte Montecatini*, Milan 1943
Milano Oggi, Milano Moderna, Milan 1957–60
From Gio Ponti's Clouds, book for Lyla Tyng at Lu Shahn, New York 1960–61

BOOKS ILLUSTRATED BY GIO PONTI

Oscar Wilde, *La ballata del carcere di Reading*, Editrice Modernissima, Milan 1919
Oscar Wilde, *La casa della cortigiana*, Editrice Modernissima, Milan 1919
(With Tomaso Buzzi), E.V. Quattrova (edited by), *La cucina elegante, ovvero il Quattrova illustrato*, Domus, Milan 1932 and 1978

SELECTED WRITINGS ON GIO PONTI

1921
P. Mezzanotte, 'La prima mostra d'architettura proposta dalla Famiglia Artistica di Milano,' *Architettura e Arti Decorative*, I, III

1925—26
P. Mezzanotte, 'Ancora del concorso per il ponte di Verona,' *Architettura e Arti Decorative*, V

1926
M. Sarfatti, in var. authors, *L'Italia alla Esposizione Internazionale di Arti Decorative e Industriali Moderne di Parigi* (Paris, 1925), Milan

1926—27
R. Papini, 'Sul concorso per una Ambasciata d'Italia,' *Architettura e Arti Decorative*, VI, VI
F. Reggiori, 'Villa a Milano in via Randaccio degli architetti Emilio Lancia e Giovanni Ponti,' *Architettura e Arti Decorative*, VI, XIII

1927
Domino (R. Giolli), 'Sottovoce — La Conversazione classica,' *1927 Problemi d'arte attuale*, October

1927—28
F. Reggiori, 'Padiglioni nuovi alla Fiera di Milano,' *Architettura e Arti Decorative*, VII

1928
'XVI Biennale Veneziana,' *Architettura e Arti Decorative*, October

1928—29
A. Maraini, 'L'architettura e le arti decorative alla XVI Biennale di Venezia,' *Architettura e Arti Decorative*, VIII

1929
'Gli specchi e le frecce di Christofle per la Biennale di Venezia,' *Domus*, 8

1930
H.A. Bull, 'Notes of the month' (on the restaurant La Penna d'Oca and Ponti at Richard-Ginori), *International Studio*, vol. 96, May
E. Persico, 'Tendenze e realizzazioni' (on the Monza Biennale, 1930), *La Casa Bella*, 29

1931
G. Muzio, 'Alcuni architetti d'oggi in Lombardia,' *Dedalo*, XI, August

1932
'Tomba Borletti dell'architetto Gio Ponti,' *Architettura*, pp. 590—93

1933
G. Pagano, 'Uno stabilimento industriale moderno a Milano,' *Casabella*, March
E. Persico, 'Il gusto italiano,' *L'Italia Letteraria*, 4 June
E. Persico, 'La Torre al Parco,' *Casabella*, August-September

1934
E. Persico, 'L'architetto Gio Ponti,' *L'Italia Letteraria*, 29 April

1935
Y. Maraini, 'Italy,' *London Studio*, vol. 9, June
G. Nelson, 'Architects of Europe Today: Gio Ponti, Italy,' *Pencil Points*, May
E. Persico, 'Un progetto di Ponti' (nursery school at Bruzzano), *Casabella*, 88

1936
M. Labò, 'Mostra Universale della Stampa Cattolica al Vaticano,' *Casabella*, 105
A. Melis, 'La scuola di Matematica alla R. Università di Roma,' *L'Architettura Italiana*, August
M. Piacentini, 'Esposizione mondiale della Stampa Cattolica nella Città del Vaticano,' *Architettura*, July
'School of Mathematics, University of Rome,' *The Architectural Review*, 80

1937
B. Moretti, 'Die eigene Wohnung eines Architekten,' *Innen-Dekoration*, 6

1939
T. Lundgren, 'Funktionalism i sin prydne,' *Svenska Hem*, 27
G. Pagano, 'Alcune note sul Palazzo della Montecatini,' *Casabella*, 138-139-140

1940
C. Malaparte, 'Un palazzo d'acqua e di foglie,' *Aria d'Italia*, May

1941
G. Pagano, 'Potremo salvarci dalle false tradizioni e dalle ossessioni monumentali?' *Costruzioni Casabella*, 157

1951
D.B., 'Across the seas collaboration for the new Singer collection,' *Interiors*, vol. 111, December
P.E. Gennarini, 'Gio Ponti: dall'architettura al disegno per l'industria,' *Pirelli*, 6

1952
J.F., 'Classicism reconsidered: the Ponti Style,' *Interiors*, vol. 111, July
O. Gueft, 'Ascetic and sybarite: the masks of Ponti,' *Interiors*, 112

1955
C. De Carli, 'La nuova sede Pirelli,' *Pirelli*, 3
R. Furneaux-Jordan, 'Skyscraper and Ox-Cart,' *The Observer*, 11 September
S. Kugler, 'Mailand baut Palazzi,' *Die Weltwoche* (Zurich), 29 July
'Free floor concrete tower,' *Architectural Forum*, November

1956
E. Kaufmann, 'Scraping the Skies of Italy,' *Art News*, 5
R.v.O., 'De hoogste Wolkencrabber van Europa,' *De Linie*, 7 July
K. Tange, (the Pirelli Office Building), *Shinkentiku*, March
V. Viganò, 'Immeuble Pirelli, Milan,' *L'Architecture d'Aujourd'hui*, 27
'Edificio Pirelli,' *Informes de la Construccion*, 84
'Pirelli Hochhaus in Mailand,' *Werk*, October
'Ponti and the Pirelli Building,' *Architectural Record*, 120

1957
A.C., 'Nowy Drapacz Nieba W Mediolanie,' *Stolica* (Warsaw), 5 July
C. Kellog, 'Apartment Plan from Italy,' *The New York Times Magazine*, 15 December
M.W. Rosenthal, 'Thoughts on Ponti's Pirelli Building,' *The Journal of the RIBA*, 64, no. 7
P.C. Santini, 'Deux gratte-ciels à Milan,' *Zodiac*, 1
'Italy' (on the Pirelli Building), *Concrete Quarterly*, 32
'Le gratte-ciel Pirelli,' *Les Nouvelles Littéraires*, Paris, 24 January
'The Pleasures of Ponti,' *Time*, 70, 9 September
'Some beautiful justifications for the decorative with Italian ceramic tiles,' *Interiors*, 116, June
'Immeuble résidentiel à Milan' (Casa Melandri), *L'Architecture d'Aujourd'hui*, October

1958
'Europe's Tallest,' *The Sunday Times*, 26 October
'Italian Skyscraper Nears Completion,' *The New York Times*, 24 August

1959
G. Veronesi, 'L'architettura dei grattacieli a Milano,' *Comunità*, 74
B. Zevi, 'Cesenatico si ribella alle vele in ferro battuto,' *Cronache di Architettura*, III, Laterza, Rome-Bari
'Powerful construction details mark Milan skyscraper,' *Progressive Architecture*, 40

1960
R. Banham, 'The newest invasion of Europe' (on the Pirelli Building), *Horizon*, November
Edilizia Moderna, 71, special issue devoted to the Pirelli Center
'Pirelli completed,' *The Architectural Review*, 127
'Bonmoschetto, Convent by Gio Ponti,' *The Architectural Review*, 127
'Nervi Ponti Design, Italian Centennial Pavilion,' *Progressive Architecture*, vol. 41, November
'Turin 1961 Exposition news: Nervi and Ponti design Exposition Palace,' *Interiors*, vol. 120, December
'The Ponti pavilion in Time and Life Building,' *Architectural Forum*, vol. 113, August

1961
R. Banham, 'Pirelli Criticism,' *The Architectural Review*, 129
R. Banham, (review of) G. Ponti, *In Praise of Architecture*, *Arts*, May
W. McQuade, 'Powerful tower, delicate shell' (on the Pirelli Building), *Architectural Forum*, February
R.M., 'Che bella voce! A review of «In Praise of Architecture,»' *Industrial Design*, 8, March

1962
'An industrial tower,' *Arts & Architecture*, 79

1966
E. McCoy, 'Ponti — In on the Ground Floor of Inspiration,' *Los Angeles Times*, 20 November

'Denver: the cage for stacking galleries,' *Architectural Record*, 139, April

1967
C. Eames, 'Ponti is one of the rare ones,' in var. authors, 'The Expression of Gio Ponti,' *Design Quarterly*, 69/70
J.R., 'Ponti programmed,' *Industrial Design*, 14, May
P. Restany, 'Un architecte italien, Gio Ponti, réinvente la maison,' *Arts/Loisirs*, 71, February
Bulletin of the Brisbane May 1967 Convention, Brisbane (Australia), May
'The 20th-century révolution: Architecture,' *The Sunday Times*, 7 May

1968
P. Restany, 'A Gio Ponti, Commissaire du Peuple à la Lumière,' *Le Livre Rouge de la révolution picturale*, Apollinaire, Milan
W. Raser, 'Triennale City,' *Home Furnishing Daily*, 27 May
S. Watson, 'Some Considerations to Gio Ponti's Theoretical Approach to Architecture,' for the course given by N.H. Shapira at the University of California, 14 March, unpublished.

1969
M. Grieg, 'Marin Villa Planned: a Modest Tycoon Luxury Home,' *San Francisco Chronicle*, 7 July
P. Restany, 'Gio Ponti,' in *L'avant-garde au XX siècle*, André Balland, Paris
'Islamabad. Pakistans unvollendete Kapitale,' *Neue Zürcher Zeitung*, 12 August

1970
F. Frontini, 'La casa a fisarmonica,' interview with Gio Ponti, *Oggi Illustrato*, May
H. Stubbs, 'Art in artificial light' (on the Denver Museum), *The Architect and Building News*, 20 May

1971
B. Chancellor, 'Denver Art Museum,' *Guestguide*, winter-spring
L. Moretti, 'Il fastigio della Cattedrale,' *Domus*, 497
'All that glitters,' *Architectural Forum*, 135, July
'Denver's new art museum,' *Design*, Autumn
'Denver Art Museum,' *Art Journal*, 31-1, Autumn

1972
E. McCoy, 'Architecture West' (on the Denver Museum), *Progressive Architecture*, 5, February
'Denver Art Museum: spirited and unconventional,' *Architectural Record*, March

1973
D. Davis, 'The Museum Explosion,' *Newsweek*, 17 September

1976
S. Wight, 'Gio Ponti,' in *The Potent Image*, Macmillan Publishing Co., New York
R.J. Vinson, 'L'architecture du troisième quart du XX siècle: vingt bâtiments qui feront date,' *Connaissance des Arts*, February

1977
'Gio Ponti. Rückblick,' *Bauen + Wohnen*, 6
R. Bossaglia, 'Gio Ponti e l'ironia déco,' *Corriere della Sera*, 27 September

1978
A. Branzi, 'Elogio della discontinuità,' *Modo*, 13
G. Corsini (edited by), 'Incontro con Gio Ponti: l'architettura è fatta per essere guardata,' *Casa Vogue*, November

1979
V. Apuleo, 'Un moderno moderato — (per la morte di Gio Ponti),' *Il Messaggero*, 18 September
F. Bellonzi, 'Gio Ponti e la bellezza,' *Il Tempo*, 18 September
F. Borsi, 'La stanza è un mondo,' *La Nazione*, 18 September
L. Carluccio, 'Era l'architetto-poeta: scriveva col cemento,' *Gazzetta del Popolo*, 8 September
C. De Carli, 'Il grattacielo e la sedia,' *L'Unità*, 18 September
C. De Seta, 'Gio Ponti: lo invidiano ma nessuno lo studia. (Non esiste un saggio sul grande architetto scomparso),' *Tuttolibri*, 29 September
A. Dragone, 'Gio Ponti, poeta del cemento armato: dal grattacielo alla posata di ogni giorno,' *Il nostro tempo*, 30 September
R. England, 'Tragic loss of a design genius,' *The Sunday Times*, 23 September
B. Gabrieli, 'L'architetto che amava inventare un cucchiaio,' *Il Secolo XIX*, 18 September
V. Gregotti, 'Da nemico del futurismo a papà del Pirellone,' *La Repubblica*, 18 September
A. Mendini, 'Gio Ponti, 1891-1979,' *Domus*, 599
L. Michel, 'La mort de Gio Ponti. Un modernisme bien tempéré,' *Le Monde*, 18 September
F. Minervino, 'Ha grattato il cielo di Milano,' *Corriere della Sera*, 17 September
P. Portoghesi, 'Tra avanguardia e cauta saggezza,' *Avanti!*, 19 September
S.R., 'Dalla architettura al design,' *La Stampa*, 18 September
M. Valsecchi, 'Gio Ponti: un eclettico a Milano,' *Il Giornale*, 18 September
L. Vergani, 'Gio Ponti, un artista caduto fra gli architetti,' *Corriere della Sera*, 17 September
B. Zevi, 'L'inventore del Pirellone,' *L'Espresso*, 7 October
C. Borngräber, *Stil Novo: design in den 50er Jahren*, Dieter Fricke, Frankfurt
A. Mendini, 'Gio Ponti,' *Modo*, December

1980
D. Baroni, 'Gio Ponti,' *Interni*, 297

1981
J. Kremerskothen, *Moderne Klassiker: Möbel die Geschichte machen*, Schöner Wohnen, Hamburg
A. Mendini, 'Master non Master,' *Space Design*, 200
L.L. Ponti, 'A retrospect of my Fa-

ther,' *Space Design*, 200
F. Raggi, 'Visto dai Japans,' *Modo*, 43
R. Rinaldi, 'L'arte della prima pagina,' *Modo*, 45

1982
R. Barilli, 'La bomboniera metafisica,' *L'Espresso*, 13 June
V. Fagone, 'Blu Ponti,' *Domus*, 630
F. Irace, *Precursors of Postmodernism*, Domus, Milan
F. Irace, 'La casa sospesa,' in var. authors, *Gli anni Trenta, arte e cultura in Italia*, Mazzotta, Milan
F. Poli, 'Piatti d'autore. Gio Ponti 1923-30,' *Il Manifesto*, 23 May
P. Portoghesi, 'Le ceramiche di Gio Ponti,' *Gio Ponti alla Manifattura di Doccia*, Sugarco, Milan
M. Spagnol, 'Svagate ragazze di ceramica,' *La Stampa*, 26 May
V. Sgarbi, 'Ma è Gio Ponti? Eccezionale,' *L'Europeo*, 31 May
'Attraverso gli anni Trenta,' *Domus*, 624

1983
M. De Giorgi, 'Il Palazzo Montecatini a Milano,' in O. Selvafolta (edited by), *Costruire in Lombardia*, Electa, Milan
G. Nicoletti, 'Gio Ponti, il designer della ceramica,' *L'Unità*, 22 March
G. Pampaloni, 'Le occasioni del gusto,' *Gio Ponti. Ceramiche 1923-1930* (Florence 1983), Electa, Florence
R. Rinaldi, 'Gio Ponti: un esempio d'eccezione,' *Ottagono*, 70
P.C. Santini, 'Gio Ponti: un innovatore,' *Gio Ponti. Ceramiche 1923-1930* (Florence 1983), Electa, Florence

1984
F. Scassellati, 'L'antiquité est contemporaine,' *Décoration Internationale*, 72

1985
A. Bangert, *Italienisches Möbeldesign: Klassiker von 1945 bis 1985*, Verlag Modernes Design Albrecht Bangert, Munich
M. Goldschmiedt, 'Gio Ponti,' *Il bagno oggi e domani*, Nov/Dec
F. Irace, 'La casa all'italiana 1928-1933: Gio Ponti e la progettazione delle case tipiche'; 'Un esempio di architettura industriale degli anni Trenta: lo stabilimento Italcima a Milano,' in O. Selvafolta (edited by), *Costruire in Lombardia*, Electa, Milan

1986
A. Avon, 'Uno stile per l'abitare: attività e architettura di Gio Ponti fra gli anni Venti e gli anni Trenta,' *Casabella*, 253
L. Bortolatto, 'Sulla cupola ridonata alla luce come Galileo Chini la ridonò a Venezia nel 1909,' *XLII Esposizione Internazionale d'Arte*, Venice
P. Farina, 'Gio Ponti: anni Trenta e dintorni,' *Ottagono*, 82
F. Irace, 'Gio Ponti e la casa attrezzata,' *Ottagono*, 82
F. Irace, 'Ovunque ponti d'oro,' *Panorama*, 1067
M. Meietta, K. Sato, 'L'architettura è un cristallo,' *Interni*, 361
L. Somaini, 'L'eredità scomoda di Gio Ponti,' *La Repubblica*, 19 November

'The Italian Taste,' *Brutus*, Tokyo, 143
'Gio Ponti,' *The Sun*, Tokyo, 299

1987
G. Dorfles, 'Torna Gio Ponti con le parole figurate,' *Corriere della Sera*, 12 March
E. Enriquez, 'Ponti d'oro,' *Panorama*, 6 September
F. Irace (edited by), 'Villa Planchart,' *Abitare*, 253
F. Irace, 'A bella posta,' *Panorama*, 1091
F. Irace, 'Domestica architettura e felicità dei tropici,' *Il Sole/24 Ore*, 18 January
C. Morone, P. Runfola, 'In cento lettere l'ingegno comunicativo di Gio Ponti,' *Il Sole/24 Ore*, 73
Johann Ossott, 'Gio Ponti y la villa Planchart,' *Revista M*, Caracas
F. Pagliari, 'Gio Ponti, l'architettura e la ceramica: poesia e materia, in G.C. Bojani *et al.* (edited by), *Gio Ponti. Ceramica e architettura*, Centro Di, Florence
A. Pizzo Greco, 'Omaggio a Gio Ponti,' *Modaviva*, 170
L.L.P., 'Arata Isozaki/Gio Ponti al Seibu Museum, Tokyo,' *Domus*, 679
Fumio Shimizu, Studio Matteo Thun, in *Descendants of Leonardo da Vinci. The Italian Design*, Graphic-sha, Tokyo

1988
P.C. Bontempi, 'Un sogno per due' (Gio Ponti and Alessandro Mendini), *Who and What's Now*, 9
G.P. Consoli, 'Questioni di stile. Gio Ponti accusato e rivalutato,' *Il Manifesto*, 25 November
S. Dal Pozzo, 'Domus, dolce Domus,' *Panorama*, 1157
F. Irace, 'L'espressione della leggerezza,' *La Gola*, September
Patrick Mauriès, 'Gio Ponti,' *City*, 40
E. Tamagno, 'Un luogo comune, il gusto all'italiana di Gio Ponti,' *Il Giornale dell'Arte*, 61
F. Pagliari (review of) 'F. Irace, *Gio Ponti. La casa all'italiana*, Milano, 1988,' *Domus*, 700
P. Mauriès, 'Gio Ponti,' *Vies Oubliées*, Rivages, Paris.

1989
G. Chiaromonte, 'Villa Planchart: Arte canoni e l'immancabile Duchamp,' *Lotus International*, 60, pp. 106—111
F. Irace, 'Corrispondenze: la villa Planchart di Gio Ponti a Caracas,' *Lotus International*, 60, pp. 84—105
L. Puppi, 'Quel pioniere del design,' *Il Giornale di Vicenza*, 6 April
A. Avon, 'Gio Ponti, architetto di stile,' *Phalaris*, 4
G. Raimondi (review of) 'U. La Pietra, *L'arte si innamora dell'industria*, Milano, 1988,' *Domus*, 702
D. Paterlini, 'Itinerario Ponti a Milano,' *Domus*, 708
A. Dell'Acqua Bellavitis (review of) 'M. Universo, *Gio Ponti designer. Padova 1936—1941*, Roma-Bari, 1989,' *Domus*, 709

1990
C. De Carli, documents on Ponti in *Creatività*, CAM, Pandino

BOOKS AND CATALOGUES ON GIO PONTI

D. Guarnati (edited by), 'Espressione di Gio Ponti,' with preface by James Plaut, *Aria d'Italia*, VIII, 1954
M. Labò (edited by), *Gio Ponti*, La Rinascente, Milan 1958
N.H. Shapira (edited by), 'The Expression of Gio Ponti,' with preface by Charles Eames, *Design Quarterly*, 69—70, 1967
N.H. Shapira (edited by), 'The Expression of Gio Ponti,' *Space Design*, 3, 40, 1968
R. Bossaglia, *Omaggio a Gio Ponti* (Milano 1980), Decomania, Milano 1980
L.L. Ponti (edited by), 'Gio Ponti,' with preface by Alessandro Mendini, *Space Design*, 200, 1981
P. Portoghesi, A. Pansera, A. Pierpaoli, *Gio Ponti alla Manifattura di Doccia* (Milan 1982), Sugarco, Milan 1982
S. Salvi, G. Pampaloni, P.C. Santini, *Gio Ponti Ceramiche 1923-1930* (Florence 1983), Electa, Florence 1983
A. Isozaki (edited by), *Gio Ponti. From the Human Scale to the Postmodernism* (Tokyo 1986), Kajima/Seibu/A.G.P., Tokyo 1986
A. Stein (edited by), *Gio Ponti. Obras en Caracas* (Caracas 1986), Caracas 1986
Bojani *et al.* (edited by), *Gio Ponti. Ceramica e architettura* (Bologna 1987), Centro Di, Florence 1987
S. Sermisoni (edited by), *Gio Ponti. Cento lettere*, with preface by Joseph Rykwert, Rosellina Archinto, Milan 1987
F. Irace, *Gio Ponti. La casa all'italiana*, Electa, Milan 1988
U. La Pietra (edited by), *Gio Ponti: l'arte si innamora dell'industria*, Coliseum, Milan 1988
M. Universo (edited by), *Gio Ponti designer. Padova 1936-1941*, with preface by Lionello Puppi, Laterza, Rome-Bari 1989
M. Ferrari, S. Castagni (edited by), *Gio Ponti. I progetti dell'Elba, 1960-1962*, Editrice Azzurra, Cavalese (Trent) 1988
U. De Marco, *La Vela di Gio Ponti*, Scorpione, Taranto 1989

LIST OF WORKS
IN CHRONOLOGICAL ORDER

1923–30 Porcelain and pottery for Richard-Ginori, at the factory in Doccia, Sesto Fiorentino, and at the factory in San Cristoforo, Milan

1925 House at no. 9, Via Randaccio, Milan (P.L.)

1926 Villa Bouilhet at Garches, Paris

1926 Competition project for the decoration of an Italian Embassy (with Tomaso Buzzi)

1927 Pavilion of the Graphics and Book Industry at the Milan Trade Fair (P.L.)

1927 Participation in the competition for the Urban Development Scheme of Milan (with the project «Forma Urbis Mediolani» of the Club degli Urbanisti, headed by De Finetti)

1927 Vestibule of the rooms of La Rinascente-Domus Nova, Milan (P.L.)

1927 Pewter and silver objects for Christofle, Paris (beginning of the collaboration with Christofle)

1927 Glassware for Venini, Murano (beginning of the collaboration with Venini)

1927–28 Furniture for the Studio L'Officina, Milan

1927–30 Furniture for La Rinascente-Domus Nova, Milan

1927–30 Furnishings for Il Labirinto, Milan

1928 Monument to the Fallen, Milan (P.L., Giovanni Muzio, Alberto Alpago Novello, Tomaso Buzzi, Ottavio Cabiati)

1928 Casa Borletti at no. 40, Via San Vittore, Milan (P.L.)

1928 Richard-Ginori stand at the Milan Trade Fair (P.L.)

1928 Decoration of the «rotunda» of the Italian Pavilion, Venice Biennale

1928 «La Penna d'Oca» restaurant, Milan (for Il Labirinto, with Tomaso Buzzi and Gigiotti Zanini)

1928 Volla furnishings, Milan

1928 Interiors of Casa Semenza, Levanto

1928 Designs for embroideries on silk (made by Countess Carla Visconti di Modrone's School in Cernobbio)

1928 Salon of the hairdresser Malagoli, on Piazza Virgilio, Milan

1929 Schejola furnishings on Via Pisacone, Milan

1930 House at no. 1, Via Domenichino, Milan (P.L.)

1930 «Casa delle Vacanze,» («Holiday Home») at the 4th Monza Triennale (P.L.)

1930 Fittings for a luxury cabin on a transatlantic liner, at the 4th Monza Triennale (made by Quarti)

1930 Large aluminum table at the 4th Monza Triennale (made by Volonté)

1930 Large pieces of crystal for Fontana, Milan (beginning of the collaboration with Fontana)

1930 Designs for the silks of Vittorio Ferrari, Milan: «balcone,» «acqua e fuoco» (beginning of the collaboration with Vittorio Ferrari)

1930 Designs for De Angeli-Frua printed fabrics, Milan

1930 Flatware for Krupp Italiana, Milan (beginning of the collaboration with Krupp)

1930 Carpet for Mita, Nervi

1931 Furniture for Turri, Varedo

1931 Borletti chapel in the Cimitero Monumentale, Milan

1931 Head office of the Banca Unione (now Banca Barclays Castellini), no. 5, Via Santa Maria Segreta, Milan (P.L.)

1931 Project for «an apartment house in town»

1931 First «Case Tipiche,» Milan (P.L.): Domus Julia, Domus Carola, Domus Fausta (nos. 25, 23, and 21, Via De Togni)

1931 Glass fittings for the Dahò store, Milan (made by Fontana)

1931 Contini-Bonacossi furnishings, Florence (with Tomaso Buzzi)

1931 Three bookcases for D'Annunzio's Opera Omnia (made by Quarti)

1931 Contini-Bonacossi furnishings, Florence (with Tomaso Buzzi)

1931 Lamp made of disks for Fontana, Milan

1932 Entrance hall with walls lined with Richard-Ginori tiles in the Ministry of Corporations (by Marcello Piacentini) on Via Vittorio Veneto, Rome

1932 Richard-Ginori ceramic panels for the Ferrario Tavern, Milan

1933 «Case Tipiche,» Milan (P.L.): Domus Aurelia, Domus Honoria, Domus Serena, Domus Livia (Via Letizia nos. 2, 10, and 8, and Via Caravaggio no. 25)

1933 «Torre Littoria» in the park, Milan (with Cesare Chiodi)

1933 Project for low-cost housing on Via Brioschi (P.L.)

1933 Casa Rasini on Corso Venezia, on the corner of Bastioni di Porta Venezia, Milan (P.L.)

1933 Furnishings for Ida Pozzi, no. 25, Via De Togni, Milan

1933 Bedroom for the 5th Triennale, Milan (made by Grazioli)

1933 Breda electric train ETR 200 (with Giuseppe Pagano)

1933 Krupp Italiana flatware for the 5th Triennale, Milan

1934 «Case Tipiche,» Milan: Domus Adele (no. 29, Viale Coni Zugna), Domus Flavia (no. 11, Via Cicognara)

1934 Casa Marmont, no. 36, Via Gustavo Modena, Milan and furnishings

1934 Competition project for the «Palazzo del Littorio» (Fascist party headquarters) on Via dell'Impero, Rome

1934 School of Mathematics at the new university campus (now «La Sapienza») Rome (with the collaboration of the engineer Zadra)

1934 Project for day nursery at Bruzzano, Milan (with the collaboration of Countess Ida Borromeo and Prof. Ragazzi)

1934 Villino Siebanec on Via Hajech, Milan

1934 Project for «Villa del Sole» housing development, Milan

1934 «Lighter-than-air» room at the Aeronautics Exhibition, Palazzo dell'Arte, Milan

1934 Project for a «Villa in the Pompeiian style»

1934 Brustio furnishings, Milan

1934 Velvet for Rubelli, Florence

1935 Hotel on Val Martello, Alto Adige (P.F.S.)

1935 Casa Buffa at no. 42, Viale Regina Margherita, Milan (P.F.S.)

1935 House at no. 12, Via Ceradini, Milan

1935 Casa Sissa at no. 9, Corso Italia, Milan (P.F.S.)

1935 De Bartolomeis villas at Bratto, Presolana (P.F.S.)

1935 Ledoga office building, at no. 32, Via Carlo Tenca, Milan (P.F.S.)

1935 Italcima factory, on the corner of Via Crespi and Via Legnone, Milan (with Luciano Baldessari)

1935 Project for an Evangelical church

1935 Cellina furnishings, Milan

1935 Standard for the Ospedale Maggiore, Milan (made by the Bertarelli Workshop, Milan)

1936 First Montecatini Building, on the corner of Via Moscova and Via Turati, Milan (P.F.S.)

1936 «Case Tipiche,» Milan: Domus Alba at no. 63, Via Goldoni (P.F.S.)

1936 Universal Exhibition of the Catholic Press, Vatican City, Rome

1936 Project for the master plan of Addis Ababa (with Giuseppe Vaccaro and Enrico Del Debbio)

1936 Project for Villa Marzotto at Valdagno (P.F.S. with Francesco Bonfanti)

1936 Furnishings for Ferrania Offices, Rome

1936 Interiors for the Italian Cultural Institute, Fürstenberg Palace, Vienna

1936 Casa Laporte at no. 12, Via Benedetto Brin, Milan.

1936 «Demonstrative dwelling» at the 6th Triennale in Milan

1936 Piccoli furnishings, Milan

1936 Pozzi furnishings, Milan

1936 Door handles, door and window frames, lamps, sanitary fixtures (later OSVA-SVAO), and design of the pneumatic post system in the Montecatini building, Milan

1936 Office furniture for Parma, Saronno

1936 Clocks for Boselli, Milan

1936 Objects for Krupp Italiana, Milan

1936–45 Furniture for «Casa e Giardino,» Milan

1936 «Volute» chair at the 6th Triennale (produced in 1969 and 1988 by Montina, San Giovanni al Natisone)

1937 Liviano building for the University of Padua (with frescoes by Massimo Campigli), on Piazza Capitaniato, Padua

1937 Furniture and ceramics in the Italian Pavilion at the Paris International Fair

1937–48 Urban development scheme for the area of the former Sempione station, Milan

1938 Victory Exhibition in Padua

1938 Project for «a hotel in the wood» on Capri (with Bernard Rudofsky)

1938 Project for the «Casa d'Italia» in Buenos Aires

1938	Villa Marchesano in Bordighera
1938	Villa Tataru in Cluj, Romania (with Elsie Lazar)
1938	Vanzetti furnishings, Milan
1938	Borletti furnishings on Via Annunciata, Milan
1938	Project for «a hotel for the Adriatic coast, a hotel for the Tyrrhenian coast» (with Guglielmo Ulrich)
1938	Standard for the University of Trieste
1938	«La pace» broad-striped fabric for Vittorio Ferrari, Milan
1939	Competition project for the Foreign Ministry, Rome (P.S. with Studio Ulrich and Studio Angeli, De Carli, Olivieri; Piero Fornasetti and Enrico Ciuti collaborated on the décor)
1939	Project for «an ideal small house»
1939	Buildings on Piazza San Babila, Milan (P.F.S. with De Min, Alessandro Rimini, and Casalis)
1939	Ferrania Building (now Fiat Building) on Corso Matteotti, on the corner of Via San Pietro all'Orto, no. 12, Milan (P.F.S.)
1939	EIAR (now RAI) Building at no. 27, Corso Sempione, Milan (P.F.S. with Nino Bertolaia)
1939	Competition project for the Palace of Water and Light at the «E42» Exhibition, Rome
1939	Project for the Palazzo Marzotto on Corso Vittorio Emanuele, on the corner of Piazza San Babila, Milan (P.F.S. with Francesco Bonfanti)
1939	Vetrocoke office furnishings, Milan
1939	Scenes and costumes for the ballet «La Vispa Teresa» by Ettore Zapparoli in San Remo
1940	House at no. 19, Via Appiani, Milan (P.F.S.)
1940	Casa Salvatelli on Via Eleonora Duse, on the corner of Piazza delle Muse, Rome (P.F.S.)
1940	Project for bungalows for the Hotel Eden Roc in Cap d'Antibes (with Carlo Pagani)
1940	Project for INA Casa house on Via Manin, Milan (P.F.S.)
1940	Villa Donegani in Bordighera
1940	Public Hall, Basilica and Rectorate in the Palazzo del Bo, University of Padua
1940	Frescoes along the grand staircase of the Rectorate in the Palazzo del Bo, University of Padua
1940	Scenes and costumes for Stravinsky's «Pulcinella» at the Teatro della Triennale, Milan
1940	Project for a cinematographic version of the unabridged text of Pirandello's «Henry IV,» for Jouvet and Anton Giulio Bragaglia (with the collaboration of Cesare Mercandino)
1940	Project for the Giustiniani furnishings, at Foro Bonaparte 35, Milan
1940	Door handles for Sassi, Milan
1940	Frescoes in the «Popolo d'Italia» Building, Milan
1940	Lamps for Lumen, Milan
1940	Panels in enameled copper executed by Paolo de Poli, Padua (beginning of the collaboration with De Poli)
1940—48	Columbus Clinic for the Missionary Sisters of the Sacred Heart of the Blessed Cabrini, at no. 48, Via Buonarroti, Milan (P.F.S.)
1941	Project for «a villa in town»
1941	Flatware for Krupp Italiana, Milan
1941	Furniture with enameled decoration executed by Paolo de Poli, Padua
1943	Project for the Mondadori factory at Rho (P.F.S.)
1943	Casa Marmont «La Cantarana,» near Lodi
1943	Furnishings for Argenteria Krupp, Milan
1943	Mosca furniture, Chiavenna
1944	Casa Ponti at Civate, Brianza (first version)
1944	Garzanti Building at nos. 28—30, Via Spiga, Milan (Studi Tecnici di Architettura Riuniti/STAR: Gio Ponti, Pier Giulio Bosisio, Gigi Ghò, Eugenio Soncini)
1944	Scenes and costumes for the ballet «Festa Romantica,» by Giuseppe Piccioli at La Scala, Milan
1945	Project for the Building and Hotel of the Ferrovie Nord (Northern Railways), Milan (P.F.)
1945	Scenes and costumes for the ballet «Mondo Tondo» by Ennio Porrino at La Scala, Milan (not performed)
1946	Designs (bottles, lamps) for Venini, Murano
1946	Brustio furnishings at no. 7, Via Marchiondi, Milan
1946	Papier-mâché frames for Enrico Dal Monte, Faenza
1946	Pottery for Melandri, Faenza
1947	Scenes and costumes for Gluck's «Orpheus» at La Scala, Milan
1947	«Labirinto» table top in enameled copper (executed by De Poli, Padua)
1947	Furniture for Spartaco Brugnoli, Cantù (the chair was produced in 1989 by Zanotta, Nova Milanese)
1948	Participation in the QT8, experimental housing development promoted by the 8th Milan Triennale
1948	House on Via Lamarmora, Milan (P.F.)
1948	Lepetit monument to concentration camp victims, at Ebensee, Austria
1948	Swimming pool at the Hotel Royal, San Remo (with Mario Bertolini)
1948	Borletti sewing machine, prototype, Milan
1948	La Pavoni espresso coffee machine, Milan
1948	New pottery for Richard-Ginori, Doccia
1948	Fabric designs for Pasini, Milan
1948	Self-illuminating furniture for the Cremaschi apartment, at no. 12, Via Alberto da Giussano, Milan
1949	Villa Plodari at Rapallo (P.F.)
1949	Furnishings for Gianni Mazzocchi, at no. 15, Via Monte di Pietà, Milan
1949	«Visetta» sewing machine, for Visa, Voghera
1949	«Leggera» chair for Cassina, Meda
1949	Interiors of the transatlantic liner Conte Grande belonging to the Gruppo Finmare Italia, Genoa (with Nino Zoncada)
1949	Interiors of the transatlantic liner Conte Biancamano belonging to the Gruppo Finmare Italia, Genoa (with Nino Zoncada)
1949	Dulciora store on the corner of Via Orefici and Via Cantù, no. 1, Milan (with Piero Fornasetti)
1950	RAS Building at no. 32, Corso Vittorio Emanuele, Milan (P.F.)
1950	Urban development scheme for the INA Casa Harrar-Dessié housing unit, Milan (with Gino Pollini and Luigi Figini)
1950	Villa Marchesano on Via del Tiro a Volo, San Remo
1950	Interiors of the San Remo Casino (with Piero Fornasetti)
1950	Interiors of Villa Cremaschi, Carate Urio, Como
1950	Ceccato furnishings, Milan
1950	Vembi-Burroughs offices in Genoa, Turin, Florence, and Padua (P.F. with Piero Fornasetti)
1950	Fabrics for the Jsa factory, Busto Arsizio, Varese (beginning of the collaboration with Jsa)
1950	Furniture for M. Singer and Sons, New York
1950	«A dining room to be looked at,» for the MUSA exhibition in U.S.A.
1951	White and yellow house in the INA Casa Harrar-Dessié housing development, Milan (with Gigi Gho)
1951	Red house with duplex apartments in the INA Casa Harrar-Dessié housing development, Milan (P.F. with Alberto Rosselli)
1951	Second Montecatini Building, at no. 2, Largo Donegani, Milan (P.F.)
1951	School complex at Chiavenna, Sondrio (P.F.)
1951	Interiors of the transatlantic liner Giulio Cesare, Genoa (with Zoncada)
1951	Bedroom at the 9th Milan Triennale (with Piero Fornasetti)
1951	Prototype of hotel bedroom at the 9th Triennale in Milan
1951	Lamps for Greco, Milan
1951	Steel flatware and silver objects for Krupp Italiana, Milan
1951	Steel flatware for Fraser, New York
1952	Edison Building at no. 5, Via Carducci, Milan (P.F.)
1952	Technical school of the Istituto Gonzaga, Crescenzago (P.F.)
1952	Villa Arata in Naples (P.F.)
1952	Edison power plant, Santa Giustina (P.F.R.)
1952	Interiors of the transatlantic liner Andrea Doria, Genoa (with Zoncada)
1952	Interiors of the ship Africa, Trieste
1952	Interiors of the ship Oceania, Trieste
1952	Lucano furnishings, no. 5, Via Washington, Milan
1952	Gio Ponti's studio at no. 49, Via Dezza, Milan
1952	Edison power plant on the Mera, Chiavenna (P.F.R.)
1952	Edison power plant on the Liri, Trent (P.F.R.)

1953	Swimming pool and interiors of the Hotel Royal, Via Partenope, Naples
1953	Project for the «Predio Italia» (Italo-Brazilian Center) in São Paulo, Brazil (with Luiz Contrucci)
1953	Project for the Faculty of Nuclear Physics at the University of São Paulo, Brazil
1953	Project for the Taglianetti house in São Paulo, Brazil
1953	Project for the Lancia Building in Turin (P.F.R. with Nino Rosani)
1953	Sanitary fixtures for Ideal Standard, Milan (with George Labalme, Giancarlo Pozzi, Alberto Rosselli)
1953	Furniture for Nordiska Kompaniet, Stockholm
1953	Furniture and «organized walls» for Altamira, New York
1953	Faucets and fittings for Gallieni, Viganò & Marazza, Milan
1953	«Distex» armchair for Cassina, Meda
1953	Furniture for Carugati, Rovellasca
1953	Automobile body proposal («diamond-line») for Carrozzeria Touring, Milan
1953	Licitra furnishings at no. 1, Via San Antonio M. Zaccaria, Milan
1954	Edison power plant on the Chiesa, Cimego (P.F.R.)
1954	Aldo Garzanti Center in Forlì (P.F.R. with Pier Giulio Bosisio)
1954	Italian Cultural Institute, Lerici Foundation, Stockholm (with Ture Wennerholm and Pier Luigi Nervi)
1954	Project for the Togni system of lightweight prefabrication at the 10th Milan Triennale (P.F.R.)
1954	«One-room apartment» at the 10th Milan Triennale
1954	Scene and costume designs for Scarlatti's «Mithridates» at La Scala, Milan (not performed)
1954	Furniture for RIV, Turin (with Alberto Rosselli)
1954	Cowhide rug for Colombi, Milan
1954	Wooden floor design for Insit, Turin (with Maria Carla Ferrario)
1954	Prototypes of striped tablecloths and plates
1955	House in the pine wood at Arenzano, Genoa
1955	Edison power plant at Plantano d'Avio (P.F.R.)
1955	Edison power plant at Vinadio, Sondrio (P.F.R.)
1955	Church of San Luca on Via Vallazze, Milan (P.F.R.)
1955	Villa Marmont at Zoagli (P.F.R.)
1955	Supermarket on Viale Zara, Milan (P.F.R.)
1955	Villa Planchart in Caracas
1955	Interiors of the Galleria del Sole, on Via Sant'Andrea, Milan
1955	Projects for «painted doors»
1955	Flatware for Christofle, Paris
1955	Metal writing-desk for Rima, Padua
1955	Writing-desk for Chiesa, Milan
1955	Furniture for the exhibition at Ferdinand Lundquist, Göteborg, Sweden
1956	Faculty of Architecture at the Milan Polytechnic (with Giordano Forti)
1956	House for RAS at no. 79, Via Vincenzo Monti, on the corner of Via Nievo, Milan (P.F.R.)
1956	Edison Stura power plant, Demonte, Cuneo (P.F.R.)
1956	Pirelli skyscraper on Piazza Duca d'Aosta, Milan (P.F.R. with the Studio Valtolina-Dell'Orto; structural consultants, Arturo Danusso, Pier Luigi Nervi)
1956	Villa Arreaza in Caracas
1956	Furnishings for Villa Beracasa, Caracas
1956	Project for «one-room apartment for four persons»
1956	Objects in enameled copper for De Poli, Padua
1956	Door handles for Olivari, Borgomanero
1956	Steel flatware for Krupp Italiana, Milan
1956	Silverware for Sabattini and Christofle, Paris
1956	Tiles for Ceramica Joo, Limito, Milan
1956	Flooring sections made of marble pebbles for Fulget, Bergamo
1956	Printed fabrics for Jsa, Busto Arsizio, Varese
1956	«Lotus,» «Round,» and «Due Foglie» easy chairs for Cassina, Meda
1957	Feal prefabricated house at the 11th Milan Triennale
1957	House at no. 49, Via Dezza, Milan (P.F.R.)
1957	Casa Melandri at no. 14, Viale Lunigiana, Milan (P.F.R.)
1957	Project for the Villa Gorrondona in Caracas (P.F.R. with Maria Carla Ferrario, and Katzuky Ivabuchi)

1957	Ponti furnishings at no. 49, Via Dezza, Milan
1957	Flatware for Reed & Barton, Newport, Mass.
1957	«Diamond-faceted» tiles for Ceramica Joo, Limito, Milan
1957	Lamps for Arredoluce, Milan
1957	«Superleggera» chair for Cassina, Meda
1957	Fabrics («tondi,» «cristalli,» «diamanti,» and «estate mediterranea») for Jsa, Busto Arsizio, Varese
1958	Carmelite convent of Bonmoschetto, San Remo (P.F.)
1958	Building for government offices in Baghdad (P.F.R. with Giuseppe Valtolina and Egidio Dell'Orto)
1958	Assolombarda Building at no. 9, Via Pantano, Milan (P.F.R.)
1958	Project for the Istituto Gallini in Voghera (P.F.R.)
1958	Project for Guzman-Blanco villa in Caracas
1958	Alitalia offices, Fifth Avenue, New York
1958	Flatware for Christofle, Paris
1958	Objects in enameled copper for Del Campo, Turin
1959	Folding chair for Reguitti, Brescia
1959	Auditorium on the eighth floor of the Time and Life Building (designed by Harrison and Abramovitz), Avenue of the Americas, New York
1959	Project for the Town Hall in Cesenatico (P.F.R.)
1959	Project for the central offices of Banca Sella, Biella
1960	Hotel Parco dei Principi in Sorrento
1960	Philips Building on Piazza Monte Grappa, Rome (P.F.R.)
1960	Villa Nemazee in Teheran
1960	Second Ponti house in Civate (Brianza)
1960	Interiors of the Alitalia Air Terminal at the Milan Central Station
1960	Fabrics for Jsa, Busto Arsizio, Varese
1960	Lamps for Lumi, Milan
1961	Architectural consultation for the Hospital of San Carlo on Via San Giusto, Milan (P.F.R.)
1961	Project for the Montreal Towers, Montreal
1961	Internal layout in Nervi's Palazzo del Lavoro, Turin, for the International Exhibition of Labor («Italia '61»)
1961	Hall in the Montecatini pavilion at the Milan Trade Fair (with Costantino Corsini and Pino Tovaglia)
1962	House for the Mother Superior of Notre-Dame de Sion at no. 38, Via Garibaldi, Rome (P.F.R.)
1962	Cassa di Risparmio di Padova e Rovigo, Padua (P.F.R.)
1962	Houses at Capo Perla, Island of Elba (with Cesare Casati)
1962	Pakistan House Hotel (for members of the Pakistan Parliament) in Islamabad (P.F.R.)
1962	Jsa workshops in Busto Arsizio, Varese (P.F.R.)
1962	RAS Building at no. 18, Via S. Sofia, Milan (P.F.R. with P. Portaluppi)
1962	Hotel Storione in Padua (P.F.R.)
1963	Cassa di Risparmio on Piazza Grande, Modena (P.F.R.)
1963	Facade of the Shui-Hing Department Store on Nathan Road, Hong Kong (P.F.R. with Harriman Realty & Co.)
1963	Villa for Daniel Koo in Hong Kong
1963	Competition project for the Anton Bruckner Cultural Center in Linz (with Costantino Corsini and Giorgio Wiskemann)
1963	Project for a housing development in Varese, for the Calzaturificio di Varese (P.F.R.)
1963	«Continuum» armchair for Bonacina, Lurago d'Erba
1964	Church of San Francesco al Fopponino, at no. 39, Via Paolo Giovio, Milan
1964	Banca del Monte Building, on Via Monte di Pietà, Milan (P.F.R.)
1964	Hotel Parco dei Principi on Via Mercadante, Rome (P.F.R. with Emanuele Ponzio)
1964	Project for the «beetle under a leaf» house (Villa Anguissola)
1964	Ministries in Islamabad, Pakistan (P.F.R.)
1964	Chair for Knoll International, Milan
1964	Tiles for Ceramica D'Agostino, Salerno
1965	Project for Saint Charles City Center, Beirut, Lebanon (P.F.R.)
1965	Tiles for Gabbianelli, Milan
1966	Church for the Hospital of San Carlo, on Via San Giusto, Milan
1966	Project for the lawcourts in Verona (P.F.R.)
1966	Ciborium in the Basilica of Oropa (with Mario Negri, sculptor)
1966	«Espressioni,» exhibition for the Ideal Standard store, Milan
1966	«Thick stained-glass windows» for Venini, Murano

1966	Armchair for Frau, Tolentino
1966	Couch for Arflex, Milan
1966	Furniture for Italbed, Pistoia
1966	Sanitary fitttings for Ideal Standard, Milan
1967	Facade of the Bijenkorf Department Store in Eindhoven, The Netherlands (with Theo Boosten and the sculptors Frans Gaast and Mario Negri)
1967	INA office building at no. 7, Via San Paolo and no. 6, Via Agnello, Milan (P.F.R.)
1967	Proposal for colored skyscrapers on a triangular plan (exhibited at the De Nieubourg gallery, Milan)
1967	«The cathedral of Los Angeles,» sculpture cut out of sheets of steel, exhibited at the De Nieubourg gallery, Milan (made by Greppi, Milan)
1967	Lamps for Fontana Arte, Milan
1967	Lamp for Artemide, Milan
1967	Lamps for Guzzini, Macerata
1967	Dinner set for Ceramica Franco Pozzi, Gallarate
1968	«Autilia,» proposal for a non-stop traffic system
1968	Low-cost housing development at Pioltello, Milan (P.F.R. with Alberto Ferrari, Gaetano Angilella, Mario De Bernardinis, Giulio Ponti, Giuseppe Turchini)
1968	Design of the «Naifs» exhibition at Palazzo Durini, Milan
1968	Furniture for Tecno, Varedo
1968	«Novedra» armchair for C&B, Novedrate
1969	Project for a villa for Daniel Koo in Marin County, California
1970	Taranto Cathedral
1970	Montedoria building on Via Pergolesi, Milan (P.F.)
1970	Competition project for an administrative center in Munich (P.F.R.)
1970	Project for «La Casa Adatta» (apartment with movable partitions) for Eurodomus
1970	«Written» fabrics for Jsa, Busto Arsizio, Varese
1970	Furniture («serie Apta») for Walter Ponti of San Biagio Pò, Mantua (now produced by Pallucco, Rome)
1971	Denver Art Museum, Denver, Colorado (with James Sudler and Joal Cronenwett)
1971	Savoia Assicurazioni e Riassicurazioni building on Via San Vigilio, Milan (P.F.R.)
1971	Competition project for the Plateau Beaubourg, Paris (with Alberto Ferrari)
1971	Proposal for multistory apartment buildings for Feal, Milan
1971	«An armchair of little seat,» for Walter Ponti, San Biagio, Mantua (now produced by Pallucco, Rome)
1971	Fabric designs for Zucchi, Milan
1972	«2 Elle» system, a proposal for prefabricated housing
1972	Consultation for the competition for the University of Salzburg (with Otto Prosinger and Martin Windish) (P.F.R.)
1973	Lamps for Reggiani, Milan
1974	Facade «with leaves» in Hong Kong
1976	Floors of special D'Agostino tiles for the head office of the Salzburger Nachtrichten, Salzburg
1978	Facade of D'Agostino tiles for the Shui-Hing Department Store in Singapore
1978	Objects made of metal plate for Sabattini, Bregnano

Gio Ponti also designed, in the thirties, for Fumagalli (Milan), Lio Carminati (Milan), Rubelli (Florence), Lavorazione Leghe Leggere (Milan), Lietti (Cantù), Mauri (Milan), Vanzetti (Milan), Salir (Murano), Croff (Milan), Ravasco (Milan), Proserpio (Barzanò), Radice (Milan), and Ferrari (Brescia); in the forties, for Ariberto Colombo (Cantù), Apem (Milan), Ambrosini (Cantù), and Ettore Colombo (Cantù), Grassotto (Milan), Calderoni (Milan); in the fifties, for Coop. Ceramica (Imola), ISA (Bergamo), Hettner (Como), Fidenza Vetraria (Milan), Cagliani e Marazza (Milan), Gosi (Cremona) and Flexa (Milan); in the sixties, for Argenteria De Vecchi (Milan), Cotonerie Meridionali (Naples), Linificio Canapificio Nazionale (Milan), Fratelli Gianoli (Vigevano), Roca (Barcelona), Childcraft (Salem, Indiana), Candle (Milan),

Abet Print (Turin), John Higgins (Bury, Lancashire), Ceramica Piemme (Sassuolo), Wilhelm Renz (Stuttgart), Consonni (Cantù), Saporiti (Besnate), Baguès (Paris), Frigerio (Cinisello), Kerasav (Naples), Lyda Levi (Milan), Sormani (Milan), and Thonet (Vienna); in the seventies, for Industria Chimica per l'Arredamento (Rome), Polymer (Milan), Avelca (Caracas), Cleto Munari (Brescia), Gaffuri (Cantù), and Balamundi (Baisieux).

This «chronological list of works» does not include any reference to a number of competitions and projects that were never carried out, whose plans and drawings are still being set in order at the Centro Studi e Archivio della Comunicazione of the Design Department (CSAC) at the University of Padua. At the CSAC is kept the entire set of documents previously belonging to the Studio P.F.R. on Via Dezza.

BIOGRAPHICAL DATA

Born in Milan on 18 November 1891 to Enrico Ponti and Giovanna Rigone. Did military service during the First World War in the Pontonier Corps, with the rank of captain, from 1916 to 1918; bronze medal and Military Cross.

Graduated with a degree in architecture in 1921 from the Milan Polytechnic, and set up a studio with the architects Mino Fiocchi and Emilio Lancia in Milan. Later he went into partnership with Lancia (Studio Ponti e Lancia, P.L.: 1926—33); then with the engineers Antonio Fornaroli and Eugenio Soncini (Studio Ponti-Fornaroli-Soncini, P.F.S.: 1933—45).

In 1921 he married Giulia Vimercati: they were to have four children (Lisa, Giovanna, Letizia and Giulio) and eight grandchildren.

In 1923 came his public debut at the first Biennial Exhibition of the Decorative Arts in Monza, which was followed by his involvement in organization of the subsequent Triennial Exhibitions in Monza and Milan.

From 1923 to 1930 he worked at the Manifattura Ceramica Richard Ginori, in Milan and Sesto Fiorentino, changing the company's whole output.

In 1928 he founded the magazine *Domus*. From 1936 to 1961 he was professor on the permanent staff of the Faculty of Architecture at the Milan Polytechnic.

In 1941 he resigned as editor of the magazine *Domus* and set up the magazine *Stile*, which he edited until 1947. In 1948 he returned to *Domus*, of which he remained the editor until the end of his life.

In 1952 he went into partnership with the architect Alberto Rosselli (Studio Ponti-Fornaroli-Rosselli, P.F.R.: 1952—76); after the death of Rosselli he continued to work with his long-time partner, Antonio Fornaroli.

He died in Milan on 16 September 1979.

AWARDS AND POSTS

1934	Award for the Arts at the Accademia d'Italia
1956	National Grand Prix Compasso d'Oro
1958	Kommendor av Kunigl. Vasaorden, Stockholm
1968	Degree Honoris Causa from the Royal College of Art, London
1968	Gold Medal of the French Academy of Architecture, Paris
1927	Member of the Council of the 3rd Biennale, Monza
1930	Member of the Board of Directors of the 4th Triennale, Monza
1933	Member of the Board of Directors of the 5th Triennale
1935	Member of the Supreme Council of Fine Arts
1936	Member of the Council of the 6th Triennale, Milan
1940	Member of the Executive Committee of the 7th Triennale, Milan
1951	Member of the Jury and Council of the 9th Triennale, Milan
1952—55	Member of the Building Commission of Milan
1961	Coordinating member of the exhibition in the Pavilion of Labor at «Italia '61,» Turin
1957—60	President of the Regional College of Architects, Milan

Corresponding member of the Royal Institute of British Architects, London
Honorary member of the American Institute of Architects, Washington
Member of the Fondation Européenne de la Culture, Amsterdam
Counseling member of the Praemium Erasmianum, Amsterdam
National Academician of San Luca, Rome
Knight of Mark Twain, Kirkwood, MO, USA, since 1968
Over the years, he gave lectures at the Faculties of Architecture in Paris, Delft, São Paulo, Athens, Ankara, Istanbul, Warsaw, Teheran, Prague, Madrid, Barcelona, Zurich, Karachi, Caracas, Lisbon, London, Stockholm, Brisbane, Tokyo, Dublin, Brussels, and Bratislava. He served on international juries for architectural competitions in Madrid, Karachi, Montreal, Barcelona, Geneva, Baghdad, Bilbao, Lourdes, and Darmstadt.

SEMINAR

'La figura e l'opera di Gio Ponti.' Debating: Lodovico Barbiano di Belgioioso, Achille Castilioni, Guido Canella, Carlo De Carli, Cesare Stevan, Vittoriano Viganò. Aula Magna, Università Statale degli Studi, Milan, 25 January 1984. Organized by the Faculty of Architecture, Politecnico di Milano, Comune di Milano, and by Cassina Spa, within the program 'Incontri di Architettura, dedicati a Gio Ponti,' 12 October 1983–25 January 1984.

ONE-MAN SHOWS BY GIO PONTI

One-man shows of paintings and drawings:
1937 Florence
1939 Galleria Gianferrari, Milan
1950 Galleria dell'Obelisco, Rome
1951 Galleria Gianferrari, Milan
1955 Galleria La Bussola, Turin
1956 Galleria del Sole, Milan
1959 Galleria del Disegno, Milan
1967 Galleria de Nieubourg, Milan
1978 Galleria Toselli, Milan

One-man shows of architecture and design:
1954 Traveling exhibition, Institute of Contemporary Art, Boston
1955 AB Ferdinand Lundquist, Göteborg, Sweden
1957 Christofle, Paris
1957 Liberty Stores, London
1966 Traveling exhibition, UCLA Art Galleries, Los Angeles

EXHIBITIONS DEVOTED TO GIO PONTI

«L'opera di Gio Ponti alla Manifattura di Doccia della Richard Ginori,» Palazzo delle Esposizioni, Faenza, 31 July — 2 October 1977; Gian Carlo Bojani, exhibition curator.
«Omaggio a Gio Ponti,» Palazzo della Permanente, Milan, 24 April—2 May 1980, an exhibition organized by Rossana Bossaglia.
«Gio Ponti alla Manifattura di Doccia,» church of San Carpoforo, Milan, April—May 1982, an exhibition organized by the Centro Internazionale di Brera.
«Gio Ponti, Ceramiche 1923–1930,» Sala d'Armi in the Palazzo Vecchio, Florence, March—April 1983, an exhibition organized by the Commune of Florence and the Richard-Ginori company.
«Gio Ponti — From the Human Scale to Postmodernism,» Seibu Museum of Art, Tokyo, September—October 1986; exhibition design by Arata Isozaki.
«Gio Ponti — Obras en Caracas,» Sala Mendoza, Caracas, 23 November 1986 — 18 January 1987, an exhibition organized by Axel Stein for the Fundacion Anala y Armando Planchart.
«Gio Ponti. Ceramica e architettura,» at the Arte Fiera di Bologna, February 1987, an exhibition organized by Gian Carlo Bojani, Claudio Piersanti, and Rita Rava.
«Gio Ponti. Cento lettere,» Antonia Jannone gallery, Milan, March—April 1987, an exhibition organized by Silvana Sermisoni.
«Gio Ponti. Grattacieli Immaginati,» Galleria Marcatré, Milan, March 1987, an exhibition organized by Silvana Sermisoni.
«Gio Ponti. Arte Applicata,» church of San Carpoforo, Milan, 15 September 1987 — 15 November 1987, an exhibition organized by the Centro Internazionale di Brera.

GIO PONTI IN MUSEUMS

Museo delle Porcellane di Doccia, Sesto Fiorentino, Florence
Museo del Tessuto, Prato
Museo della Ceramica, Faenza
Museo della Scala, Milan
The Metropolitan Museum, New York
The Brooklyn Museum, Brooklyn, New York
Vitra Design Museum, Weil-am-Rhein, Germany

AUCTIONS OF WORKS BY GIO PONTI

Galleria Salamon-Agustoni-Algranti, Milan: «Mobili di Gio Ponti,» 11 April 1984.
Finarte, Milan: «Gio Ponti: arte e design,» 27 October 1988.
Finarte, Milan: «Arti decorative del Novecento (comprendenti l'arredo di casa Lucano a San Remo, progettato da Gio Ponti),» 29 May 1989.

Photographs

Alinari, Florence	Farabola, Milan	Porta, Milan
Ballo, Milan	Fortunari, Milan	Pozzi, Milan
Bombelli, Milan	Gasparini, Caracas	Publifoto, Milan
Bricarelli, Bordighera	Host-Ivessich Mangani, Milan	Rosselli, Milan
Cartoni, Rome	Licitra, Milan	Scherb, Vienna
Casali, Milan	Moncalvo, Turin	Sorrentino, Padua
Chiolini e Turconi, Pavia	Monti, Milan	Stefani, Milan
Clari, Milan	Mulas, Milan	Talani, Florence
CSAC, Parma	Neroblù, Milan	Vender, Milan
Danesin, Padua	Ornati, Milan	Villani, Bologna

The photographs reproduced in this book are largely taken from the Archivio Ponti, Milan.